The Making of Europe

THE

MAKING

OF

EUROPE

An Introduction to the History of European Unity

by CHRISTOPHER DAWSON

A MERIDIAN BOOK

NEW AMERICAN LIBRARY

TIMES MIRROR

NEW YORK, LONDON AND SCARBOROUGH, ONTARIO

Originally published June 1932.
Reprinted without bibliography by arrangement with
Sheed & Ward from the fifth printing, November 1952

Library of Congress Catalog Card Number: 56-10016

MERIDIAN TRADEMARK REG. U.S. PAT. OFF. AND FOREIGN COUNTRIES
REGISTERED TRADEMARK—MARCA REGISTRADA
HECHO EN CLINTON, MASS., U.S.A.

SIGNET, SIGNET CLASSICS, MENTOR, PLUME AND MERIDIAN BOOKS
are published *in the United States* by
The New American Library, Inc.,
1301 Avenue of the Americas, New York, New York 10019,
in Canada by The New American Library of Canada Limited,
81 Mack Avenue, Scarborough, 704, Ontario,
in the United Kingdom by The New English Library Limited,
Barnard's Inn, Holborn, London, E.C. 1, England.

First Printing/World Publishing Company, August, 1956
First Printing/New American Library, May, 1974

2   3   4   5   6   7   8   9   10

PRINTED IN THE UNITED STATES OF AMERICA

To V. M. D.

Contents

8   *Contents*

NOTE ON THE ILLUSTRATIONS

THE NEW PEOPLE. Painting from the Cemetery of St. Priscilla
in the Catacombs, Rome. Wilpert, *Die Katakombenge-
mälde und ihrer alten copien* (Herder, Freiburg i.B)

The art of the catacombs is the first outward manifestation
of Christian culture, and shows in a remarkable way how the
external forms of the old Roman-Hellenistic culture were
assimilated and modified by the new spiritual forces. Early
Christian art took over the traditional commonplaces of the
Hellenistic house-decorator, and infused them with a profound spiritual meaning. The subjects are mere generalised
types or symbols—a fish, a dove, or a figure borrowed from
heathen mythology—the value of which consists entirely in
their hieratic and mystical significance to the initiated. Of
these figures the most popular is that of a woman in an
attitude of prayer—the *orans*—a figure that symbolised at
once the soul of the deceased, the freed and enlightened
spirit of man, and also the Virgin Church, the Bride of the
Spirit.

The figure shown in the illustration differs from the majority
of *orantes* by its more individual character, which suggests
that it is a portrait of the deceased. According to Wilpert's
view it is the figure of a consecrated virgin, who is shown
again in the background receiving the veil from a bishop,
while other writers have interpreted it as representing the
different states of life—marriage, motherhood, and virginity.
But it also retains a general symbolic character, so that the
scenes may equally be understood as referring to the mystery
of regeneration—the birth and consecration and consummation of the New Man.

JULIUS CÆSAR. From the Palazzo dei Conservatori, Rome

CHRISTUS RHETOR. From the Museo Nazionale delle Terme,
Rome

This statue, which dates from the third or fourth century,
is so thoroughly classical in style that its Christian character

9

has been questioned. It appears, however, to represent Christ as Teacher in the dress and attitude of a Hellenistic schoolmaster. Here again, as in the frontispiece, we see Christian art appropriating the motives of secular art and giving them a new religious significance.

CHRISTIAN-BARBARIAN ART: THE FRANKS CASKET. Front and top from the British Museum; right side from the Bargello, Florence

This casket is of Anglian origin, probably dating from the close of the seventh century, and thus belongs to the great age of Northumbrian culture (cp. Pl. X, the Lindisfarne Gospels). It is a striking example of the way in which Christian and barbarian elements were blended in the new art of the northern peoples. The front panel shows, on the right, the adoration of the Magi, and on the left, apparently, the story of Wayland the Smith. The top depicts a hero, Egil, probably the brother of Wayland, defending his house against an attack.

The right side, which shows a horse-headed figure seated on a mound, and a number of other figures, is the most obscure of all: and though attempts have been made to connect it with the story of Sigurd and Brynhild, its real interpretation and that of the runic inscription are uncertain. The other scenes not reproduced represent the story of Romulus and Remus and the capture of Jerusalem by Titus. Here the runes leave no doubt as to the meaning.

THE KING AND THE GOD. Sassanian rock-carving from Shapur. Sarre & Herzfeld, *Iranische Felsreliefs* (Ernst Wassmuth, Berlin), plate xli

This scene of the King face to face with the God from whom he receives the sacred emblems of royalty is one of the most ancient subjects of oriental art and the classic representation of sacred monarchy. It appears first in Egypt, in the figures of Pharaoh receiving the gifts of Horus; and the same idea underlies the ceremony of royal investiture in Babylonia, in which the King "takes the hands of Bel," and thus acquires the right to world-dominion. A rock-carving of the first century B.C. at Nimrud Dagh in Asia Minor, which represents Antiochus I of Commagene taking the hands of Mithras, shows that the motive was still current among the Iranian peoples in the Hellenistic period. But it is in the Sassanian reliefs of the third century A.D. that the most impressive representation

of the subject is to be found. Although these reliefs, like that
of Nimrud Dagh, show the influence of Hellenistic art, they
are at the same time intensely national in spirit, and express
the reawakening of Persian culture and the triumph of oriental religion and oriental monarchy over the alien forces of
the West.

THE BYZANTINE CHRIST. Mosaic from the apse of San Vitale,
Ravenna

The mosaics in the Church of S. Vitale at Ravenna, dating
from the years 540-550, are perhaps the finest existing examples of the classical period of Byzantine art. It is not, as
in the catacombs, the anonymous art of a persecuted minority,
but the triumphant expression of the Christian imperialism
of the Byzantine monarchy. The dominant spiritual force in
the new art comes from the East, above all from Syria, where,
as Mr. Dalton writes, the traditions of the ancient oriental
monarchies had taught men to regard art as an instrument for
the exaltation of royal and divine power. "The association of
kingship with divinity, so far-reaching in its effects upon life
under the ancient monarchies, was not forgotten in the Semitic
East of Christian times, which could not dissociate the idea
of godhead from that of sombre and tremendous power. The
Aramaeans saw Christ as the Ruler of All (Pantocrator) rather
than as the carpenter's son, or as the serene youth of Hellenistic art." (O. M. Dalton, *East Roman Art*, p. 228.) This
ideal finds expression in the great monumental art of S. Vitale,
which is devoted to the glorification of the two Monarchies,
the Heavenly and the Earthly. In the apse Christ is shown
seated in majesty on the orb of the world, with the four rivers
of Paradise flowing from beneath his feet, while below, on
either side of the choir, the Emperor and the Empress appear
in state, surrounded by their court.

But, on the other hand, this art also inherited the tradition
of the Hellenistic world with its love of nature and its ideal
of beauty and harmony. This element is shown above all
in the figure of Christ, which is Hellenic rather than oriental
in spirit, and is a striking contrast to the tremendous figure
of the Pantocrator in the cathedral of Monreale.

THE HOMAGE OF THE EAST. Mosaic from the nave of S. Apollinare Nuovo, Ravenna

The earlier mosaics in S. Apollinare Nuovo date from the

Gothic period, when this was the Arian court church. But the two great processions of saints in the nave—that of the Virgins led by the Magi on the left, and that of the Martyrs on the right—belong to the Byzantine period under Bishop Agnellus (*d.* 589 A.D.). The figures of the Magi were restored in the last century.

IRISH CHRISTIAN ART: THE ST. GALL GOSPELS. From the Stifts-
   bibliothek, St. Gall

This manuscript dates from the close of the eighth century, and is perhaps the finest example of Irish art outside the British Isles. It was either written or completed on the continent, as the script changes towards the end to continental minuscule.

The Irish Christian art of the eighth century is by far the most original and creative achievement of the barbaric peoples, and though it owes something to foreign influence, it subdued these alien elements in accordance with its own formal principles. Thus the scene of the crucifixion shown in this illustration was probably based on a Byzantine-Syrian model; but its spirit has been entirely changed, and the figures are subordinated to the decorative scheme. Elsewhere, as in the Book of Kells, the human figure is used as pure ornament without any regard for natural representation or human sentiment, with the result that the design conveys an extraordinarily magical and fantastic impression. Although barbaric, it is by no means a "young" or naïve art: it is rather the mature product of a highly elaborate and sophisticated tradition, which has no more in common with that of the Mediterranean world than the art of the Aztecs or the Maya.

ANGLIAN CHRISTIAN ART: THE LINDISFARNE GOSPELS. From
   the British Museum

According to the colophon (which is not, however, contemporary) this manuscript was the work of "Eadfrith, bishop of the church of Lindisfarne (698-721 A.D.), who first wrote this book for God and St. Cuthbert and all the saints who are in the island." With the exception of the book of Kells, which is somewhat later in date, it is by far the finest example in existence of the Irish style of calligraphy and ornament. Hence Professor Macalister has rejected the statement of the colophon and argued for a purely Irish origin for the manuscript. On the other hand, the figure subjects are far more classical in design and more representational in treatment than those of the Irish manuscripts. That shown is apparently a copy of a figure in the Codex Amiatinus (Ceolfrid's Bible) which is itself said to be a reproduction of a South Italian portrait of Cassiodorus in his library. The Calendar of feasts also derives from South Italy, from the church of Naples; and all these features point to Northumbria, where Celtic influences met those of Byzantine Italy, introduced into England by Hadrian, who had been Abbot of Nisida near Naples, and by St. Benedict Biscop.

THE CAROLINGIAN EMPEROR: CHARLES THE BALD. From the *Codex Aureus*, in the Staatsbibliothek, Munich

From the Codex Aureus, made for Charles the Bald in 870 by Beringer and Liuthard, and afterwards presented by Arnulf of Carinthia to the abbey of St. Emmeran at Regensburg. A magnificent example of the most highly developed school of Carolingian art, usually described as the School of Corbie, but now attributed to 'the Scriptorium of the Emperor at St. Denis. The later Carolingian Empire did not possess the material resources for monumental works of art, and consequently the imperial culture found expression in these sumptuous manuscripts, on which all the resources of Carolingian calligraphy and painting were lavished. The illustration shown here is a good example of the classical-Byzantine element in Carolingian art, and shows the Emperor enthroned, wearing a short blue tunic and a violet mantle. The two female figures on either side represent the peoples of the empire, and are labelled Francia and Gothia.

THE CAROLINGIAN BISHOP. From S. Ambrogio, Milan, Hauttmann, *Die Kunst des Mittelalters* (Propyläenverlag, Berlin), p. 174

This forms the ciborium to the elaborately decorated altar of S. Ambrogio at Milan, which is one of the most magnificent examples of Carolingian metal-work. It was the work of a certain Master Wolvinus under Bishop Angilbert II of Milan (824-859 A.D.). But there is some doubt whether it was actually produced at Milan or at Rheims, an important centre of Carolingian art.

THE CONVERSION OF THE NORTH: KING CANUTE. From the British Museum (Stowe MSS. 944)

From the Newminster Register of 1016-24 (*Liber Vitae*)

from Winchester, now in the British Museum (Stowe Manuscript 944). The drawing illustrates the mediaeval conception of the divine origin of royal authority (symbolised by the angel setting the crown on the King's head), and is also of interest as a contemporary drawing of the greatest of Scandinavian rulers.

LEWIS THE PIOUS. From the Vatican Library. Goldschmidt, *German Illumination* (Pegasus Press), I, 56

From the manuscript of Rabanus Maurus, *De Laudibus Sanctae Crucis*, written in gold on purple at Fulda in the second quarter of the ninth century. The emperor is shown in Roman dress as a type of the Christian Soldier. It is by far the most realistic and individual portrait in the art of the early Middle Ages.

THE HOLY ROMAN EMPIRE: OTTO III RECEIVING THE HOMAGE OF THE PEOPLES OF THE EMPIRE. From the Staatsbibliothek, Munich

From the Gospels of Otto III, produced at Reichenau about 1000 A.D. This is one of the masterpieces of the school of Reichenau, the centre of what has been called the Ottonian Renaissance. It is a striking witness to the importance of the reign of Otto III in the history of mediaeval culture; for in spite of its connection with the Byzantine tradition, it is profoundly original in style, and shows the birth of the new art of the mediaeval West. A modern German critic (Hans Karlinger) writes of this art: "It is the product of the renewed relation between North and South—the union of the imperial art of Byzantium and the so-called popular art of the post-Carolingian age." "It arose exclusively in the Middle Kingdom on German soil. There is nothing comparable to it in the South or West, and contemporary Byzantium has nothing greater. The pupil has become a master and his imagery realises what the dream of Otto III imagined: a Christian world-empire over all the countries of the age." (*Die Kunst des frühen Mittelalters*, 63.)

CONSTANTINE THE GREAT. From a colossal head in the Palazzo dei Conservatori, Rome

The Making of Europe

INTRODUCTION

I do not think that it is necessary to make any apology for writing a book on the period usually known as the Dark Ages, for in spite of the general progress in mediaeval studies and the growing interest in mediaeval culture, this still remains a neglected and unappreciated subject. The later mediaeval centuries—the eleventh, for example, or the thirteenth—have each of them a distinctive individual character; but to most of us the centuries between the fall of the Roman Empire and the Norman Conquest present a blurred and vague outline which has no real significance to our minds. We are apt to speak of Anglo-Saxon England, for example, as though it was the same all through, not remembering that the age of Edward the Confessor is separated from that of the Anglo-Saxon conquest by as wide a gap as that which divides it from the time of Cromwell and Mazarin, or as that which separates our own age from the age of Edward III and Chaucer.

In reality that age witnessed changes as momentous as any in the history of European civilisation; indeed, as I suggest in my title, it was the most creative age of all, since it created not this or that manifestation of culture, but the very culture itself—the root and ground of all the subsequent culture achievements. Our difficulty in understanding and appreciating that age is due in part to the creative nature of its activity. It was an internal organic process which did not manifest itself in striking external achievements, and consequently it lacks the

15

superficial attractiveness of periods of brilliant cultural expansion, like that of the Renaissance or the Augustan Age.

Nevertheless it is not the "easy" periods of history that are the most worth studying. One of the great merits of history is that it takes us out of ourselves—away from obvious and accepted facts—and discovers a reality that would otherwise be unknown to us. There is a real value in steeping our minds in an age entirely different to that which we know: a world different, but no less real—indeed more real, for what we call "the modern world" is the world of a generation, while a culture like that of the Byzantine or the Carolingian world has a life of centuries.

History should be the great corrective to that "parochialism in time" which Bertrand Russell rightly describes as one of the great faults of our modern society. Unfortunately, history has too often been written in a very different spirit. Modern historians, particularly in England, have frequently tended to use the present as an absolute standard by which to judge the past, and to view all history as an inevitable movement of progress that culminates in the present state of things. There is some justification for this in the case of a writer like Mr. H. G. Wells, whose object it is to provide the modern man with an historical background and a basis for his view of the world; but even at the best this way of writing history is fundamentally unhistorical, since it involves the subordination of the past to the present, and instead of liberating the mind from provincialism by widening the intellectual horizon, it is apt to generate the Pharisaic self-righteousness of the Whig historians or, still worse, the self-satisfaction of the modern Philistine.[1]

There is, of course, the opposite danger of using history as a weapon *against* the modern age, either on account of a romantic idealisation of the past, or in the interests of religious or national propaganda. Of these the latter is the most serious, since the romanticist at least treats history as an end in itself; and it is in fact to the romantic historians that we owe the first attempts to study mediaeval civilisation for its own sake rather than as a means to something else. The propagandist historian, on the other hand, is inspired by motives of a non-historical order, and tends unconsciously to falsify history in the interests of apologetics. This is a danger to which Catholic historians of the Middle Ages are peculiarly exposed, since the romantic revival first brought in the conception of the Middle

Ages as "The Ages of Faith," and of mediaeval culture as the social expression of Catholic ideals. In the past this was not so, and Catholic historians, like Fleury, often tended to err in the opposite direction by adopting the current prejudices of the post-Renaissance period against the "Gothic" barbarism and ignorance of the Dark Ages. But for the last century and more there has certainly been a tendency among Catholic writers to make history a department of apologetics and to idealise mediaeval culture in order to exalt their religious ideals. Actually this way of writing history defeats its own ends, since as soon as the reader becomes suspicious of the impartiality of the historian he discounts the truth of everything that he reads.

Yet, on the other hand, it is impossible to understand mediaeval culture unless we have a sympathy and appreciation for mediaeval religion, and here the Catholic historian possesses an obvious advantage. To the secular historian the early Middle Ages must inevitably still appear as the Dark Ages, as ages of barbarism, without secular culture or literature, given up to unintelligible disputes on incomprehensible dogmas or to savage wars that have no economic or political justification. But to the Catholic they are not dark ages so much as ages of dawn, for they witnessed the conversion of the West, the foundation of Christian civilisation, and the creation of Christian art and Catholic liturgy. Above all, they were the Age of the Monks, an age which begins with the Fathers of the Desert and closes with the great movements of monastic reform that are associated with the names of Cluny, in the West, and of Mount Athos in the East. The greatest names of the age are the names of monks—St. Benedict and St. Gregory, the two Columbas, Bede and Boniface, Alcuin and Rabanus Maurus, and Dunstan, and it is to the monks that the great cultural achievements of the age are due, whether we look at the preservation of ancient culture, the conversion of the new peoples or the formation of new centres of culture in Ireland and Northumbria and the Carolingian Empire.

It is very difficult for anyone who is not a Catholic to understand the full meaning of this great tradition. There have, indeed, been a few scholars, like the late Heinrich Gelzer, who have been led by their interest in Byzantine or mediaeval studies to an intuitive realisation of the monastic ideal.[2] But such men are rare; to the ordinary secular historian monasticism must remain as alien and incomprehensible a phenomenon as the Lamaism of Thibet or the temple priesthood of the ancient Sumerians. To the Catholic, on the other hand, the monastic institution still forms an integral part of his spiritual world. The Benedictine Rule still governs the lives of men as it did in the days of Bede. Men still perform the same Divine office and follow the same ideals of discipline and contemplation. And thus the monastic tradition supplies a living bridge by which the mind can travel back to that strange antediluvian society of the sixth century without losing contact entirely with the world of actual experience.

Even this, however, is of minor importance in comparison with a comprehension of the faith which was the ultimate spiritual inspiration of that age. If that age was an age of faith, it was not merely on account of its external religious profession; still less does it mean that the men of that age were more moral or more humane or more just in their social and economic relations than the men of to-day. It is rather because they had no faith in themselves or in the possibilities of human effort, but put their trust in something more than civilisation and something outside history. No doubt, this attitude has much in common with that of the great oriental religions, but it differs essentially in that it did not lead to quietism or fatalism in regard to the external world, but rather to an intensification of social activity. The foundations of Europe were laid in fear and weakness and suffering—in such suffering as we can hardly conceive to-day, even after the disasters of the last eighteen years. And yet the sense of despair and unlimited impotence and abandonment that the disasters of the time provoked was not inconsistent with a spirit of courage and self-devotion which inspired men to heroic effort and superhuman activity.

This was the spirit of the great men who were the makers of the new age—of St. Augustine, who saw the vanity and futility of the cult of human power; of St. Benedict, who created a nucleus of peace and spiritual order amidst the disasters of the Gothic wars; of St. Gregory, who carried the cares of the whole world on his shoulders while civilisation was falling in ruins around him; of St. Boniface, who in spite of profound discouragement and disillusion gave his life for the increase of the Christian people.

Diem hominis non desideravi—that is the essential conviction of the age, and it is one that it is difficult for the modern who views all history *sub specie humanitatis* to appreciate, since to him "the Day of Man" is the only possible object of a reasonable man's devotion. Nevertheless, if we do not realise this point of view, the highest and most permanent achievement of that age becomes as unintelligible as a Buddhist monastery would have been to a Victorian man of business. We are cut off from the European past by a spiritual barrier and are forced to study it from outside with the disinterested curiosity of the archaeologist who disinters the relics of a dead culture.

Consequently, if the non-religious reader should feel that an undue amount of space or of emphasis has been given in this book to theological or ecclesiastical matters, he must remember that it is impossible to understand the past unless we understand the things for which the men of the past cared most. The very fact that these things are still matters of interest to theologians is apt to lead to their neglect by the historians, with the result that the latter devote more space to secondary movements that make some appeal to the modern mind than to the central issues that were of vital interest to the men of the past and governed not only their inner life but also their social institutions and their practical activities. If I have written at length on these matters, it is not to prove a theological point or to justify a religious point of view, but to explain the past. This is not a history of the Church or a history of Christianity; it is a history of a culture, of the particular culture that is ancestral to our own. The world of the early Middle Ages is the world of our not very distant ancestors, the world from which we have come and which has formed our national being. Many of us even have in our veins the blood of the makers of the mediaeval world.[8]

Modern scientists rightly insist on the way in which the existence of modern man is conditioned by the inheritance of his prehistoric past. But if this is true of our remote neolithic ancestors, it is much more so of those immediate ancestors whose influence still directly moulds our lives and determines the very language that we speak and the names of the places in which we live. For this was the period in which the age-long prehistoric tradition of our race emerges into the full light of history and acquires consciousness through its first contact with the higher civilisation. Without this creative process there would have been no such thing as European civilisation, for that civilisation is not an abstract intellectual concept, like the "civilisation" of the eighteenth-century philosophers, it is a concrete social organism, which is just as real and far more important than the national unities of which we talk so much.

The fact that this truth is not generally realised is due, above all, to the fact that modern history has usually been written from the nationalist point of view. Some of the greatest of the nineteenth-century historians were also apostles of the cult of nationalism, and their histories are often manuals of nationalist propaganda. This influence shows itself in the philosophic historians, who were affected by the Hegelian idealisation of the State as the supreme expression of the universal idea, as well as in writers like Treitschke and Froude, who were the representatives of a purely political nationalism. In the course of the nineteenth century this movement permeated the popular consciousness and determined the ordinary man's conception of history. It has filtered down from the university to the elementary school, and from the scholar to the journalist and the novelist. And the result is that each nation claims for itself a cultural unity and self-sufficiency that it does not possess. Each regards its share in the European tradition as an original achievement that owes nothing to the rest, and takes no heed of the common foundation in which its own individual tradition is rooted. And this is no mere academic error. It has undermined and vitiated the whole international life of modern Europe. It found its nemesis in the European war, which represented a far deeper schism in European life than all the many wars of the past, and its consequences are to be seen to-day in the frenzied national rivalries which are bringing economic ruin on the whole of Europe.

To-day there is no lack of thinkers who realise the dangers of this state of things, but with few exceptions they are as oblivious of the European tradition as their opponents. They put their faith in an abstract internationalism which has no historic foundation, and consequently they provoke a fresh outburst of nationalist sentiment which is in some respects more excessive than anything the nineteenth century experienced.

The evil of nationalism does not consist in its loyalty to the traditions of the past or in its vindication of national unity and the right of self determination. What is wrong is the identification of this unity with the ultimate and inclusive unity of culture which is a supernational thing.

The ultimate foundation of our culture is not the national state, but the European unity. It is true that this unity has not hitherto achieved political form, and perhaps it may never do so; but for all that it is a real society, not an intellectual abstraction, and it is only through their communion in that society that the different national cultures have attained their actual form.

No doubt it was easy to lose sight of this unity during the eighteenth and nineteenth centuries, when European civilisation had attained such prestige that it seemed to have no rivals and to be identical with civilisation in general. But the case is very different to-day, when the hegemony of Europe is challenged on every side; when Russia and America can no longer be regarded as colonial extensions of European culture, but are beginning to rival Europe in population and wealth and to develop independent cultures of their own; when the peoples of the East are reasserting the claims of oriental culture, and when we ourselves are losing confidence in the superiority of our own traditions.

Unfortunately it is nobody's business to defend the cause of Europe. Every national state creates a thousand vested interests that are concerned in its defence, and the cause of internationalism also has its champions in the forces of Liberalism and Socialism and international finance. Even the oriental cultures have attained self-consciousness by borrowing the forms of western nationalism and developing a nationalist propaganda after the western model. But nobody has ever thought of calling Europe a nation, and so the cause of Europe goes by default.

Yet if our civilisation is to survive it is essential that it should develop a common European consciousness and a sense of its historic and organic unity. We need not fear that this will prejudice the cause of international peace or cause an increase of hostility between Europe and the non-European cultures. What the oriental resents is the arrogant claim that our civilisation is the only kind of civilisation that matters, and he is far more likely to view it with sympathy if he sees it as a spiritual whole than if, as at present, he regards it as an incomprehensible material power that is seeking to control his life. If a true world-civilisation is ever to be created, it will not be by ignoring the existence of the great historic traditions of culture, but rather by an increase of mutual comprehension.

But before it is possible to give European culture its due place in the international society of the future, it is first necessary to undo the false view of the past that has gained currency during the last century and to recover an historic sense of the European tradition. We must rewrite our history from the European point of view and take as much trouble to understand the unity of our common civilisation as we have given hitherto to the study of our national individuality. This is what I have tried to do in an elementary way in the present volume. It does not attempt to identify the cause of civilisation with that of any race or people or to exalt Europe at the expense of other civilisations. In fact, the period that I have chosen is one in which Western culture is obviously inferior to its great oriental neighbours and has no external splendour with which to impress us. Yet for that very reason—because it is small and weak and rudimentary—it is, I think, easier to see it as a whole and to understand the different elements that have gone to its formation. No doubt it is a far cry from the barbarism of the eighth century to the mechanical perfection of the twentieth, but we must remember that, so far as the externals of life are concerned, we are further from the world of our great-grandparents than they were from the world of Charlemagne. The social life of to-day, as distinct from its technical equipment, has its roots in the remote past, and there is a vital connection between the society of modern Europe and that of the early mediaeval world. They are both phases of a single process, which is not the product of blind material and economic forces, but which is none the less an organic development that must be studied as a whole before it can be understood in part.

PART ONE:

The Foundations

THE ROMAN EMPIRE

We are so accustomed to base our view of the world and our whole conception of history on the idea of Europe that it is hard for us to realise what the nature of that idea is. Europe is not a natural unity, like Australia or Africa; it is the result of a long process of historical evolution and spiritual development. From the geographical point of view Europe is simply the north-western prolongation of Asia, and possesses less physical unity than India or China or Siberia; anthropologically it is a medley of races, and the European type of man represents a social rather than a racial unity. And even in culture the unity of Europe is not the foundation and starting-point of European history, but the ultimate and unattained goal, towards which it has striven for more than a thousand years.

In prehistoric times Europe possessed no cultural unity. It was the meeting-place of a number of different streams of culture, which had their origin, for the most part, in the higher civilisations of the ancient East and were transmitted to the West by trade and colonisation or by a slow process of culture-contact. In this way, the Mediterranean, the Danube, the Atlantic and the Baltic were the main channels of cultural diffusion, and each of them was the basis of an independent development that in turn became the starting-point of a number of local cultures.

But the creation of a truly European civilisation was due not so much to the parallelism and convergence of these separate streams of culture as to the formation of a single

25

centre of higher culture that gradually dominated and absorbed the various local developments. This movement had its starting-point in the Ægean, where, as early as the third millennium, B.C., there had arisen a centre of culture comparable to the higher civilisations of Western Asia rather than to the barbaric cultures of the West. And on the foundation of this earlier development there finally arose the classical civilisation of ancient Greece, which is the true source of the European tradition.

It is from the Greeks that we derive all that is most distinctive in Western as opposed to Oriental culture—our science and philosophy, our literature and art, our political thought and our conceptions of law and of free political institutions. Moreover, it was with the Greeks that there first arose a distinct sense of the difference between European and Asiatic ideals and of the autonomy of Western civilisation. The European ideal of liberty was born in the fateful days of the Persian war, when the navies of Greece and Aisa met in the Bay of Salamis and when the victorious Greeks raised their altar to Zeus the Giver of Freedom after the battle of Platæa.

Apart from Hellenism, European civilisation and even the European idea of man would be inconceivable. Nevertheless Greek civilisation itself was far from being European in the geographical sense. It was confined to the Eastern Mediterranean, and while Asia Minor played a great part in its development from the beginning, continental Europe and even parts of continental Greece lay outside its zone of influence. Throughout its history it retained this intermediate character; for, though it extended westward to Sicily and Southern Italy, its chief movement of expansion was eastward into Asia. Hellenism had its first beginnings in Ionia and its end in Alexandria, Antioch and Byzantium.

The extension of this tradition of higher civilisation to the West was the work of Rome, whose mission it was to act as the intermediary between the civilised Hellenistic world of the Eastern Mediterranean and the barbaric peoples of Western Europe. At the same time as Alexander and his generals were conquering the East and sowing the seeds of Hellenistic culture broadcast over the East from the Nile to the Oxus, Rome was slowly and painfully building up her compact military peasant state in Central Italy. A single generation, in the years from 340 to 300 B.C., saw the rise of two new social organisms, the Hellenistic monarchy and the Italian confederation, differing entirely from one another in spirit and in organisation, but, nevertheless, destined to be so drawn together that they ultimately absorbed one another and passed into a common unity.

The result of this process, no doubt, represents a victory for the Roman sword and the Roman genius for organization, but socially and intellectually it was the Greeks who conquered. The age of the Romanisation of the Hellenistic East was also the age of the Hellenisation of the Roman West, and the two movements converged to form a cosmopolitan civilisation, unified by the Roman political and military organisation, but based on the Hellenistic tradition of culture and inspired by Greek social ideals.

But this cosmopolitan civilisation was not as yet European. In the first century B.C. Europe had not come into existence. Rome herself was a Mediterranean Power, and up to this point her expansion had been confined to the Mediterranean coast lands. The incorporation of continental Europe in the Mediterranean cultural unity was due to the personal initiative and military genius of Julius Cæsar—a remarkable instance of the way in which the whole course of history may be transformed by the will of an individual. When Cæsar embarked on his enterprise in Gaul his primary motive was, no doubt, to strengthen his hold over the army and to provide a counterpoise to the conquests of his rival, Pompey, in the East. But it would be a mistake to judge his achievement as though it were an accidental bye-product of his political ambitions. As Mommsen says, it is the peculiar characteristic of men of genius, like Cæsar and Alexander, that they have the power to identify their interests and ambitions with the fulfilment of a universal purpose, and thus Julius Cæsar used the temporary circumstances of Roman party politics to open a new world to Mediterranean civilisation. "That there is a bridge connecting the past glory of Hellas and Rome with the prouder fabric of modern history; that Western Europe is Romanic and Germanic Europe classic; that the names of Themistocles and Scipio have to us a very different sound from those of Asoka and Salmanassar; that Homer and Sophocles are not merely like the Vedas and Kalidasa attractive to the literary botanist, but bloom for us in our garden—all this is the work of Cæsar; and while the creation of his great predecessor in the East has been almost wholly reduced to ruin by the tempests of the Middle Ages, the structure of Cæsar has outlasted those thousands of years which have changed religion and polity for the human race and even shifted for it the centre of civilisation itself, and it still stands erect for what we may designate as eternity." [1]

This conception of the work of Cæsar and of the importance of the Roman contribution to modern culture has indeed been widely challenged in recent times. The modern cult of nationalism had led men to revise their historical scale of values and to look on the native cultures of barbaric Europe with very different eyes from those of our humanist predecessors. First the Germanic peoples and then the Celts have leant to exalt the achievements of their ancestors—or rather of those whom they suppose to be their ancestors—and to minimise the debt that the Western peoples owe to Rome. Like M. Camille Jullian in his great History of Gaul, they regard the Roman Empire as an alien militarism that destroyed with brutal force the fair promise of a budding culture. And no doubt there is some ground for this view inasmuch as the Roman conquest was, in itself, brutal and destructive, and the imperial culture that it brought was stereotyped and lacking in originality. But it is very difficult to find any justification for M. Jullian's belief that Celtic Gaul would have accepted the higher civilisation of the Hellenistic world without the intervention of Rome, or for the view of the modern German writers who believe that the Germanic world would have developed a brilliant native culture under the influence of the Asiatic world.[2]

There is no inevitable law of progress that must force the barbarians of the West to create civilisations for themselves. Without any strong external influence, a simple tribal culture will remain unchanged for centuries, as we see in Morocco or in Albania. The creation of a new civilisation cannot be accomplished without a great deal of hard work, as Virgil himself says in the famous line: "Tantae molis erat Romanam condere gentem"—"it was such a toil to found the Roman people."

We cannot tell if the Celts or the Germans were capable of such an effort if they had been left to their own devices, or if some other power—Persian, or Arab or Turk—would have intervened to do the work for them. All that we know is that the work was actually done, and done by Rome. It was the act of Rome that dragged Western Europe out of its barbaric isolation and united it with the civilised society of the Mediterranean world. And the decisive factor in this achievement was supplied by the personality of Julius Cæsar, in whom the Roman genius for conquest and organisation found its supreme representative.

It is indeed difficult to say what was the ultimate aim of Cæsar's life work: whether, as Mommsen held, he desired to retain the civic traditions of the Roman state, or whether, as Eduard Meyer and many other modern writers believe, he aimed at the creation of a new monarchical state on Hellenistic lines. It is probable that there is some truth in both of these opinions and that the Alexandrine monarchy of Mark Antony and the principate of Augustus each represent one aspect of the Cæsarian idea. However this may be, there can be no doubt about the aims and ideas of the man who was actually destined to complete Cæsar's work, his adopted son and heir, the great Augustus. In his struggle against the Alexandrine monarchy of Antony and Cleopatra, Augustus stood forth as the conscious champion not only of Roman patriotism but of specifically Western ideals. In the eyes of his supporters, Actium, like Marathon and Salamis, was a battle of East and West, the final victory of the European ideals of order and liberty over oriental despotism. Virgil's great passage in the eighth book of the Æneid shows us the formless hosts of oriental barbarism arrayed not only against the Penates and the divine guardians of the Roman state, but against the great gods of Greece—Poseidon, Aphrodite and Athene:

> Omnigenumque deum monstra et latrator Anubis
> Contra Neptunum et Venerem contraque Minervam
> Tela tenent.

and the victory is due not so much to the Roman Mars as to the Hellenic Apollo:

> Actius haec cernens arcum intendebat Apollo
> Desuper: omnis eo terrore Aegyptus et Indi
> Omnis Arabs omnes vertebant terga Sabaei.

In actual fact the victory of Augustus saved European civilisation from being absorbed by the ancient East or overwhelmed by the Western barbarians and inaugurated a new period of expansion for classical culture. In the East the Roman Empire co-operated with the forces of Hellenism to extend Greek civilisation and municipal life. In the West, it brought Western and Central Europe into the orbit of Medi-

terranean civilisation and created a solid bulwark against barbarian invasion. Augustus and his generals completed the
work of Cæsar by advancing the frontiers of the empire to
the Danube from its source to the Black Sea, and though they
failed in their great project for the conquest of Germany as
far as the Elbe, they at least made southern Germany and the
Rhineland a part of the Roman world.

Henceforward for more than four hundred years Central
and Western Europe was submitted to a process of progressive
Romanisation which affected every side of life and formed an
enduring basis for the later development of European civilisation. The Roman Empire consisted essentially in the union of
a military dictatorship with a society of city states. The latter
inherited the traditions of the Hellenistic culture, whether in
a pure or a latinised form, while the former represented both
the Latin military tradition and that of the great Hellenistic
monarchies which it had replaced.

At first sight it is the military aspect of Rome's work which
is most impressive, but the civil process of urbanisation is even
more important in the history of culture. It was Rome's
chief mission to introduce the city into continental Europe,
and with the city came the idea of citizenship and the civic
tradition which had been the greatest creation of the Mediterranean culture. The Roman soldier and military engineer
were the agents of this process of expansion: indeed the army
itself was organised by Augustus as a preparation for citizenship and an agent for the diffusion of Roman culture and
institutions in the new provinces.

Moreover, not only the colonies of veterans, such as Cologne, Treves, Aquileia and Merida, but also the fortresses
and legionary headquarters, such as Sirmium or York or
Mainz, became centres of Roman influence and of urban
life. In the majority of cases, however, the urbanisation of the
new lands was carried out by reorganising the existing Celtic
tribal communities on the model of an Italian municipality
or by attaching the more backward tribal territories to a town
that already existed. In this way there was created a regular
hierarchy of communities reaching from the barbaric tribe
or *populus* at one end of the scale through the provincial
city and the municipality with Latin rights up to the citizen
colony at the other. Thus a continual process of assimilation
and levelling up went on throughout the empire, by which
client states were converted into provinces, provincial cities

into colonies, and citizen rights were granted to provincials.

Each city was the political and religious centre of a rural territory, and the land-owning class was the governing body of citizens. It was the normal process for the freedman and the man who had enriched himself by trade to invest his money in land, and thus to become inscribed as a decurion on the roll of those who were eligible for municipal office, while the wealthy decurion normally obtained Roman citizenship, and according to his financial position on the census rolls, might eventually rise to knighthood or to the senatorial rank. The great senatorial properties, and still more those of the emperor and the imperial fisc, were organised independently of the local city territory, but it was a point of honour with the Roman senator to use his wealth for the adornment or service of his native city, as we see in the case of Pliny or Herodes Atticus. Moreover, the central government was far from being a mere tax-gatherer. Nerva and Trajan established a fund for providing Italian landowners with loans at a low rate of interest, the profits of which were used to promote the growth of the population by grants to poor parents and to orphans, and this system was afterwards extended to the provinces.

The ordinary well-to-do citizen was as much a country as a city dweller, for in addition to his town house, he had his rural estate with its staff of slaves and dependent *coloni* centring in the villa, which combined the farm building of the domain with the often luxurious residence of the owner. In Britain, and in the north of France, the city was little more than an administrative centre, and the so-called citizens lived mainly on their estates, but their culture formed part of the regular urban civilisation of the rest of the Empire, as we can see from the plentiful villa remains in England, with their baths and central heating and mosaic floors. In Northern France and Belgium, these country estates preserved their identity through the Barbarian invasions and the Middle Ages, and even at the present day bear names which are derived from those of their original Gallo-Roman proprietors.

During the first two centuries of the Empire this system led to an extraordinarily rapid development of urban life and economic prosperity in the new provinces. In Gaul and Spain not only the external forms of civic life, but the social and intellectual culture of the Roman-Hellenistic world were diffused throughout the country, while on the Rhine and the

Danube there was an equally rapid development of agricultural colonisation and commercial prosperity. Even the outlying regions, such as Britain and Dacia, shared in the general prosperity and became initiated into the higher civilisation of the Mediterranean world. The whole empire was bound together socially by common laws and a common culture, and materially by the vast system of roads, which rendered communications easier and safer than at any time before the seventeenth century.

In the second century, under the wise rule of the great Flavian and Antonine emperors, this movement of expansion attained its full development. Never had the ancient world seemed more prosperous, more civilised, or more peaceful. Rome seemed to have realised the Stoic ideal of a world state in which all men should live at peace with one another under the rule of a just and enlightened monarchy. Yet appearances were deceptive.

All this brilliant expansion of urban civilisation had in it the seeds of its own decline. It was an external and superficial development, like that of modern European civilisation in the East or in eighteenth-century Russia. It was imposed from above and was never completely assimilated by the subject populations. It was essentially the civilisation of a leisured class, the urban bourgeoisie and their dependents, and though the process of urbanisation promoted the advance of civilisation, it also involved a vast increase of unproductive expenditure and a growing strain on the resources of the empire. As Professor Rostovtzeff has said, every new city meant the creation of a new hive of drones. The expansion of urban civilisation in the imperial age was, in fact, to an even greater extent than that of modern industrialism, a great system of exploitation which organised the resources of the newly conquered lands and concentrated them in the hands of a minority consisting of capitalists and business men; and since the basis of the system was landed property rather than industry, it was less elastic and less capable of adapting itself to the requirements of a growing urban population. So long as the empire was expanding the system paid its way, for every new war resulted in fresh territories to urbanise and new supplies of cheap slave labour. But as soon as the process of expansion came to an end and the empire was forced to stand on the defensive against new barbarian invasions, the economic balance was destroyed. The resources of the empire began to diminish, while its expenditure continued to increase. The imperial government was obliged to raise the taxes and the other burdens of the cities, and the wealthy municipal aristocracy, which supplied the cities with unpaid magistrates and administrators and was corporately responsible for the payment of taxes, was gradually ruined

And at the same time the progress of urbanisation also weakened the military foundations of the imperial system. The army was the heart of the Empire. All the cosmopolitan medley of races and religions, with their divergent interests of classes and cities, was in the last resort held together by a comparatively small but highly trained army of professional soldiers. But it was an ever-present source of danger; for this tremendous fighting machine was too strong and too highly organised to be controlled by the constitutional organs of a city state. Already, at the beginning of the first century B.C., the old citizen army of the Roman Republic had become a professional army of mercenaries led by generals who were half politicians and half military adventurers. It was the greatest of all the achievements of Augustus to overcome the monstrous development of Roman militarism and to restore the ideal of a citizen army, not, indeed, in the old sense, but in the only form that was possible in the new conditions. According to the design of Augustus the legionary army was to be a school of citizenship, officered by Roman citizens of Italian origin and recruited in part from Italy and in part from the urban communities of the most Romanised parts of the Empire.[3] Enlistment in the army carried with it the right of citizenship, and when the long term of military service—sixteen or twenty years—had expired, the soldier received a grant of money or land and re-entered civil life either in his native city or as a member of one of the military colonies that were continually being established as centres of Roman culture and influence in the outlying provinces. Thus, in spite of the hard conditions of service, the army offered a sure path to social and even economic advancement, and it attracted volunteers from the best elements in the population. In every Italian city, and after the time of Vespasian in the provincial cities as well, the guilds of cadets—*collegia juvenum*—trained the sons of citizens for military service, while the veterans held an honoured and influential place in municipal life.

By degrees, however, this system lost its efficacity. The population of Italy and of the more Romanised provinces grew steadily more unsuitable for military service, and the army began to lose its connection with the citizen class in the towns. From the time of Vespasian the army, with the exception of the praetorian guard, which was stationed at Rome, became entirely provincial in composition, and Italians no longer served in the legions, while in the second century, from the reign of Hadrian onwards, the principle of local recruiting became general, and the legions gradually became identified with the frontier provinces in which they were quartered. Thus the army gradually lost contact with the citizen population of the more urbanised parts of the Empire and became a separate class with a strong sense of social solidarity. Even in the first century the *esprit de corps* of the armies of the Rhine and the Danube and the Eastern provinces had been responsible for the disastrous civil war of the year A.D. 69, and it became an even more serious danger when the troops began to be drawn from a lower social stratum. By the end of the second century the army consisted almost entirely of men of peasant origin who were only half-Romanised, and whose whole interest and loyalty centred in their corps and their commanders. But the commanders, who were members of the upper classes—senators and knights—and not permanently connected with the army, were often mere figureheads. The real power in the army was the corps of company officers—the centurions—most of whom had risen from the ranks and whose whole life was devoted to their profession. In the civil wars that followed the fall of Commodus in A.D. 193, the army became conscious of its power, and Septimius Severus was obliged to increase their privileges, especially those of the centurions, who were granted the rank of knighthood and thus became eligible for the higher commands.

Henceforward the emperors were driven to adopt the maxim of Septimius Severus: "Enrich the soldiers and scorn the rest." The old opposition between the city state and the mercenary army, between the ideals of citizenship and military despotism—the opposition that had already destroyed the Roman Republic and had been for a time removed by the work of Augustus—now reappeared in a more serious form than ever before and destroyed the social balance of the imperial system. The Empire gradually lost its constitutional character as a community of city states governed by the twofold authority of the Roman Senate and Princeps, and became a pure military despotism. Throughout the third century, and above all in the disastrous fifty years from 235 to 285, the legions made and unmade emperors at their pleasure, and the civilised world was torn to pieces by civil war and barbarian invasions. Many of these emperors were good men and gallant soldiers, but they were almost without exception ex-centurions—for the most part men of humble origin and little education, who were called from the barrack-yard to control a situation that would have taxed the powers of the greatest of statesmen.

It is therefore not surprising that the economic conditions of the Empire went from bad to worse under the rule of a succession of sergeant-majors. In order to satisfy the demands of the soldiers and the needs of war, an enormous increase of taxation was necessary, and at the same time the inflation of the coinage, which had reached vast proportions by the second half of the century,[4] led to a disastrous rise in prices and a loss of economic stability. Hence the government was driven to resort to a system of forced levies in kind and compulsory services which increased the distress of the subject population.

Thus the military anarchy of the third century produced a profound change in the constitution of Roman society. According to the view of Professor Rostovtzeff, this change was nothing less than a social revolution in which the exploited peasant class avenged itself by means of the army on the rich and cultured city bourgeoisie.[5] This is perhaps an overstatement, but even if there was no conscious class conflict the issue was the same. The provincial cities and the wealthy classes were ruined, and the old senatorial aristocracy was replaced by a new military caste that was largely of peasant origin.

At last the military anarchy was brought to an end and the Empire was restored by the Dalmatian soldier, Diocletian. But it was no longer the same empire. The foundations on which Augustus had built—the Roman senate, the Italian citizen class, and the city states of the provinces—had all of them lost their strength. There remained only the imperial government and the imperial army, and, accordingly, the work of restoration had to be carried out from above by a bureaucratic organisation of the most absolute kind. The seeds of this development had been present in the Empire from the beginning; for, although in the West the Emperor was theoretically merely the first magistrate of the Roman Republic and the commander of the Roman armies, in the East he occupied a different position. He was the heir of the tradition of the great Hellenistic monarchies, which in their turn had inherited the traditions of the ancient oriental states.

This was, above all, the case in Egypt, which had never been annexed by the Republic, and which was acquired by Augustus as the personal dominion of the Emperor and administered directly by imperial officials. Thus the Roman emperors stepped into the place of the Ptolemies and the Pharaohs and took over the control of a society that embodied the most complete system of state socialism that the ancient world had known. "In direct opposition to the structure of economic life in Greece and Italy," writes Professor Rostovtzeff, "the whole economic organisation of Egypt was built up on the principle of centralisation and control by the Government, as well as the nationalisation of all production in agricultural and industrial life. Everything was for the State and through the State, nothing for the individual. . . . Nowhere in the whole evolution of mankind can be found so far reaching and so systematic limitations as those that applied to private property in Ptolemaic Egypt." [6]

The social and economic history of the later Empire is the history of the extension to the rest of the provinces of the main principles of this Egyptian Hellenistic system. The administration of the vast imperial estates, the development of the official hierarchy, the régime of tribute in kind and of forced services, above all the fixation of status in the hereditary guilds, and the binding of the cultivator to his holding and the craftsman and the trader to his calling, were already fully developed institutions in Egypt centuries before they came to be applied to the rest of the Empire. The system of compulsory state services—*liturgies or munera*—was, however, common to the Hellenistic East, and it had begun to make its influence felt in the West as early as the second century. What Diocletian did, therefore, was not to introduce a new principle, but to make these oriental institutions an essential part of the imperial system. The old institutions of the city state, which rested on private property and a privileged citizen class, had become an anachronism, and in their place there arose a bureaucratic unitary state based on the principle of universal service.

It was the task of Diocletian and his successors to reorganise the administration and the finances of the Empire on these foundations. And though this undoubtedly led to an enormous increase in the economic burdens of the population and a decline of social and political freedom, we who live in the fourth decade of the twentieth century are in a better position than the historians of the eighteenth and nineteenth centuries to realise the problems of the age and to do justice to the grim tenacity with which these tough Illyrian emperors fought against the social and economic forces that threatened to overwhelm ancient civilisation. At least Diocletian succeeded in his primary tasks of warding off barbarian invasion and putting an end to the state of military anarchy that was destroying the Empire. He did this by a drastic reorganisation of the Roman military system. From the beginning it had been the fundamental principle of the Roman state that authority—*imperium*—was indivisible and that the supreme magistrates—the consuls—and their representatives in the provinces—the proconsuls—were *ex officio* the commanders of the Roman armies; and under the Empire the same conditions obtained with regard to the emperor and his provincial representatives—the legates. In theory this principle secured the control of the army by the state, but it actually resulted, both at the close of the Republic and during the third century of the Empire, in the control of the state by the army. Diocletian put an end to this state of things by the radical separation of civil and military command. The army and the civil service were constituted as two independent hierarchies which were united only in their common head— the emperor. The provincial governor was no longer a sort of viceroy in his province. He had no control over the troops, and his province, which under Diocletian's successors became much reduced in size, was grouped with several others so as to form a *diocese* under the supervision of a new official, the vicar, who was himself responsible to the Prætorian Prefect, the chief minister of the Empire. In the same way the army underwent a similiar process of reorganisation. The great frontier armies of the Rhine, the Danube and the East, whose rivalries and revolts had led to so many civil wars, were replaced by second-line troops, consisting of an hereditary class of peasant soldiers, while the best troops were stationed behind the frontiers as a field army which could be used as a striking force wherever it was needed. At the same time the historic legion of 5,400 men with its auxiliaries was reduced to a regiment of 1,000 to 1,400 men under a tribune, and was put under the control not of the civil governor, but of a new military officer—the duke. The supreme command was in the hands of the emperor himself, and since Diocletian could not be everywhere at the same time, he returned to the old Roman principle of collegiate authority and associated with himself, first his comrade Maximian, to whom he entrusted the defence of the western frontiers, and then the sub-emperors, the Cæsars Constantius and Galerius. There was now an emperor to each frontier. From Treves Constantius watched the Rhine and Britain; Galerius at Sirmium, west of Belgrade, controlled the Danube; while the senior partners occupied the key positions of the second line—Maximian at Milan to defend Italy, and Diocletian at Nicomedia, the stragetic centre of the Empire, whence he could keep his eyes on the Danube to the north and the Persian frontier in the east. Thus Rome was no longer the centre of the Empire. She was left to nurse the memory of her past glory, while the tide of civilisation ebbed back to the east. The work of Diocletian found its completion in that of Constantine, who gave the new Empire a new capital and a new religion, and thus inaugurated a new civilisation which was not that of the classical world.

Yet, in spite of these profound changes the work of Rome was not undone. In fact it was only in this later period that the social unity of the Empire was completely realised and that men became fully conscious of the universal character of the Roman state. The early Empire outside Italy had been a foreign power imposed from above on a number of conquered societies; its relations were primaily not with the individual but with the subject community. To the ordinary man the *state* was not the Roman Empire but his native city. It was only in proportion as the imperial bureaucracy encroached on the old city administration that a man's local citizenship became subordinated to his membership of the Empire.

Thus the decay of the old city constitution was not an unmitigated misfortune, for it was accompanied by a development of imperial citizenship. The third century, which saw the rise of a centralised bureaucratic state, also saw the extension of Roman citizenship to the provincials and the transformation of Roman law from the possession of a privileged class to the common law of the Empire. And this de-

velopment rested not merely on the desire of the central
government to increase its control over its subjects; it also
had a basis in the social and political ideals of the age. These
ideals already find expression in the writings of Greek men
of letters, such as Dio Chrysostom and Aelius Aristides, who
were the leaders of that somewhat academic revival of classical culture which characterised the second century A.D. They
saw in the Roman Empire the realisation of the traditional
Hellenistic idea of the unity of the civilised world—the *oecu-
mene*—and they held up to the emperors the Stoic ideal of
an enlightened monarchy in which the ruler dedicates his life
to the service of his subjects and regards government, not as
a privilege, but as a duty. Thus the great emperors of the
second century, from Trajan to Marcus Aurelius, who laid the
foundations of the bureaucratic régime, had no intention of
destroying civic liberty. Their ideal was that which was expressed by Marcus Aurelius as "the ideal of a polity in which
there is the same law for all, a polity administered with regard to equal rights and equal freedom of speech, and the
ideal of a kingly government which respects most of all the
freedom of the governed." [7] And the same ideal inspired the
great jurists of the following century, such as Ulpian and
Papinian, through whom the humane and enlightened principles of the Antonine period became incorporated in the
traditions of later Roman law. Even in the darkest period of
the later Empire these ideas never entirely disappeared. The
Roman felt that the Empire stood for all there was in the
world of civilisation and justice and freedom, and down to
the seventh century they still loved to repeat the old saying
that alone among the rulers of the earth the Roman emperor
ruled over free men while the chiefs of the barbarians lorded
it over slaves.[8]

We must not suppose that Roman patriotism had disappeared because the institutions of the city state were moribund, and the Empire itself seemed falling into decay. On the
contrary it is just in this period that we find the clearest realisation of what the world owed to the work of Rome. It runs
through all the literature of the fifth century and is common
alike to Christian and pagan writers.[9] It was the cult of
Rome rather than a belief in the pagan gods that explains the
attachment of aristocratic conservatives like Symmachus to
the old religion and brings a note of genuine passion and
conviction into the artificial poetry of Claudian and Rutilius

Namatianus. There is something touching in the devotion of the Gallic senator Namatian to Rome, "the mother of gods and men," in her misfortunes and in his belief that she would surmount the disasters that had overtaken her—ordo renascendi est crescere posse malis—"it is the law of progress to advance by misfortune."

But the supreme claim of Rome upon the loyalty of Namatian and Claudian, the Gaul and the Egyptian, is to be found in the generosity with which she had given the conquered peoples a share in her laws and has made the whole world into one city.[10] "She it is," writes Claudian, "who alone has received the conquered into her bosom and fostered the human race under a common name." [11] And these ideas are not peculiar to the defenders of the lost cause of the old religion; they are equally characteristic of Christian writers such as Ambrose, Orosius and Prudentius. In fact, Prudentius gave a still wider significance to the conception of Rome's universal mission, since he brought it into organic relation with the ideals of the new world religion. "What," he asks, "is the secret of Rome's historical destiny? It is that God wills the unity of mankind, since the religion of Christ demands a social foundation of peace and international amity. Hitherto the whole earth from east to west had been rent asunder by continual strife. To curb this madness God has taught the nations to be obedient to the same laws and all to become Romans. Now we see mankind living as citizens of one city and members of a common household. Men come from distant lands across the seas to one common forum, and the peoples are united by commerce and culture and intermarriage. From the intermingling of peoples a single race is born. This is the meaning of all the victories and triumphs of the Roman Empire: the Roman peace has prepared the road for the coming of Christ. For what place was there for God or for the acceptance of truth, in a savage world in which men's minds were at strife and there was no common basis of law?" And he concludes:

> En ades, omnipotens, concordibus influe terris!
> jam mundus te, Christe, capit, quem congrege nexu
> Pax et Roma tenent.[12]

And thus, although Prudentius had no more idea of the approaching fall of the Western Empire than had Claudian or Namatian, he had divined with almost prophetic insight the true significance of the changes that had come upon the ancient world. The new Christian Rome, whose advent Prudentius had hailed, was indeed destined to inherit the Roman tradition and to preserve the old ideal of Roman unity in a changed world. For it was to Rome that the new peoples owed the very idea of the possibility of a common civilisation. Through all the chaos of the dark ages that were to follow, men cherished the memory of the universal peace and order of the Roman Empire, with its common religion, its common law and its common culture; and the repeated efforts of the Middle Ages to return to the past and to recover this lost unity and civilisation led the new peoples forward to the future and prepared the way for the coming of a new European culture.

II

THE CATHOLIC CHURCH

The influence of Christianity on the formation of the European unity is a striking example of the way in which the course of historical development is modified and determined by the intervention of new spiritual influences. History is not to be explained as a closed order in which each stage is the inevitable and logical result of that which has gone before. There is in it always a mysterious and inexplicable element, due not only to the influence of chance or the initiative of the individual genius, but also to the creative power of spiritual forces.

Thus in the case of the ancient world we can see that the artificial material civilisation of the Roman Empire stood in need of some religious inspiration of a more profound kind than was contained in the official cults of the city-state; and we might have guessed that this spiritual deficiency would lead to an infiltration of oriental religious influences, such as actually occurred during the imperial age. But no one could have foretold the actual appearance of Christianity and the way in which it would transform the life and thought of ancient civilisation.

The religion which was destined to conquer the Roman Empire and to become permanently identified with the life of the West was indeed of purely oriental origin and had no roots in the European past or in the traditions of classical civilisation. But its orientalism was not that of the cosmopolitan world of religious syncretism in which Greek philosophy mingled with the cults and traditions of the ancient East, but that of a unique and highly individual national tradition which held itself jealously aloof from the religious influences of its oriental environment, no less than from all contact with the dominant Western culture.

The Jews were the one people of the Empire who had remained obstinately faithful to their national traditions in spite of the attractions of the Hellenistic culture, which the other peoples of the Levant accepted even more eagerly than their descendants have received the civilisation of modern Europe. Although Christianity by its very nature broke with the exclusive nationalism of Judaism and assumed a universal mission, it also claimed the succession of Israel and based its appeal not on the common principles of Hellenistic thought, but on the purely Hebraic tradition represented by the Law and the Prophets. The primitive Church regarded itself as the second Israel, the heir of the Kingdom which was promised to the People of God; and consequently it preserved the ideal of spiritual segregation and the spirit of irreconcilable opposition to the Gentile world that had inspired the whole Jewish tradition.

It was this sense of historic continuity and social solidarity which distinguished the Christian Church from the mystery religions and the other oriental cults of the period, and made it from the first the only real rival and alternative to the official religious unity of the Empire. It is true that it did not attempt to combat or to replace the Roman Empire as a political organism. It was a supernatural society, the polity of the world to come, and it recognised the rights and claims of the state in the present order. But, on the other hand, it could not accept the ideals of the Hellenistic culture or cooperate in the social life of the Empire. The idea of citizenship, which was the fundamental idea of the classical culture, was transferred by Christianity to the spiritual order. In the existing social order Christians were *peregrini*—strangers and foreigners—their true citizenship was in the Kingdom of God, and even in the present world their most vital social relationship was found in their membership of the Church, not in that of the city or the Empire.

Thus the Church was, if not a state within the state, at least an ultimate and autonomous society. It had its own organisation and hierarchy, its system of government and law, and its rules of membership and initiation. It appealed to all those who failed to find satisfaction in the existing order, the poor and the oppressed, the unprivileged classes, above all those who revolted against the spiritual emptiness and corruption of the dominant material culture, and who felt the need of a new spiritual order and a religious view of life. And so it became the focus of the forces of disaffection and opposition to the dominant culture in a far more fundamental sense than any movement of political or economic discontent. It was a protest not against material injustice but against the spiritual ideals of the ancient world and its whole social ethos.

This opposition finds an inspired expression in the book of the Apocalypse, which was composed in the province of Asia at a time when the Church was threatened with persecution owing to the public enforcement of the imperial cult of Rome and the Emperor in the time of Domitian. The state priesthood that was organised in the cities of the province is described as the False Prophet that causes men to worship the Beast (the Roman Empire) and its image, and to receive its seal, without which no man might buy or sell. Rome herself, whom Virgil described as "like the Phrygian Mother of the Gods, crowned with towers, rejoicing in her divine offspring," [1] now appears as the Woman sitting upon the Beast, the mother of harlots and abominations, drunken with the blood of the saints and the blood of the martyrs of Jesus. And all the heavenly hosts and the souls of the martyrs are shown waiting for the coming of the day of vengeance when the power of the Beast shall be destroyed and Rome shall be cast down for ever, like a mill-stone into the sea.

This is an impressive witness to the gathering forces of spiritual hostility and condemnation that were sapping the moral foundations of the Roman power. The Empire had alienated the strongest and most living forces in the life of the age, and it was this internal contradiction, far more than war or external invasion, that caused the downfall of ancient civilisation. Before ever the barbarians had broken into the Empire and before the economic breakdown had taken place, the life had passed out of the city-state and the spirit of classical civilisation was dying. The cities were still being built with their temples and statues and theatres as in the Hellenistic age, but it was a sham façade that hid the decay within. The future lay with the infant Church.

Nevertheless, Christianity won the victory only after a

long and bitter struggle. The Church grew under the shadow of the executioner's rods and axes, and every Christian lived in peril of physical torture and death. The thought of martyrdom coloured the whole outlook of early Christianity. It was not only a fear, it was also an ideal and a hope. For the martyr was the complete Christian. He was the champion and hero of the new society in its conflict with the old, and even the Christians who had failed in the moment of trial—the *lapsi*—looked on the martyrs as their saviours and protectors. We have only to read the epistles of St. Cyprian or the *Testimonia* which he compiled as a manual for the "milites Christi," or the treatise *de Laude Martyrum* which goes under his name, to realise the passionate exaltation which the ideal of martyrdom produced in the Christian mind. It attains almost lyrical expression in the following passage of St. Cyprian's epistle to Nemesianus, which is deservedly famous: "O feet blessedly bound, which are loosed not by the smith but by the Lord! O feet blessedly bound, which are guided to paradise in the way of salvation! O feet bound for the present time in the world that they may be always free with the Lord! O feet lingering for a while among the fetters and crossbars but to run quickly to Christ on a glorious road! Let cruelty, envious or malignant, hold you here in its bonds and chains as long as it will, from this earth and from these sufferings you shall speedily come to the Kingdom of Heaven. The body is not cherished in the mines with couch and cushions, but it is cherished with the refreshment and solace of Christ. The frame wearied with labours lies prostrate on the ground, but it is no penalty to lie down with Christ. Your limbs unbathed are foul and disfigured with filth; but within they are spiritually cleansed, though the flesh is defiled. There the bread is scarce, but man liveth not by bread alone but by the Word of God. Shivering, you want clothing; but he who puts on Christ is abundantly clothed and adorned." [2] This is not the pious rhetoric of a fashionable preacher; it is the message of a confessor, who was himself soon to suffer death for the faith, to his fellow bishops and clergy and "the rest of the brethren in the mines, martyrs of God."

In an age when the individual was becoming the passive instrument of an omnipotent and universal state it is difficult to exaggerate the importance of such an ideal, which was the ultimate stronghold of spiritual freedom. More than any other factor it secured the ultimate triumph of the Church, for it rendered plain to all the fact that Christianity was the one remaining power in the world which could not be absorbed in the gigantic mechanism of the new servile state.

And while the Church was involved in this life-and-death struggle with the imperial state and its Hellenistic culture, it also had to carry on a difficult and obscure warfare with the growing forces of oriental religion. Under the veneer of cosmopolitan Hellenistic civilisation, the religious traditions of the ancient East were still alive and were gradually permeating the thought of the age. The mystery religions of Asia Minor spread westwards in the same way as Christianity itself, and the religion of Mithras accompanied the Roman armies to the Danube and the Rhine and the British frontier. The Egyptian worship of Isis and the Syrian cults of Adonis and Atargatis, Hadad of Baalbek, and the Sun-God of Emesa, followed the rising tide of Syrian trade and migration to the West, while in the oriental underworld new religions, like Manichaeanism, were coming into existence, and the immemorial traditions of Babylonian astral theology were appearing in new forms.[3]

But the most characteristic product of this movement of oriental syncretism was the Gnostic theosophy, which was an ever-present danger to the Christian Church during the second and third centuries. It was based on the fundamental dualism of spirit and matter and the association of the material world with the evil principle, a dualism which derived more, perhaps, from Greek and Anatolian influences than from Persia, since we find it already fully developed in the Orphic mythology and in the philosophy of Empedocles. But this central idea was enveloped in a dense growth of magic and theosophical speculation which was undoubtedly derived from Babylonian and oriental sources.

This strange oriental mysticism possessed an extraordinary attraction for the mind of a society which, no less than that of India six centuries before, was inspired with a profound sense of disillusionment and the thirst for deliverance. Consequently, it was not merely an exterior danger to Christianity; it threatened to absorb it altogether, by transforming the historical figure of Jesus into a member of the hierarchy of divine Aeons, and by substituting the ideal of the deliverance of the soul from the contamination of the material world for the Christian ideals of the redemption of the body and the realisation of the Kingdom of God as a social and historical reality. And its influence was felt not only directly in the great Christian-Gnostic systems of Valentinus and Basilides, but also indirectly through a multitude of minor oriental heresies that form an unbroken series from Simon Magus in the apostolic age down to the Paulicians of the Byzantine period. In the second century this movement had grown so strong that it captured three of the most distinguished representatives of oriental Christianity, Marcion in Asia Minor, and Tatian and Bardesanes, who were the founders of the new Aramaic literature, in Syria.

If Christianity had been merely one among the oriental sects and mystery religions of the Roman Empire it must inevitably have been drawn into this oriental syncretism. It survived because it possessed a system of ecclesiastical organisation and a principle of social authority that distinguished it from all the other religious bodies of the age. From the first, as we have seen, the Church regarded itself as the New Israel, "an elect race, a royal priesthood, a holy nation, a people set apart." [4] This holy society was a theocracy inspired and governed by the Holy Spirit, and its rulers, the apostles, were the representatives not of the community but of the Christ, who had chosen them and transmitted to them His divine authority. This conception of a divine apostolic authority remained as the foundation of ecclesiastical order in the post-apostolic period. The "overseers" and elders, who were the rulers of the local churches, were regarded as the successors of the apostles, and the churches that were of direct apostolic origin enjoyed a peculiar prestige and authority among the rest.

This was the case above all with the Roman Church, for, as Peter had possessed a unique position among the Twelve, so the Roman Church, which traced its origins to St. Peter, possessed an exceptional position among the churches. Even in the first century, almost before the close of the apostolic age, we see an instance of this in the authoritative intervention of Rome in the affairs of the Church of Corinth. The First Epistle of Clement to the Corinthians (c.A.D. 96) gives the clearest possible expression to the ideal of hierarchic order which was the principle of the new society.[5] The author argues that order is the law of the universe. And as it is the principle of external nature so, too, is it the principle of the Christian society. The faithful must preserve the same discipline and subordination of rank that marked the Roman army. As Christ is from God, so the apostles are from Christ, and the apostles, in turn, "appointed their first converts, testing them by the spirit, to be the bishops and deacons of the future believers. And, knowing there would be strife for the title of bishop, they afterwards added the codicil that if they should fall asleep other approved men should succeed to their ministry." Therefore it is essential that the Church of Corinth should put aside strife and envy and submit to the lawfully appointed presbyters, who represent the apostolic principle of divine authority.[6]

The doctrine of St. Clement is characteristically Roman in its insistence on social order and moral discipline, but it has much in common with the teaching of the Pastoral Epistles, and there can be no doubt that it represents the traditional spirit of the primitive Church. It was this spirit that saved Christianity from sinking in the morass of oriental syncretism.

In his polemic against the Gnostics in the following century St. Irenaeus appeals again and again to the social authority of the apostolic tradition against the wild speculations of Eastern theosophy. "The true Gnosis is the teaching of the apostles and the primitive constitution of the Church throughout the world." And with him also it is the Roman Church that is the centre of unity and the guarantee of orthodox belief.[7]

In this way the primitive Church survived both the perils of heresy and schism and the persecution of the imperial power and organised itself as a universal hierarchical society over against the pagan world-state. Thence it was but a step to the conquest of the Empire itself, and to its establishment as the official religion of the reorganised Constantinian state. Whether Constantine himself was moved by considerations of policy in his attitude to Christianity is a debatable question.[8] No doubt he was sincere in the conviction he expresses in his letter to the provincials: that he had been raised up by the Divinity from the far west of Britain to destroy the enemies of Christianity, who would otherwise have ruined the Republic; and this belief may well have been reinforced by a conviction that the order and universality of the Christian Church predestined it to be the spiritual ally and complement of the universal Empire. In any case, this was the light in which the official Christian panegyrist of Constantine, Eusebius of Caesarea, interpreted the course of events. "One God," he writes, "was proclaimed to all mankind; and at the same time one universal power, the Roman Empire, arose and flourished. The enduring and implacable hatred of nation for nation was now removed; and as the knowledge of one God and one way of religion and salvation, even the doctrine of Christ, was made known to all mankind; so at the selfsame period, the entire dominion of the Roman Empire being vested in a single sovereign, profound peace reigned throughout the world. And thus, by the express appointment of the same God, two roots of blessing, the Roman Empire and the doctrine of Christian piety, sprang up together for the benefit of mankind." [9]

In fact the official recognition of the Church and its association with the Roman state became the determining factor in the development of a new social order. The Church received its liberty and in return it brought to the Empire its resources of spiritual and social vitality. Under the later Empire the Church came more and more to take the place of the old civic organisation as the organ of popular consciousness. It was not itself the cause of the downfall of the city-state, which was perishing from its own weakness, but it provided a substitute through which the life of the people could find new modes of expression. The civic institutions which had been the basis of ancient society had become empty forms; in fact, political rights had become transformed into fiscal obligations. The citizenship of the future lay in the membership of the Church. In the Church the ordinary man found material and economic assistance and spiritual liberty. The opportunities for spontaneous social activity and free co-operation which were denied by the bureaucratic despotism of the state continued to exist in the spiritual society of the Church, and consequently the best of the thought and practical ability of the age was devoted to its service.

Thus in every city of the later Empire, side by side with the old citizen body, we find the new people of the Christian Church, the "plebs Christi," and as the former lost its social privileges and its political rights, the latter gradually came to take its place. In the same way the power and prestige of the clergy—the Christian *ordo*—increased as those of the civil *ordo*—the municipal magistracy—declined, until the bishop became the most important figure in the life of the city and the representative of the whole community. The office of the bishop was indeed the vital institution of the new epoch. He wielded almost unlimited power in his diocese, he was surrounded by an aura of supernatural prestige, and yet, at the same time, his was an essentially popular authority, since it sprang from the free choice of the people. Moreover, in addition to his religious authority and his prestige as a representative of the people, he possessed recognised powers of jurisdiction not only over his clergy and the property of the Church, but as a judge and arbitrator in all cases in which his decision was invoked, even though the case had already been brought before a secular court. Consequently, the episcopate was the one power in the later Empire capable of counterbalancing and resisting the all-pervading tyranny of the imperial bureaucracy. Even the most arrogant official feared to touch a bishop, and there are numerous instances of episcopal intervention not only on behalf of the rights of individuals, but also of those cities and provinces.

So, too, the Church came to the economic help of the people in the growing material distress and impoverishment of the later Empire. Its vast endowments were at that time literally "the patrimony of the poor," and in great cities like Rome and Alexandria the Church by degrees made itself responsible for the feeding of the poor as well as for the maintenance of hospitals and orphanages.

St. Ambrose declared that it was a shameful thing to have gold vessels on the altar when there were captives to be ransomed, and at a later period when Italy was devastated by the famine and barbarian invasion St. Gregory is said to have taken his responsibilities so seriously that when a single poor man was found dead of hunger in Rome, he abstained from saying Mass as though he were guilty of his death.

This social activity explains the popularity of the Church among the masses of the people and the personal influence of the bishops, but it also involved new problems in the relation of the Church to secular society. The Church had become so indispensable to the welfare of society, and so closely united with the existing social order, that there was a danger that it would become an integral part of the imperial state. The germs of this development are already to be seen in Origen's theory of the Church.[10] He draws an elaborate parallel between the Christian society and that of the Empire. He compares the local church to the body of citizens in each city—the *Ecclesia*—and as the latter had its *Boulè* or *Curia* and its magistrates or archons, so, too, the Christian Church has its *ordo* or clergy, and its ruler, the bishop. The whole assembly of churches, "the whole body of the synagogues of the Church," corresponds to the unity of the cities in the Empire. Thus the Church is, as it were, "the cosmos of the cosmos," and he even goes so far as to envisage the conversion of the Empire to Christianity and the unification of the two societies in one universal "city of God."

In the fourth century the ecclesiastical organisation had become closely modelled on that of the Empire. Not only did each city have its bishop, the limits of whose see corresponded with those of the city territory, but the civil province was also an ecclesiastical province under a metropolitan who resided in the provincial capital. By the end of the fourth century an effort was even being made to create an ecclesiastical unity or "exarchate" corresponding to the civil diocese or group of provinces that was governed by an imperial *vicar*.

The logical culmination of this development was to make the capital of the Empire also the centre of the Church. The solution indeed might seem to have been already provided by the traditional primacy of the Church of Rome, the imperial city. But in the fourth century Rome no longer occupied the same unique position that it had held in the previous centuries. The centre of the Mediterranean world had shifted back once more to the Hellenistic east. Since the reorganisation of the Empire by Diocletian, the emperors no longer resided at Rome, and the importance of the old capital rapidly declined, especially after the foundation of the new capital at Constantinople in 330.

These changes also affected the position of the Roman Church. Under the early Empire Rome had been an international city and Greek was the language of the Roman Church. But from the third century A.D., Rome and the Roman Church gradually became Latinised,[11] and East and West tended to drift apart. The ecclesiastical aspect of this centrifugal tendency is already visible in the middle of the third century, in the opposition of the Eastern bishops, under St. Firmilian, to Pope Stephen on the question of the re-baptism of heretics, and the tendency became still more marked in the following century. From the time of Constantine onwards the Eastern churches began to look to Constantinople rather than to Rome for guidance, and it was the imperial court rather than the Apostolic See that was the centre of unity. This was already evident in the later years of Constantine himself, and his successor, Constantius II went so far as to anticipate the Caesaropapism of later Byzantine history and to transform the Church of the Eastern provinces into a State Church closely dependent on the imperial government.

The essential organ of the ecclesiastical policy of Constantine and his successors was the General Council, an institution which was not, like the earlier provincial councils, of purely ecclesiastical origin, but owed its existence to the imperial power.[12] The right of convocation was vested in the emperor, and it was he who decided what was to be discussed and ratified the decisions by his imperial sanction. But, though in the hands of a crowned theologian like Constantius or Justinian, the General Council was an instrument of the imperial control of the Church rather than an organ of ecclesiastical self-government, it was also a representative institution, and the great ecumenical councils were the first representative deliberative assemblies that had ever existed.[13] Moreover, the Eastern churches in the fourth century were far from being the passive servants of an Erastian government. They were full of independent spiritual and intellectual life. If the Western Church takes a second place in the ecclesiastical history of the time, it is largely because the great religious forces of the age had their centre in the East.

It was in the East that there arose the monastic movement which created the dominant religious ideals of the new age, and though it spread rapidly from one end of the Empire to the other, it continued to derive its inspiration from the hermits and ascetics of the Egyptian desert.

It was the East also that created the new liturgical poetry and the cycle of the liturgical year which was to become the common possession of the Christian Church.[14]

Above all, it was the East that united the Christian tradition with that of Greek philosophical culture and embodied Christian doctrine in a scientific theological system. The foundations of this development had already been laid in the third century, above all by Origen and the catechetical school of Alexandria, and the work was carried on in the following century by Eusebius in Palestine, by Athanasius at Alexandria, and finally, by the three great Cappadocian Greeks, St. Basil, St. Gregory of Nazianzus, and St. Gregory of Nyssa. Thanks to their work the Church was able to formulate a profound and exact intellectual statement of Christian doctrine and to avoid the danger of an unintelligent traditionalism on the one hand, and on the other, that of a superficial rationalisation of Christianity, such as we find in Arianism.

No doubt this process of theological development was accompanied by violent controversies and the intellectualism of Greek theology often degenerated into metaphysical hairsplitting. There is some justification for Duchesne's remark that the Eastern Church would have done well to think less of speculative questions about the Divine Nature and more about the duty of unity[15]; but the development of scientific theology was not the only or even the principal cause of heresy and schism, and without that development the whole intellectual life of Christendom would have been immeasurably poorer.

In order to realise what the West owed to the East, we have only to measure the gap that divides St. Augustine from St. Cyprian. Both of them were Westerners, and Africans, both of them owed much to the older Latin tradition of Tertullian. But, while Cyprian never indulges in philosophical speculations and is not even a theologian in the scientific sense of the word, Augustine yields nothing to the greatest of the Greek Fathers in philosophical profundity. He is, as Harnack puts it, an Origen and an Athanasius in one, and something more as well.

This vast progress is not to be explained as a spontaneous development of Western Christianity, even though we admit the supreme personal genius of Augustine himself. The theological development of the West in the century that followed Tertullian was in fact a retrograde one, and writers such as Arnobius and Commodian possess no theology, but only a millennarist traditionalism.[16]

The change came with the introduction into the West of Greek theological science during the second half of the fourth century. The agents of this transformation were the Latin Fathers, Hilary of Poitiers, Ambrose of Milan, Jerome, Rufinus of Aquileia, and the converted rhetorician, Victorinus; while at the same time St. Martin of Tours and Cassian of Marseilles, both of them natives of the Danube provinces, brought to the West the new ideals of oriental asceticism and monasticism.[17]

The Latin Fathers, apart from St. Augustine, were not profound metaphysicians nor even original thinkers. In theological matters they were the pupils of the Greeks, and their literary activity was mainly devoted to making the intellectual riches that had been accumulated by the Christian East available in the Latin world. Yet at the same time they were the heirs of the Western tradition, and they combined with their newly acquired knowledge the moral strength and the sense of discipline that had always characterised the Latin Church. Their interest in theological problems was always subordinated to their loyalty to tradition and to the cause of Catholic unity. In the Western provinces the Christians were still but a small minority of the population, and consequently the Church was less exposed to internal dissensions and still preserved the spiritual independence that it had possessed in pre-Constantinian times.

This is very evident in the case of the Arian controversy, for Arianism appeared in the West as not so much an internal danger to Christian orthodoxy as an attack from without on the spiritual liberty of the Church. The Western attitude is admirably expressed in the remonstrance which Hosius, the great bishop of Cordova, addressed to the Emperor Constantius II: "I have been a confessor," he wrote, "in the persecution that your grandfather Maximian raised against the Church. If you wish to renew it you will find me ready to suffer all rather than to betray the truth and to shed innocent blood. . . . Remember that you are a mortal man. Fear the day of judgment. . . . Do not interfere in ecclesiastical affairs, or dictate anything about them to us, but rather learn from us what you ought to believe concerning them. God has given to you the government of the Empire and to us that of the Church. Whosoever dares to impugn your authority, sets himself against the order of God. Take care lest you likewise render yourself guilty of a great crime by usurping the authority of the Church. We are commanded to give unto Caesar the things that are Caesar's and to God the things that are God's. It is not lawful for us to arrogate to ourselves the imperial authority. You also have no power in the ministry of holy things." [18]

St. Hilary of Poitiers goes still further and attacks the emperor with all the resources of his classical style. "We are fighting today," he writes, "against a wily persecutor, an insinuating enemy, against Constantius the antichrist, who does not scourge the back, but tickles the belly, who does not condemn to life but enriches to death, who instead of thrusting men into the liberty of prison, honours them in the slavery of the palace . . . who does not cut off the head with the sword, but slays the soul with gold . . ." [19]

The language of Lucifer of Cagliari is still more uncompromising, and the very titles of his pamphlets, "On royal apostates," "On not sparing the persons of those who offend against God," or "On the duty of martyrdom," breathe a spirit of hostility and defiance against the secular powers that recalls that of Tertullian.

Thus the Western Church was far from being dependent upon the state; the danger was rather that it might have become permanently alienated from the Empire and from the traditions of ancient civilisation, like the Donatist Church in Africa, or the Church in Egypt after the fifth century.

This danger was averted, on the one hand, by the return of the Western Empire to orthodoxy under the house of Valentinian, and on the other, by the influence of St. Ambrose and the new development of Christian culture. In St. Ambrose, above all, the Western Church found a leader who could maintain the rights of the Church no less vigorously than St. Hilary, but who was at the same time a loyal friend of the emperors and a devoted servant of the Empire.

Ambrose was indeed a Roman of the Romans, born and trained in the traditions of the imperial civil service, and he brought to the service of the Church the public spirit and the devotion to duty of a Roman magistrate. His devotion to Christianity did nothing to weaken his loyalty to Rome, for he believed that the true faith would be a source of new strength to the Empire and that as the Church triumphed over paganism so the Christian Empire would triumph over the barbarians.

"Go forth," he wrote to Gratian, on the eve of his expedition against the Goths, "go forth under the shield of faith and girt with the sword of the Spirit; go forth to the victory promised of old time and foretold in the oracles of God." . . . "No military eagles, no flight of birds here lead the van of our army, but Thy Name, Lord Jesus, and Thy worship. This is no land of unbelievers, but the land whose custom it is to send forth confessors—Italy; Italy oft times tempted but never drawn away; Italy whom your Majesty has long defended and now again rescued from the barbarian." [20]

Thus Ambrose is the first exponent in the West of the ideal of a Christian state, as was Eusebius of Caesarea in the East. But he differs utterly from Eusebius in his conception of the duties of the Christian prince and the relations between the Church and the state. Eusebius' attitude to Constantine is already that of a Byzantine court bishop, and he surrounds the figure of the emperor with a nimbus of supernatural authority such as had always characterised the theocratic monarchies of the ancient East. But Ambrose belongs to a different tradition. He stands midway between the old classical ideal of civic responsibility and the mediaeval ideal of the supremacy of the spiritual power. He has something of the Roman magistrate and something of the mediaeval pontiff. In his eyes the law of the Church—the *jus sacerdotale*—could only be administered by the magistrates of the Church—the bishops, and even the emperor himself was subject to their authority. "The Emperor," he wrote, "is within the Church, not over it"; and "in matters of faith bishops are wont to be the judges of Christian emperors, not emperors of bishops." [21] And accordingly, while Eusebius addresses Constantine as a sacred being exalted above human judgment,[22] Ambrose did not hesitate to rebuke the great Theodosius and to call him to account for his acts of injustice. "Thou art a man, temptation has come upon thee. Conquer it. For sin is not removed save by tears and repentance." [23]

The authority of St. Ambrose had a far-reaching influence on the ideals of the Western Church, for it helped to strengthen the alliance between the Church and the Empire, while at the same time it preserved the traditional Western conception of authority in the Church. In the East the Church was continually forced to turn to the Emperor and to the councils which he convoked in order to preserve its unity; in the West the conciliar system never attained such importance, and it was to the Roman See that the Church looked as the centre of unity and ecclesiastical order. The attempts to define the jurisdiction of the Papacy by the Council of Sardica in 343, and by the Emperor Gratian in 378, are of minor importance in comparison with the traditional belief in the apostolic prerogative of the Roman See and in the "Romana fides" as the norm of Catholic orthodoxy. In the fifth century this development was completed by St. Leo, who united the conviction of St. Ambrose in the providential mission of the Roman Empire with the traditional doctrine of the primacy of the Apostolic See; while, earlier in the same century, St. Augustine had completed the Western theological development and endowed the Church with a system of thought which was to form the intellectual capital of Western Christendom for more than a thousand years.

And thus, when the Western Empire fell before the barbarians, the Church was not involved in its disaster. It was an autonomous order which possessed its own principle of unity and its own organs of social authority. It was able at once to become the heir and representative of the old Roman culture and the teacher and guide of the new barbarian peoples. In the East it was not so. The Byzantine Church became so closely bound up with the Byzantine Empire that it formed a single social organism which could not be divided without being destroyed. Anything that threatened the unity of the Empire also endangered the unity of the Church. And so it was that while the Eastern Empire resisted the attacks of the barbarians, the Eastern Church lost its unity owing to the re action of the oriental nationalities to the ecclesiastical centralisation of the Byzantine state. Among the oriental peoples, nationality took on a purely religious form and the state was ultimately swallowed up by the Church.

But although from the fifth century the two halves of the Empire drifted apart in religion as well as in politics, the division was not complete. The Papacy still preserved a certain primacy in the East, for as Harnack says, "even in the eyes of the Orientals there attached to the Roman Bishop a special something, which was wanting to all the rest, a nimbus which conferred upon him a special authority." [24] And similarly, the Western Church still regarded itself as in a sense the Church of the Empire, and continued to recognise the ecumenical character of the General Councils which were convoked by the Byzantine Emperor.

These conditions characterised the whole period with which we are about to deal. It was not until the eleventh century that the religious bond which united East and West was finally destroyed and Western Christendom emerged as an independent unity, separated alike in culture and religion from the rest of the old Roman world.

III

THE CLASSICAL TRADITION
AND CHRISTIANITY

If Europe owes its political existence to the Roman Empire and its spiritual unity to the Catholic Church, it is indebted for its intellectual culture to a third factor—the Classical Tradition—which is also one of the fundamental elements that have gone to the making of the European unity.

It is indeed difficult for us to realise the extent of our debt, for the classical tradition has become so much a part of Western culture that we are no longer fully conscious of its influence on our minds. Throughout European history this tradition has been the constant foundation of Western letters and Western thought. It was first diffused through the West by the cosmopolitan culture of the Roman Empire. It survived the fall of Rome and remained through the Middle Ages as an integral part of the intellectual heritage of the Christian Church, and in the age of the Renaissance it arose with renewed strength to become the inspiration and model of the new European literatures and the basis of all secular education.

Thus for nearly two thousand years Europe had been taught in the same school and by the same masters, so that the schoolboy and undergraduate of the nineteenth century were still reading the same books and conforming their minds to the same standards as their Roman predecessors eighteen hundred years before.

It is almost impossible to overrate the cumulative influence of so ancient and continuous a tradition. There is nothing to be compared with it in history except the Confucian tradition in China, and it is curious to reflect that both of them seem finally in danger of coming to an end at the same moment and under the influence of the same forces.

But the classical tradition of Europe differs from that of China in one important particular. It is not of indigenous origin, for though it is so closely linked with the Roman tradition Rome was not its creator, but rather the agent by which it was transmitted to the West from its original home in the Hellenic world. The classical tradition is, in fact, nothing else than Hellenism, and perhaps the greatest of all the services that Rome rendered to civilisation is to be found in her masterly adaptation of the classical tradition of Hellenism to the needs of the Western mind and the forms of Western speech, so that the Latin language became not only a perfect vehicle for the expression of thought but also an ark which carried the seed of Hellenic culture through the deluge of barbarism. And thus the great classical writers of the first century B.C., above all, Cicero, Virgil, Livy and Horace, have an importance in the history of Europe that far outweighs their intrinsic literary value, great as this is, for they are the fathers of the whole Western tradition of literature and the foundations of the edifice of European culture.

At the very moment when Rome had succeeded in extending her Empire over the Hellenistic world, the empire of the Greek classical tradition over the Western mind was assured by the Latin literature of the Augustan age, and the influence of Hellenism continued to increase and spread throughout the first two centuries of the Roman Empire. On the one hand, the first and second centuries A.D. witnessed a renaissance of the Hellenic tradition in its strictly classical form throughout the Greek world; and on the other, the Latin form of Hellenism, which had already reached its full development in the first century B.C., above all in the work of Cicero, was communicated to the Western provinces and became the foundation of their culture. Classical education was widely diffused throughout the Empire, and not only great cities like Rome and Antioch and Alexandria and Carthage, but provincial towns such as Madaura in Africa, Autun and Bordeaux in Gaul, Cordova in Spain, and Gaza and Berytus in Syria became the centres of an intense educational activity. Juvenal writes of the universal mania for education which was extending even to the barbarians:—

> Nunc totus Graias, nostrasque habet orbis Athenas,
> Gallia causidicos docuit facunda Britannos,
> De conducendo loquitur jam rhetore Thule.[1]

This culture was indeed purely literary. Science had little place in it, except at Alexandria. The rhetorical ideal of education, inaugurated by Gorgias and the Sophists of the fifth century B.C. and developed in the schools of the Hellenistic world, was completely dominant, and the successful rhetorician was the idol of the educated public. But rhetoric had a much wider scope than anything which we understand by the name. It was the culmination of the whole cycle of liberal studies—arithmetic, geometry, astronomy, music, grammar, rhetoric and dialectic—the so-called "artes liberales," which were the fore-runners of the mediaeval Quadrivium and Trivium.[2] Even apart from this wide ideal of oratory, which was upheld by Cicero and Tacitus, the pure rhetorician, such as Quintilian or Aristides, was far from being a mere pedant. He aimed at something wider than technical scholarship—at a broad literary culture which is nothing less than humanism. In fact, the humanist ideal of culture, which has dominated modern education since the Renaissance, owes its existence to a deliberate revival of the old rhetorical training. But even in the Middle Ages the latter survived to a far greater extent than is usually realised; indeed there is no period of European history in which its influence is not perceptible. The very type of the publicist—the man of letters who addresses himself to the educated public in general—a type which is almost unknown in other cultures, is a product of this tradition: Alcuin, John of Salisbury, Petrarch, Erasmus, Bodin, Grotius and Voltaire were all of them the successors and disciples of the ancient rhetoricians, and this is but one aspect of that classical tradition which has been one of the chief creative forces in European culture.

In the fourth century, however, the supremacy of the classical tradition seemed gravely threatened by the victory of the new religion. Christianity was founded on an oriental tradition which had nothing in common with Hellenism, and its spirit and ideals were sharply opposed to those of the pagan rhetorician and man of letters. The Christians acknowledged no debt to the classical tradition. They had their own classics

—the Christian Scriptures—which were so fundamentally different in form and spirit from pagan literature that there was at first no room for mutual comprehension. "What has Athens to do with Jerusalem?" writes Tertullian, "what concord is there between the Academy and the Church?" St. Paul himself expressly disavowed all claim to the graces of style and the wisdom of secular philosophy. "Where is the wise? Where is the scribe? Where is the disputer of this world? Hath not God made foolish the wisdom of this world? For the Jews require signs, and the Greeks seek after wisdom; but we preach Christ crucified, unto Jews a stumbling-block and unto the Gentiles foolishness; but with them that are called, both Jews and Greeks, Christ the power of God and the wisdom of God." [3]

Thus Christianity made its appeal not to the sophisticated and sterile mind of cultivated society, but to the fundamental needs of the human soul and to the religious experience of the common man. "Stand forth, O soul, and give thy witness," says Tertullian. "But I call thee not as when, fashioned in schools, trained in libraries, fed up in Attic academies and porticoes, thou belchest forth thy wisdom. I address thee simple and rude and unlettered and untaught, such as they have thee who have thee only, that very thing, pure and entire, of the road, the street, the workshop." [4]

In fact the early Christians were for the most part men of little education and culture. In the cities they belonged mainly to the lower and lower middle classes, while in the country they were often drawn from a peasantry which was almost unaffected by classical culture and which preserved its native Syriac or Coptic or Punic speech. In these circumstances it was but natural that the official representatives of the classical tradition should look on Christianity as the enemy of culture and, like the Emperor Julian or Porphyry, should identify the cause of Hellenism with that of the old religion. The "golden mediocrity" of the classical scholar could have little sympathy with the fanaticism of the martyrs and the desert monks, who condemned everything that made life delightful and proclaimed the approaching doom of all secular civilisation. Maximus of Madaura, the pagan rhetorician who corresponded with St. Augustine, speaks of Christianity as a resurgence of oriental barbarism which sought to replace the worship of the gracious figures of the classical deities by the cult of executed criminals with horrid Punic names. [5]

Nevertheless, though it was ignored by the leaders of culture, there was going on all the time a process of assimilation by which the Church was preparing for the reception of the classical tradition and for the formation of a new Christian culture. As early as the second century, educated converts such as Justin Martyr and Athenagoras were beginning to address the cultivated public in their own language, and attempting to show that the doctrines of Christianity were in harmony with the rational ideals of ancient philosophy. The most remarkable of these attempts is the *Octavius* of Minucius Felix, a Ciceronian dialogue which is purely classical both in form and spirit. It is true that the greatest of the Latin apologists—Tertullian—wrote in a very different spirit, but even he, for all his neglect of the classical tradition, was a rhetorician to his very marrow, and appropriated the methods of the Roman barrister to the service of the new religion.

The tendency which is already visible in the Apologists to assimilate Hellenic thought and culture reaches its highest development in the school of Alexandria in the third century. Origen and his predecessor Clement were the first to conceive the mediaeval ideal of a hierarchy of sciences culminating in Christian theology. As the Greeks had treated the arts and sciences as a propaedeutic to rhetoric and philosophy, so Origen proposed to make philosophy itself a propaedeutic to theology—"that what the sons of the philosophers say about geometry and music and grammar and rhetoric and astronomy —that they are the handmaidens of philosophy—we may say of philosophy itself in relation to theology." [6] He taught, writes his disciple, Gregory Thaumaturgus, "that we should philosophise and collate with all our powers every one of the writings of the ancients, whether philosophers or poets, excepting and rejecting nothing," save the writings of the atheists, "but giving a fair hearing to all." [7] The result of this programme was a far-reaching synthesis of Christianity and Hellenic thought which had a profound influence in the whole subsequent development of theology, but which from the first provoked considerable opposition on the ground that it was inconsistent with traditional orthodoxy, as indeed in some respects it certainly was. It is, however, important to note that this opposition to Origen did not necessarily imply any hostility to Hellenic culture as distinct from Hellenic philosophy. There were Hellenists in both camps; in fact Origen's chief opponent, Methodius of Olympus, went further than Origen himself in his allegiance to the classical tradition.[8]

Thus, by the beginning of the fourth century, classical culture had gained a sure foothold within the Church, and the establishment of the Christian Empire was actually followed by a considerable literary revival. The leaders of this movement—the great rhetoricians of the fourth century, Himerius, Themistius and Libanius—were themselves pagans, but they found no lack of pupils and imitators among the Christians; indeed even from a purely literary point of view the Christian writers of the period often surpassed their teachers. The Fathers of the fourth century, alike in the East and the West, were essentially *Christian rhetoricians* who shared the culture and traditions of their pagan rivals, but whose art was no longer an endless elaboration of the worn-out themes of the lecture-room, but had become the instrument of a new spiritual force. Three centuries earlier Tacitus had pointed out that rhetoric had become empty and unreal, because it no longer fulfilled a vital function in political life. "Great oratory, like fire, needs fuel to feed it and movement to fan it; it brightens as it burns." [9] Through the Church, rhetoric had recovered this vital relation to social life: in place of the old *ecclesia* of the Greek city it had found the new ecclesia of the Christian people. Once more the most profound issues were debated with passionate earnestness before an audience drawn from every class; as when St. John Chrysostom delivered his great homilies to the people of Antioch, while the fate of the city was hanging in the balance. Even the most abstruse theological questions were a matter of burning interest to the man in the street, and the man who could speak or write of them with eloquence and skill was assured of an almost world-wide influence.

This, of course, is primarily true of the Greek-speaking world, the world of Athanasius and Arius, of Basil and Eunomius, of Cyril and Theodoret; but in the Latin West the rhetorical tradition was equally powerful, though it was the tradition of the Roman magistrate and orator rather than of the Hellenic sophist and demagogue. No doubt the Hellenic world still retained its cultural leadership. Eusebius of Caesarea, St. Basil and the two Gregories, of Nyssa and Nazianzus, possessed a wider and deeper culture, alike in literature and philosophy, than any of their Western contemporaries. They preserved the traditions of the school of

Origen, whereas the Western tradition inherited something of the legal and authoritative spirit of Tertullian and Cyprian. But in the fourth century the rise of the new Christian culture tended to draw East and West together once more. St. Ambrose was a diligent student of Greek literature, and owes infinitely more to the writings of the Greek Fathers than to Tertullian and Cyprian, whom he entirely ignores. St. Jerome acquired his theological learning in the East as the pupil of St. Gregory Nazianzen and Apollinarius of Laodicea, and the student of Origen and Eusebius.

Moreover, the tendency of the Church to come to terms with secular culture and to assimilate classical literature and thought manifests itself in the West no less than in the East. St. Ambrose adorns his sermons with quotations from Virgil and Horace, and takes Cicero as his model and guide in his most famous work, *De Officiis Ministrorum*. The Ciceronian tradition forms an essential part of the new Christian culture and influences patristic literature from the time of Lactantius to that of Augustine. St. Jerome, it is true, speaks strongly of the dangers of pagan literature, and the famous vision in which he was condemned for being "a Ciceronian not a Christian" is often quoted as an example of the hostility of Christianity to classical culture.[10] But the true significance of the episode is that Jerome's devotion to classical literature was so intense that it had become a spiritual temptation. Had he not reacted against it, he might have become a rhetorician and nothing more. And in that case the Middle Ages would have lost the greatest of their spiritual classics—the Latin Vulgate. For in his translation of the Bible Jerome makes no attempt to adhere to Ciceronian standards, but allows the primitive grandeur of the Hebrew original to reflect itself in his style, so that he enriched the Latin language with a new range of expression. But though he attempted to moderate his ardour, he never lost his passionate devotion to the greatest of the rhetoricians—"Tullius qui in arce eloquentiae romanae stetit rex oratorum et latinae linguae illustrator." [11] Rufinus relates, not without malice, that he would in his later years pay his copyists more highly for the transcription of Cicero's dialogues than for that of ecclesiastical works,[12] and that he taught the children at Bethlehem to read Virgil and the poets. In fact, far from being an enemy to the classical tradition, Jerome is of all the Fathers the most steeped in pagan literature and the most deeply influenced by the rhetorical tradi-

tion. Even the intolerance and pugnacity which have scandalised so many modern critics do not spring from the fanaticism of a bigot, but from the irascibility of a scholar, and his
literary vendettas are often curiously similar to those of the
humanists of the Renaissance, who were themselves among
his warmest admirers.[18]

The influence of Jerome was indeed second to none, not
even to that of Augustine, but it was the influence of a
scholar, not of a thinker or a theologian. In him the two great
spiritual traditions of the classics and the Bible meet together,
and from him they flow out again in a single stream to
fertilise the culture of the Middle Ages.

The influence of the classical tradition is even more clearly
discernible in the rise of a new Christian poetry; in the East,
however, save in the case of St. Gregory Nazianzen, the servile imitation of classical models destroyed all spontaneity of
feeling and found its supreme expression in the attempt of
Apollinarius of Laodicea and his son to translate the Bible
into the forms and metres of classical poetry. In the West,
the same tendency produced the Biblical paraphrases of
Juvencus and the ingenious but misguided attempts to com-
pose poems on Biblical subjects entirely made up of passages
from Virgil detached from their context. But the West possessed a far more living poetical tradition than the East, and
during the fourth and fifth centuries this tradition was fully
assimilated by the new Christian culture. Paulinus of Nola,
who found a kindred spirit in his English biographer, Henry
Vaughan, was a genuine Christian humanist, the spiritual ancestor of Vida and Mantuanus. He was not a great poet, but
he was a man of high culture and of noble and attractive character, and his influence did more even than that of Jerome or
Augustine to popularise the ideals of the new Christian culture among the educated classes in the Western provinces.

But the greatest of the Christian poets was Paulinus' Spanish contemporary, Prudentius, whom Bentley termed "the
Christian Virgil and Horace." Of all the Christian writers,
Prudentius shows the fullest appreciation of the classical tradition in both its literary and its social aspects. He yields to
none of the pagan poets in his civic patriotism and his devotion to the great name of Rome. He does not look on Rome
with the eyes of Tertullian and Augustine as a mere manifestation of human pride and ambition. Like Dante, he sees in
the Empire a providential preparation for the unity of man-

kind in Christ. The Fabii and the Scipios were the uncon-
scious instruments of the divine purpose, and the martyrs
gave their lives for Rome no less than the legionaries. The
last words of St. Laurence in the *Peristephanon* are a prayer
for Rome. "O Christ, grant to thy Romans that the city by
which Thou hast granted to the rest to be of one mind in
religion should itself become Christian. . . . May it teach
lands far apart to come together in one grace; may Romulus
become faithful and Numa himself believe." [14] Now this
prayer had been fulfilled; the Rome of the consuls and the
Rome of the martyrs had become one. "To-day the lights of
the Senate kiss the threshold of the temple of the apostles.
The Pontiff who wore the sacred fillets bears on his brow the
mark of the cross, and the Vestal Claudia kneels before the
altar of St. Laurence." [15]

In the poems of Prudentius and in those of Paulinus of
Nola we see how the cult of the martyrs, which had its origins
in the protest of the Christian mind against the anti-spiritual
claims of the secular power, had become transformed into a
social institution and a manifestation of civic piety. To Prudentius, the old local patriotism of the city-state finds a new
justification through the cult of the local saints. He shows us
the cities of Spain presenting themselves before the judg-
ment-seat of God, each bearing the relics of its native martyrs.
The saint has become the representative and guardian of the
city and imparts to it a share in his glory.

> Sterne te totam generosa sanctis
> Civitas mecum tumulis; deinde
> Mox resurgentes animas et artus
> Tota sequeris.[16]

The reconciliation between Christianity and the classical
tradition in the fourth and fifth centuries, which finds expression in the patristic culture and the new Christian poetry, had
a profound influence on the formation of the European mind.
The modern is apt to regard the whole rhetorical tradition as
empty pedantry, and to dismiss Cicero himself as a pompous
bore. But, as I have already pointed out, it is to the rhetorician and his educational work that we owe the survival of
classical literature and the whole tradition of humanism.
Without them European culture would not only have been
poorer, it would have been fundamentally different. There
would have been no tradition of secular learning, no secular

literature, save that of the minstrel and the saga-writer. The
higher culture would have been entirely religious, as it has
tended to be in the oriental world outside China. The survival
of classical literature and the rhetorical tradition not only
made possible the rise of the modern European literatures;
they also formed the European habit of mind, and rendered
possible that rational and critical attitude to life and nature
which is peculiar to Western civilisation. The coexistence of
these two spiritual and literary traditions—that of the Church
and the Bible on the one hand, and that of Hellenism and the
classics on the other—has left a profound mark on our culture, and their mutual influence and interpenetration has enriched the Western mind in a way that no single tradition,
however great, could have done by itself.

It is true that this rhetorical and literary habit of mind has
its defects, and it is perhaps partially responsible for that
artificiality which is one of the greatest weaknesses of our
civilisation. Moreover, the coexistence of two intellectual traditions of disparate origin has tended to produce a certain
dualism and disharmony in European culture that is absent in
civilisations of a simpler or more uniform type. Nor can it be
said that the rhetorical tradition was a complete embodiment
of the intellectual achievement of the ancient world. It was a
partial and one-sided development, which represents one aspect of the Hellenic genius, but fails to do justice to its
scientific and metaphysical achievements. The true responsibility for the failure of mediaeval culture to preserve the inheritance of Greek science rests not on the Church, but on the
rhetoricians. The scientific tradition of the Greek world had
become separated from the literary tradition of the rhetoricians during the Hellenistic period, and consequently it was
never assimilated by the Latin West as was the literary side of
Greek culture. The only Latin contributions to science were
the encyclopaedias of cultivated amateurs like Varro and Pliny
and the technical works of engineers and surveyors (*gro-
matici*). All the real scientific work of the age was due to
Greeks, such as Galen and Claudius Ptolemaeus (Ptolemy) in
the second century A.D., who were the last creative minds in
ancient science; but it is significant that although Galen lived
and worked at Rome, his writings were never translated into
Latin until the Middle Ages.

The scientific tradition still survived during the later Empire, but it was confined to the East and flourished mainly in

the schools of Alexandria and Athens, which were at this period almost monopolised by the Neoplatonists. It was the aim of the latter, from the fourth century onwards, to combine the whole body of Greek science in an organic unity based on their own metaphysical and theological doctrines. Above all, they aimed at the reconciliation of Aristotle with Plato and Ptolemy with Aristotle, and consequently their energies were directed not to original research but to interpreting and commentating the older authorities. Their curriculum was based on the works of Euclid and Nicomachus, Ptolemy and Geminos, Aristotle and Plato, but the importance of Aristotle steadily increased and reached its climax in the Alexandrian philosophers of the sixth century—Ammonius, Simplicius, Damascius and the Christian John Philoponus, all of whom show an extraordinarily wide knowledge of ancient science. This Aristotelian revival, which had begun as early as the beginning of the third century with the great commentator Alexander of Aphrodisias, was of the greatest importance for the future; but it did not reach the Latin West, save in a very rudimentary form through Boethius, until the twelfth and thirteenth centuries.

But although the later scientific development of Greek culture failed to affect the West, later Greek philosophy, as represented by Neoplatonism, had a direct influence on the new Latin Christian culture. Up to this point, philosophy in the West had been represented mainly by the Stoic ethics embodied in the rhetorical tradition, above all in the writings of Cicero and Seneca. There had been no creative metaphysical thought and no original psychological observation. Now at the very close of the imperial epoch the Latin world produced in St. Augustine a profoundly original genius, in whose thought the new Christian culture found its highest philosophic expression. Augustine also was a rhetorician by profession, and it was from Cicero that his mind first received an impulse towards the study of philosophy. But the turning-point in his life was eleven years later, when he came under the influence of the writings of the Neoplatonists that had been translated into Latin by the converted rhetorician Marius Victorinus. By them he was first convinced of the objective existence of spiritual reality, and from them he derived the two fundamental principles which remained the poles of his philosophy—the idea of God as the source of being and intelligence, the Sun of the intelligible world; and the idea of the soul as a

spiritual nature which finds its beatitude in the participation
of the Uncreated Light.

But Augustine was not contented with the intellectualism
of Greek philosophy. He demanded not a speculative theory
of truth, but its experimental possession. "The Platonists," he
says, "indeed saw the Truth fixed, stable, unfading, in which
are all the forms of all created things, but they saw it from
afar . . . and therefore they could not find the way by which
they might attain to so great and ineffable and beatific a possession." [17]

This *way* he found only in Christianity—in the supernatural
wisdom which not only shows man the truth, but gives him
the means of attaining to its fruition. His philosophy acquired
its final character from the experience of his own conversion,
the realisation of the intervention of a spiritual power which
was strong enough to change his personality and to transform
the notional order of intelligence into a vital order of charity.
The spiritual evolution which began with the *Hortensius* of
Cicero ends in the *Confessions*, and the *sapientia* of the Roman rhetorician finds its fulfillment in the *contemplatio* of
the Christian mystic.

Thus the philosophy of Augustine differs from that of Origen, the greatest Christian thinker of the Greek world, in its
intensely personal character. It remains Hellenic in its insistence on the existence of a rational order pervading the world,
and in its sense of the goodness and beauty of all created
being.[18] But it was both Western and Christian in its moral
preoccupations and by reason of the central position which it
accords to the will.

The philosophy of Augustine is essentially a philosophy of
spiritual experience, and as such it is the source of Western
mysticism and of Western ethics, as well as of the Western
tradition of philosophic idealism.

In the fifth and sixth centuries, the influence of Augustine
became dominant throughout the Christian West. Orosius,
Prosper of Aquitaine, Leo the Great, Fulgentius of Ruspe,
were all of them Augustinians; and finally through St. Gregory the Great the Augustinian tradition in a simplified form
became the intellectual patrimony of the mediaeval Church.
But this theological tradition was accompanied by a growing
alienation from classical culture. The very profundity of Augustinian thought tended to narrow the range of intellectual
activity and to concentrate all attention on the two poles of

the spiritual life—God and the soul. This religious absolutism left no room either for pure literature or for pure science. For, to St. Augustine, the knowledge "wherein men desire nothing but to know" is an unprofitable curiosity that distracts the mind from its one true goal—the knowledge and the love of God. It is better for a man to know God than to number the stars or to seek out the hidden secrets of nature. "Surely unhappy is he who knoweth all these and knoweth not Thee, but happy whoso knoweth Thee, though he know not these. And whoso knoweth both Thee and them is not happier for them, but for Thee only." [19]

This view was destined to dominate the clerical and monastic culture of the Latin West for many centuries. Nevertheless, so long as the West preserved the Roman-Byzantine tradition of an educated bureaucracy trained in the schools of rhetoric, there was no risk of classical culture being undervalued. Even the temporary recovery of secular culture that accompanied the Byzantine revival of the sixth century was not without its counterpart in the West. This is especially the case in Africa, where the court of the last Vandal kings was frequented—surprisingly enough—by the swarm of minor poets whose verses are preserved in the four-and-twenty books of the Salmasian anthology, and where the subsequent period produced the respectable epic of Corippus—the *Johannis*—perhaps the last genuine representative of the classical tradition in Latin poetry. So, too, in Italy under the rule of Theodoric the civil administration was still in the hands of highly cultivated officials like Boethius, Symmachus and Cassiodorus, and they did all that was in their power to preserve the inheritance of classical learning. Boethius was not only the last of the classics, he was also the first of the scholastics, a great educator, through whom the mediaeval West received its knowledge of Aristotelian logic and the rudiments of Greek mathematics. His tragic death put an end to the work of philosophical translation that he had planned, but in compensation it gave the world the *De Consolatione Philosophiae*—a masterpiece which, in spite of its deliberate reticence, is a perfect expression of the union of the Christian spirit with the classical tradition.

The same ideal inspired the work of Cassiodorus, who did even more than Boethius to build a bridge between the culture of the ancient world and that of the Middle Ages. In the first part of his life, as a minister of state in the service of the

Gothic régime, he devoted himself to the promotion of religious unity and the reconciliation of the Germanic invaders to Roman culture, while his later life was dedicated to the service of the Church and to the reconciliation of classical culture with the needs of the new ecclesiastical society and the ideals of the monastic life. It is as though he realised that the state could no longer serve as an organ of the higher culture and that the inheritance of classical civilisation could be saved only by being placed under the tutelage of the Church. In the last years of Gothic rule he planned, in co-operation with Pope Agapitus, to found a Christian school at Rome which should perform somewhat the same function for the West that the catechetical school of Alexandria had fulfilled in the East at an earlier period.

These plans were frustrated by the outbreak of the Gothic wars, which had a more disastrous effect on Italian culture than all the invasions of the previous century. But Cassiodorus refused to be discouraged. Though he was forced to abandon public life and to take refuge in the cloister, he found an opportunity for the realisation of his ideal in the monastery that he founded in his great Calabrian estates at Vivarium. Here he collected a library and drew up his two programmes of monastic studies—the *Institutes of Divine and Secular Letters* —which are one of the fundamental documents for the history of mediaeval culture. The first and most important of these works deals with religious learning and insists on the need for a high standard of scholarship in the study and reproduction of the Sacred Text; the second is an encyclopaedic compendium of the seven Liberal Arts, especially grammar, rhetoric and dialectic. It is the old curriculum of the later Empire adapted to the needs of the new religious society. As with Gregory Nazianzen and Augustine, the arts are regarded as an instrument of religious education, not as an end in themselves. But they are a necessary instrument, since the neglect of them involves the weakening and impoverishment of the theological culture that they serve. Even the study of the pagan poets and prose writers is regarded as legitimate and even necessary, since without them it was impossible to receive a complete training in the Liberal Arts.

Thus Vivarium was the starting-point of the tradition of monastic learning that was afterwards to become the glory of the Benedictine Order. Western monasticism entered into the heritage of the classical culture and saved it from the ruin that overwhelmed the secular civilisation of the Latin West at the end of the sixth century. It is to the monastic libraries and scriptoria that we owe the preservation and translation of almost the entire body of Latin classical literature that we possess to-day. It is true that Italian monasticism was itself affected by this collapse, and Cassiodorus left no successors in his own land. His work was taken up and completed by the children of a new world—the Irish and Anglo-Saxon monks, who prepared the way for that revival of Christian classicism which finally emerged in the Carolingian period.

IV

THE BARBARIANS

The three elements that have been described above are the true foundations of European unity, but they do not of themselves constitute Europe. They are the formative influences which have shaped the material of our civilisation, but the material itself is to be found elsewhere, in the obscure chaos of the barbarian world. For it is the barbarians who provided the human material out of which Europe has been fashioned; they are the *gentes* as against the *imperium* and the *ecclesia*—the source of the national element in European life.

In the past the importance of this element was minimised by the scholars and ecclesiastics who controlled education and thought, for their attention was concentrated on the traditions of the higher culture, whether literary or religious, of which they were the appointed guardians, and they were naturally hostile to anything which savoured of barbarism. It was not until the nineteenth century that the vital importance of the national contribution to European civilisation was fully realised. Then at last there came a sweeping reaction, and the new current of romantic nationalism led writers to minimise the classical and Christian elements in our culture and to derive everything from the native energy of the national genius. This is the spirit which dominates the Teutonic school of nineteenth-century historians, both in Germany and in this country, the Pan-Slavonic writers in Eastern Europe, and the adherents of the Celtic revival in Ireland and France. And to-day the tendency finds its culmination in the theories of writers like Strzygowski, who argue that European history has been progressively falsified by the malign influence of the classical tradition and of the Catholic Church, both of them originating in the Mediterranean—that forcing-house of effete and artificial culture—and who find the true affinities of the Nordic European spirit in the art and culture of the barbarians of the Asiatic steppes.

And, in spite of such exaggerations, this reaction has its justifications. For the barbarian peoples were not merely a passive and negative background for the creative activities of the higher culture. They had cultural traditions of their own, and we are only now beginning to learn from prehistoric research how ancient and deeply rooted these traditions were. As far back as the Bronze Age, and even earlier, there were centres of culture in Central and Northern Europe which had an autonomous development and which exerted an influence not only on the surrounding peoples but even on the higher culture of the Eastern Mediterranean.

It may seem at first sight unjustifiable to describe ancient cultures of this kind as barbaric. But barbarism in the sense in which we are using the word is by no means the same thing as savagery. It is applied to any stage of social development which has not acquired the higher organisation of a settled urban and territorial state—in short, to the culture of the tribe as against that of the city. The essence of barbaric society is that it rests on the principle of kinship rather than on that of citizenship or that of the absolute authority of the state. It is true that kinship is not the only element in tribal society; in practically every case the territorial and the military factors also intervene. But whereas in a civilised state the unit is the individual or the economic group, the unit of tribal society is the group of kinsmen. A man's rights depend not on his direct relation to the state, but on his position in the kindred, and in the same way crime is not conceived as an offence against the state, but as an occasion of feud or negotiation between two groups of kinsfolk. The guilt of blood lies on the whole kindred of the slayer and must be atoned by compensation to the kindred of the slain. It is true that the higher political unit of the tribe or clan does not necessarily consist of men of common blood, though they are apt to claim such unity by some genealogical fiction. It is usually a territorial or military union of groups of kinsmen.

Consequently, in spite of the protests of patriotic Irish scholars, such as Professor MacNeil and Professor Macalister, it is legitimate to describe the social organisation of Celtic Ireland as a tribal one, since it was, no less than that of the ancient Germans, based on kinship-groups, such as the sept or the clan.[1] The reluctance to accept this definition is, of course, due to the suggestion of cultural inferiority which the word "tribe" carries with it. Nevertheless, though the tribe is a relatively primitive form of social organisation, it possesses virtues which many more advanced types of society may envy. It is consistent with a high ideal of personal freedom and self-respect and evokes an intense spirit of loyalty and devotion on the part of the individual tribesman towards the community and its chief. Consequently its moral and spiritual development is often far in advance of its material culture. The tribal ideal, at least in the case of the more warlike pastoral peoples, is essentially of the heroic type. In fact, we may say that all the great heroic traditions which are the inspiration of epic poetry and national legend, whether Greek, Celtic, Germanic or Arab, owe their existence to the tribal culture, though as a rule only at the moment when it has come into contact with the higher culture and is itself in process of dissolution.

At the time when Roman civilisation came into contact with the barbarian world, this warlike tribal culture of the Celts and the Germans was dominant throughout continental Europe and gave it a superficial appearance of national and cultural unity. Nevertheless, barbarian culture was never a single or uniform thing. There was an extreme variety of local types which crossed with one another and produced new mixed forms of culture. Just as in West Africa to-day we may see native states with a relatively high type of social and political organisation existing side by side with tribes whose way of life was hardly changed since remote prehistoric ages, so it was in barbarian Europe. The way in which we map out ancient Europe among a comparatively small number of historic people—Celts, Germans, Thracians and so on—gives a very misleading idea of the real situation. For these peoples were not, as we are apt to imagine, nations, but loose tribal groups which might embrace or overlie the remnants of numerous older peoples and cultures. A group of warlike tribes might overrun a great territory and give their name to it, but they did not thereby create a unified state and culture. Underneath the ruling society and the conquering warriors the life of the conquered peasants still went on, sometimes possessing its own language and religion, and always tending to preserve a distinct social and cultural tradition.

Consequently, the more warlike a society is, the more superficial and disunified in its culture. Successive waves of conquest do not necessarily involve a change of population; in many cases they amount to no more than the substitution of one warrior aristocracy for another. The ruling class is often responsible for the introduction of the development of a new and higher type of culture, but it has no permanence and it may pass away without leaving any permanent impression on the life of the peasant population. On the other hand, in those regions which have been little affected by war and conquest, there are no sharp contrasts between the different elements of society. The whole people tends to possess a uniform culture, though it is often of simple and primitive type. Cultures of this type are naturally deep rooted and are not easily changed, but as a rule they are to be found only in the more backward and unfertile regions which do not attract the greed of a conqueror. The richest and most favoured lands are those which undergo the most frequent invasions, and these are consequently the regions which possess the least social unity and experience the most rapid changes of culture.

These factors were of exceptional importance in barbarian Europe owing to the warlike character of the population and the numerous movements of invasion. In fact, we shall see that the duality of culture—the contrast between the warrior noble and the peasant serf—was not confined to the age of the Barbarians, but was transmitted to later periods, and had an important influence on the development of mediaeval culture.

Of all these warrior cultures the greatest and the most typical is that of the Celts. Starting from their homelands in south-western Germany and north-eastern France, the Celtic warriors with their broad swords and their war chariots swept over the whole breadth of Europe, sacking Rome and Delphi and conquering every people between the Atlantic and the Black Sea. Their outlying settlements were established in the heart of Asia Minor and in the Ukraine, and the whole of Central Europe, including the valleys of the Rhine and the Rhone, the Danube, and the Upper Elbe, the Po and the Dniester, were in their possession.[2]

Obviously this vast extent of territory was not occupied by a homogeneous Celtic population. The Celtic tribesmen formed a warrior aristocracy who governed their conquered territories from the great hill camps or *duns* whose remains are still scattered over Europe. Wherever they went they brought with them a distinctive type of culture and art which was developed in the Alpine lands in the sixth and fifth centuries B.C., and which takes its name from the Swiss station of La Tene. Thus for the first time in history the greater part of continental Europe was united in a common culture. From the Atlantic to the Black Sea there was one ruling race, speaking the same language, possessing the same type of social organisation and the same manners and way of life. But it was a culture of chieftains and warriors which did not deeply affect the lives of the subject populations or entirely replace the older local traditions of culture. Only in the extreme west, in Ireland, where the Celtic conquerors remained in undisturbed possession for a thousand years, did their culture permeate the whole society. Elsewhere it passed away as quickly as it had come before the advent of a stronger power —that of the Roman Empire, which reaped the fruits of the Celtic conquests. The Gauls who sacked Rome in the fourth century did not guess how the whole fortunes of their races were bound up with that of this contemptible little Italian city-state. Yet so it was to be.

Beginning with the Gallic tribes of North Italy, Rome gradually encroached on the territory of the Celts until the whole of their great empire was destroyed. Where the Celts had broken down the resistance of the local cultures, Rome followed. But when she came into contact with the simpler and more homogeneous society of the Germanic peoples her progress was stayed. In fact, the extension of the Roman Empire in Europe coincides to a remarkable extent with that of the Celtic territories.[3]

There was, however, an important exception. Owing to the fact that the Romans adopted the line of the Danube as their frontier, two of the most ancient and important centres of culture in continental Europe—Bohemia-Moravia and Transylvania-Wallachia—remained outside the Empire. Nevertheless in these regions also the Celtic hegemony disappeared in the first century B.C., and new states were founded as a result of Germanic invasions and of the reassertion of the native element in the population. In 68 B.C. Burebista founded the Dacian kingdom on the Lower Danube, and seventy-four years later Marboduus, the King of the Marcomanni, conquered Bohemia and organised a powerful state. These kingdoms, and especially the latter, were the chief intermediaries between the barbarian world and the Roman Empire. They were in close contact with the Roman provinces and adopted many elements of the higher culture from the Roman traders and craftsmen who established themselves in their territories.

In this way there arose a mixed Roman-barbarian type of culture which spread far and wide through Continental Europe. Even in the far north the whole material culture of Scandinavia, which had remained in a backward state during the earlier part of the Iron Age, was now transformed by the influence of Mediterranean civilisation, which reached the Baltic not only by the maritime trade route from Northern Gaul and the mouth of the Rhine, but also directly from Central Europe by way of the Elbe and the Vistula. The use of classical ornament in design, such as the meander pattern which characterises the art of the period in Jutland, the adoption of Roman types of weapons and armour, the importation of Roman glass-ware, bronzes and coins, all testify to the strength of the current of influence from the south which was at this time affecting Nordic culture. Professor Shetelig even goes so far as to suggest that the appearance in southeast Norway and in Gotland of a new type of burial and tomb-furniture resembling that of the Roman borderlands is to be attributed to northern warriors who had returned to their homes after having served as mercenaries in the armies of the Marcomanni. And the same writer believes that the earliest Teutonic system of writing—the Runic alphabet—originated in the Marcomannic kingdom in the second century A.D. rather than, as it has usually been supposed, in the Gothic kingdom of South Russia in the following century.[4]

But however this may be, there can be no doubt that South Russia was the principal channel through which the influence of Mediterranean civilisation reached the eastern part of the barbarian world. From the first age of Greek colonisation down to the Byzantine period the Greek cities of the Crimea and the neighbouring regions—especially Olbia and Chersonesus together with the Hellenised native state of Bosporus—carried on an active trade with the peoples of the Russian steppe. South Russia was one of the chief sources of corn supply in the ancient world, and the Greek, Scythian and Sarmatian tombs of the region are full of the finest products of Greek, Campanian and Alexandrian art and industry.[5] During the Roman period the Sarmatians, an Iranian people from Central Asia, had taken the place of the Scythians as the dominant power in the steppes, and Iranian influences began to affect the Graeco-Scythian culture of the coastland. But the Greek cities still flourished under Roman protection, and the products of Mediterranean industry continued to find their way far into the heart of Russia.

Thus, in the second century A.D., the barbarian world was exposed from every side to influences coming from the higher civilisation of the Mediterranean world, and the whole of Continental Europe seemed in a fair way to become Romanised. By the following century, however, the situation had completely changed. The influence of Roman civilisation was no longer in the ascendant, and the increasing pressure of the barbarian world threatened the very existence of the Empire. Henceforward Rome stands on the defensive, and even her own civilisation begins to show traces of barbarian influences.

Nevertheless, this reassertion of the barbaric element in European life was itself in a large measure due to the work of Rome. The pressure which the Empire had exerted for centuries on the Germanic peoples by its military power and its civilising influence had transformed their culture and changed the conditions of their national life. They had acquired new methods of warfare and had been forced to combine in resistance to the disciplined power of Rome. Moreover, their natural tendency towards expansion had been checked by a relentless pressure from the Roman frontiers, so that the border peoples had been forced back on the interior. Already in the second century A.D. the whole of the outer lands were seething with the suppressed agitation of forces which could only find their outlet by some violent explosion. The wars on the Danube in the time of Trajan and Marcus Aurelius, though apparently successful, did nothing to allay this agitation. On the contrary they brought the crisis nearer by the destruction of Dacia and the Marcomannic Kingdom, which were the only stable elements in the barbaric world and the main channels for the diffusion of Roman cultural influence. Henceforward the screen of half-civilised buffer states is destroyed, and the Empire is brought into immediate contact with the moving forces of barbarism of the interior.

From the time of the Marcomannic wars the Germanic world begins to assume a new form. The old peoples of whom we read in Caesar and Tacitus have vanished and in their place we find new groups of peoples formed either by the coming of new peoples from the north or by the fusion of the broken remnants of the older tribes in new warlike confederations or national leagues.

On the lower Rhine the Franks make their appearance, in Southern Germany the Allemanni are the dominant power, while to the east there are the federation of the Hermunduri, the Vandals in Silesia and, greatest of all, the Goths in the Ukraine and South Russia.

The latter had migrated in the second century from their old homes on the Baltic to South Russia, where they came into contact with the Iranian Sarmatians of the steppe. Early in the third century they advanced to the Black Sea and founded a powerful state of mixed Germanic and Sarmatian elements. The Greek cities of the Crimea, the third great centre of civilising influence in the barbarian world, lost their independence. Olbia and Tyras were destroyed, while Cherson and the Hellenised kingdom of Bosporus were subjugated. Henceforward the region ceased to be the main source for the diffusion of Graeco-Roman culture in Eastern Europe and became instead the centre of a new barbaric culture from which new oriental, and especially Iranian, influences were transmitted to the whole of the Germanic world.

For together with these changes there was taking place a general shifting of the axis of culture which had a profound influence on European civilisation. On the one hand the culture and economic life of the Empire was progressively losing its vitality owing to the causes that have already been described, and on the other the Oriental world was awakening to new cultural activity. The foundation of the new Persian kingdom of the Sassanids in A.D. 226 was the most epoch-

making event of the third century, for it marks not only the
rise of a new oriental world-power but even more the reassertion of the native Iranian tradition of culture against the
hegemony of Western, or rather Hellenistic civilisation
which had dominated both East and West for five hundred
years. The Mediterranean world was now threatened not only
by the Northern Barbarians but by the challenge of a civilisation even older than its own, which had recovered its vitality
and now sought to impose its supremacy on its former conquerors.

In the middle of the third century the storm burst. The
Empire, weakened by civil war and continual mutinies, was
attacked by its enemies on every frontier—by the Persians in
the East, by the Goths and Sarmatians on the Danube, and by
the Franks and the Allemanni on the Rhine.

Throughout the reign of Gallienus (253-268) the Empire
was devastated from end to end by the ravages of barbarian
invasions, civil war and pestilence. Antioch was sacked by the
Persians, Athens was taken by the Goths, and the temple of
Diana at Ephesus was burnt by the Sarmatians. The Franks
and the Allemanni ravaged Gaul and Italy, and even in distant Spain the rich city of Tarracona was destroyed. Nevertheless Rome did not perish. It was saved by the Illyrian
soldier-emperors, Claudius, Aurelian and Probus, who beat
back the barbarians, defeated the attempts of provincial
usurpers to disintegrate the Empire, and re-established the
frontiers of the Rhine and the Danube, sacrificing only the
outworks of Dacia and south-west Germany.

But, as we have seen, it was no longer the same empire.
The new empire of Diocletian and Constantine was a semi-
oriental state that resembled the Persian monarchy more than
the Roman republic. It no longer rested on the foundation of
a citizen army, but on a semi-barbaric militia, supported by
barbarian auxiliaries from beyond the frontiers. And, in the
same way, the emperors were no longer the presidents of the
Roman Senate and the representatives of the old civic tradition, like Augustus and the Antonines. They lived either on
the frontiers, surrounded by their barbarian men-at-arms, like
Valentinian I, or surrounded by their eunuchs and officials in
the oriental seclusion of the court life of Constantinople or
Ravenna, like Honorius and Theodosius II. In fact the Empire
itself had changed its orientation. It no longer looked inwards

to the Mediterranean world of city-states with its centre at Rome, but outwards from its new capitals of Treves and Milan and Sirmium and Constantinople to the frontiers of the Rhine, the Danube and Euphrates. The great age of Mediterranean culture was over and a new period of continental development had begun.

V

THE BARBARIAN INVASIONS AND THE FALL OF THE EMPIRE IN THE WEST

The age of the barbarian invasions and the foundation of the new Germanic kingdoms in the West has always been regarded as one of the great turning-points in world history; and as the boundary between the ancient and mediaeval worlds. It may be compared with the age of invasion which destroyed the Mycenean civilisation of the Ægean world in that it marks the appearance of a new racial element and the beginning of a new cultural development. Nevertheless it is easy to exaggerate the catastrophic character of the change. The breach with the old tradition of culture was far less sudden and less complete than that which occurred at the beginning of the Iron Age.

As we have already seen, the life had passed out of the ancient classical civilisation as early as the third century, and a new culture had arisen which was due not to the coming of the Germanic barbarians but to the infiltration of new influences from the East. The old culture of the city-state with its civic religion passed away owing to a gradual process of internal change, and its place was taken by a theocratic monarchy in close alliance with the new world-religion—Christianity. But while in the East this development was closely linked with a native oriental tradition of immense antiquity, in the West it was entirely new, with no basis in past history; and here, accordingly, it failed to strike root. In

its place we find the old European type of tribal society tending to reassert itself, and on the ruins of the provincial city-
states there re-appears a rural society of noble landowners
and peasant serfs, such as had existed in Central Europe before the coming of Rome. Consequently the new age in the
West is not to be explained solely by the forcible intrusion of
the Germanic peoples, but also to the renaissance of an older
type of society on the soil of the Empire itself, as we see with
special clearness in Western Britain. In fact, the break-up of
the imperial system and the rise of the new territorial states
might have followed very much the same course, even without the intervention of the barbarian invaders.

This transformation of society in the Western provinces of
the Empire had already begun as far back as the end of the
second century A.D. Its leading feature was the decline of the
municipalities and of the middle classes, and the reformation
of society on the basis of the two classes of landowner and
peasant. We have already seen how the increasing pressure of
taxation and of governmental control crushed the life out of
the self-governing municipalities which had been the living
cells of the earlier Roman imperial organism. The government
did all in its power by forced measures to galvanise the machinery of municipal life into artificial activity and to prevent
the middle classes from deserting the city or escaping their
obligations by entering the ranks of the senatorial aristocracy
or buying a privileged sinecure in the imperial service. But
what they tried to build up with one hand, they destroyed
with the other, since they rendered the life of the middle class
economically impossible. Consequently the government was
forced to supplement the decaying city magistracy both by an
imperial official—the count—who was directly responsible to
the central government and stood outside the municipal constitution, as well as by transferring responsibility to influential individuals such as neighbouring landowners or Christian
bishops.

The city was, in fact, no longer a vital organ in the life of
the Empire. Economically, the state was becoming purely
agrarian and the primary concern of the government was to
maintain the numbers of the rural population and the prosperity of agriculture. The whole finance of the Empire depended on the land tax, which was assessed not upon income
but on a definite unit—the *jugum* or, in the western provinces, the *centuria*—which represented the holding of a single

peasant. It was the same principle as the old English hide—in theory, the land of a single family, which was at once a fiscal unit and a rough measure of land.[1] In both cases the unit was based on the amount of land which could be cultivated with a single team of oxen, but in the West this was very much larger than in the East, owing partly to the use of a team of eight oxen instead of two, partly to the lower standard of cultivation and taxation. The size of the Roman unit differed according to its productivity. In the East it might be 5 acres of vineyard, and of good arable land, or 60 acres of poorer quality, while in the West the Centuria consisted of 200 *jugera*, i.e., 120 acres. But, in any case, it was a definite unit, actually measured and registered by the officers of the cadastral survey. The assessment was known as *capitatio* (poll-tax) as well as *jugatio* (land tax), which shows the close connection between the land and the labourer. If a single one of these units went out of cultivation it was a direct loss to the revenue; and consequently the government, following the Egyptian precedent, not only bound the free farmer and his heirs to their holding, but forbade landlords to sell land without the slaves that cultivated it, or *vice versâ*. Moreover, if a holding went out of cultivation owing to the death or disappearance of its owner, the neighbouring landowners were obliged to add it to their own holdings and became liable for the tax upon it. The policy of the government, however, defeated its own ends. The pressure of taxation was so great (at times it amounted to as much as 50 per cent. of the produce) that the small landowner was crushed out of existence, and driven to flight or to the slavery of debt.

All this favoured the expansion of the senatorial aristocracy, which alone had the power to protect itself and its dependents from the oppression of the fisc, since its members were assessed not by the magistrates of the neighbouring city, but by the governor himself. It is true that the power of the landlord over his slaves was considerably limited. They were no longer chattels to be bought and sold; they were serfs—*ascripticii glebae*—who could not be separated from their holdings, and who consequently enjoyed their own family life. But, on the other hand, in compensation, the power of the landlord over his free tenants was enormously increased. Their tenure, as a rule, involved not only the payment of rent, but also a specified period of work on the lord's own land. Since he was responsible for their tax, they also, no less than the slaves, were bound to the soil. And since the lord represented them to the revenue, he also came to represent them before the law. He possessed police powers, and in many cases he held his own local court and executed justice among his dependents. Thus slaves and tenants became fused in a single class of semi-servile peasants, in absolute political and social dependence on their lord, and to these were joined a growing number of small landowners, who sought to escape the oppression of the tax-gatherer by recommending themselves to the patronage of a neighbouring noble and resigning to him the property of their land, on condition that they should continue to enjoy the use of it.

Thus already before the fall of the Empire, a semi-feudal condition of society was establishing itself. In the fifth century we hear of nobles like Ecdicius, who could support 4,000 poor in time of famine, and raise his own troop of horse in time of war; and the fortified "Burgus" of Pontius Leontius, which is described by Sidonius Apollinaris, with its walls and towers, might be the castle of a mediaeval baron. As the Roman organisation weakened, the old conditions of pre-Roman Gallic society, which was based on the relation of the noble "patron" to his dependent "clients," re-asserted themselves in a new guise. The senatorial noble lived on his lands, surrounded by the villages of his dependents. Part of his land was in his own hands, cultivated by the household slaves (*casarii*) and by the labour that was due from the tenants (*coloni*). The rest consisted of peasant holdings which paid rent and service to him.

This self-sufficient system of rural economy had grown up on the great imperial estates, which were administered as autonomous units by the procurators of the Empire and were jealously protected from all interference on the part of the municipalities or the provincial authorities. In Africa, especially, we find the system already fully developed as early as the second century A.D., and under the later Empire it spread to the great estates of the senatorial aristocracy. In many respects it resembles the later mediaeval manor, and in France, at least, the majority of villages are derived not from the Roman *vici* or from barbarian settlements, but as their names denote, from a private or imperial estate of the later Empire. In fact, throughout a great part of Gaul the land-owning nobility and the corresponding system of agrarian organisation survived the Germanic conquest and supplied one of the

main links of continuity between the Roman and the mediaeval worlds.

This social order did not pass away with the fall of the
Western Empire. On the contrary, the Barbarian Invasions
tended, on the whole, to favour its development by destroying
the complicated machinery of the imperial bureaucracy, and
thus increasing the centrifugal tendencies in society.

It is important to remember that, apart from a few exceptional crises, the Germanic settlement was a gradual process of
infiltration rather than a sudden catastrophe. As far back as
the second century A.D., the Roman government had adopted
the practice of settling barbarian captives in the provinces,
and during the fourth century enormous numbers of Germans
and Sarmatians were established in devastated areas, especially
in the Balkans and Northern Gaul, as agricultural and military colonists; so that the barbarian invaders usually found
the frontier districts occupied by men of their own blood, who
were familiar with Roman civilisation and had, to some extent, gone through a process of superficial Romanisation.

The army itself was largely recruited from these barbarian settlers, as well as from mercenaries and allies from beyond the frontiers, who, in the fourth century, came to form
the *élite* of the Roman troops. To many of the barbarians, in
fact, the Empire was, as Fustel de Coulanges has said, "not an
enemy but a career." This is true, above all, of the *foederati*,
the "allied peoples," who stood in the same relations to the
Empire as the tribes of the North-West Frontier to the Government of India, and supplied tribal levies to the imperial
army in return for regular subsidies. In the West the most
important of these peoples were the Franks, especially of the
Salian branch. After their defeat by Julian in 358, this people were allowed to settle in Toxandria or Northern Belgium
as *foederati* or allies. But even before this date Franks had
entered the army in large numbers. Constantine is said to
have favoured them, and Silvanus, the master of the troops,
who revolted against Constantine in 355, was the son of a
Frankish officer. In the second half of the fourth century many
of the leading figures in the history of the Western Empire
were Franks, such as Merobaudes, the minister of Gratian,
Arbogast, the king-maker and the most dangerous rival of
Theodosius, and Bauto, the father-in-law of the Emperor Arcadius.

Even more important was the position of the Goths in the

East; indeed, they were the true makers of history throughout
the period that we are considering. The Visigoths, who were
settled on the Lower Danube in Dacia and the neighbouring
regions, had become *foederati* of the Empire in 332, and
thenceforward remained at peace with the Romans for a generation. The Visigoths were the first of the Germanic peoples
to receive Christianity through the preaching of Ulfilas, a
Roman citizen of Gothic descent, who was the founder not
only of Germanic Christianity, but also of Teutonic literature
through his Gothic translation of the Bible. Owing, however,
to the domination of Arianism in the Eastern Empire at this
period, the Visigoths accepted an Arian form of Christianity,
and, through their influence, Arianism became the national
religion of all the East German peoples.

Meanwhile, the eastern section of the Gothic people, the
Ostrogoths, who had remained behind in South Russia, had
established a powerful independent kingdom, the supremacy
of which was recognised by all the peoples of Eastern Europe
from the mouth of the Vistula to the Caucasus. The culture
of this state, as we have seen, was not purely Germanic, but
owed its distinctive features to the conquered or allied Sarmatians, who were themselves strongly influenced by the culture of Iran and Central Asia.[2] In this way the Gothic peoples
acquired the new style of art and the new system of warfare
that they afterwards transmitted to the other Germanic peoples. The Sarmatians were essentially a people of horsemen,
and it is to them that we owe the invention (or at least the
introduction into Europe) of the use of stirrups and spurs.
This invention had a revolutionary effect on tactics by rend-
ering possible the development of heavy cavalry, which was
to dominate European warfare for the next thousand years.
In fact, the mail-clad Sarmatian and Gothic horseman, armed
with lance and sword, was the true ancestor and prototype of
the mediaeval knight.

But the Ostrogothic kingdom did not only exert a powerful
influence on the culture of the barbarian peoples; it was the
direct source of the movement which destroyed the unity of
the Roman Empire and created the new barbarian kingdoms
in the West. Throughout the period of invasions it was South
Russia and the Danube frontier, rather than Germany and the
Rhine, that were the storm-centre of Europe. It was here that
the southward migration of Germanic peoples from the Baltic
met the westward movement of Asiatic peoples from the

steppes, and their combined forces, pushed onwards by the pressure of new hordes of East Mongolian nomads in the rear, broke in an irresistible wave on the defences of the Roman Empire.

The ultimate source of this movement is to be found in the far East, on the frontiers of the Chinese Empire, whence the Huns, the age-long scourge of civilised China, had been expelled by the efforts of the Han emperors and the establishment of the great line of frontier defences from North China to Eastern Turkestan. The flood which was thus dyked back in the East flowed westwards until it piled up against the barriers of the Roman West.

In 49 B.C. the West Huns left their old homes and set out towards the West, followed a century and a half later by the remnants of the Northern Huns. By the third century they had driven the Sarmatians from the Volga region, and in the following century they invaded Europe. In A.D. 375 they overwhelmed the Ostrogothic Kingdom and advanced against the Visigoths. The latter threw themselves on the mercy of Rome and were allowed to cross the Danube and settle in Moesia, but the oppression of the Roman officials caused them to mutiny, and, reinforced by Ostrogoths and Sarmatian Alans from across the Danube, they invaded the Balkan provinces. In 378 they met the Emperor Valens and his army in front of Adrianople, and their victory was due to the irresistible onslaught of the Sarmatian and Ostrogothic horsemen, led by the Alan kings, Alatheus and Saphrax. This is one of the decisive battles of history, since it marks the definite victory of the barbarian cavalry over the Roman infantry.[3] Gratian and Theodosius were able to restore the power of the Empire, but they could not restore the prestige of the Roman legions. The Goths remained quartered in the Empire, the Visigoths in Moesia and the Ostrogoths in Pannonia, and Gothic and Alan contingents, serving under their own leaders, became the mainstay of the Roman armies. The favour which Gratian and Theodosius showed to their Alan and Gothic mercenaries was unpopular in the West and was one of the chief causes of the successive attempts of the Gallic armies, supported by conservative and pagan elements, to assert the independence of the Western Empire against Constantinople. The resultant civil wars had a disastrous effect on the fortunes of the Empire in the West. Not only were the Western armies weakened and demoralised by their defeats, but Theodosius was forced to transfer the capital of the Western Empire from Gaul to North Italy. From Milan and Ravenna the emperors were able to keep in touch with their colleagues in the East, but they could no longer guard the Western frontiers as they had done at Treves. Gaul was the vital centre of the Roman defensive system, and the withdrawal of the government to Italy prepared the way for the disintegration of the Western Empire.[4]

With the death of Theodosius the forces of destruction were finally unleashed. The Visigoths quartered in Moesia revolted, and after ravaging the Balkans, marched westward into Italy, followed by fresh hordes of barbarians from across the Upper Danube. The barbarian commander of the Western armies, Stilicho, the Vandal, succeeded in repelling the invaders for the moment, but the Rhine was left unguarded, and on the last day of A.D. 406 a horde of peoples, Vandals and Suevi, headed by the ubiquitous Alans, burst into Gaul, and after ravaging the country from end to end, passed on into Spain. The whole of the West was a chaos in which Roman generals, barbarian chiefs, and peasant insurgents fought one another indiscriminately. Far away at Bethlehem St. Jerome wrote: "A remnant of us survives not by our merits, but by the mercy of God. Innumerable savage peoples have occupied the whole of Gaul. All that lies between the Alps and the Pyrenees, the Rhine and the Ocean is devastated by the barbarian. . . . Formerly from the Julian Alps to the Black Sea our property was no longer our own, and for the space of thirty years the frontier of the Danube was broken and men fought over the lands of the Empire. Time has dried our tears, and save for a few greybeards, the rest, born in captivity and siege, no longer regret the liberty of which the very memory is lost. But who could believe that Rome, on her own soil, fights no longer for glory, but for her existence; and no longer even fights, but purchases her life with gold and precious things."[5]

Certainly in the second and third decades of the fifth century the last days of the Empire seemed to have come. Rome herself had been sacked by Alaric, his successor had established a Visigothic Kingdom in Southern France, the Vandals had conquered Africa, and the Franks, the Burgundians and the Allemanni had occupied the west bank of the Rhine, while the Huns devastated both the Eastern and the Western provinces. Nevertheless, as the turmoil subsided, the invaders found that it was not to their interest to destroy the Empire. The Goths had been allies of the Empire almost for a century, and during the last thirty years had been quartered on the Roman provinces. Consequently when they had conquered their new kingdoms in the West, they found no difficulty in establishing a *modus vivendi* with the Roman population and in admitting the nominal supremacy of the Empire. Athaulf the Visigoth himself declared that he had once wished to destroy the name of Rome and to be the founder of a new Gothic Empire, but he had come to realise that the undisciplined barbarism of the Goths was powerless to create a state without the laws of Rome, and he now preferred the glory of using the Gothic power to restore the Roman name.[6]

This programme was most fully realised in the Ostrogothic Kingdom which Theodoric established in Italy in 493. No other barbarian state reached so high a level of culture or assimilated the Roman tradition of government to the same extent. But, with the exception of the Vandals in Africa, who remained the irreconcilable enemies of Rome, the other East German peoples—the Visigoths in Spain and Southern Gaul, the Suevi in Spain and the Burgundians in Eastern Gaul—came to terms with the Empire and accepted the nominal status of allies or *foederati*.

They were quartered on the Roman provincials, as a kind of permanent garrison, in the same way in which they had been temporarily settled in the Danube provinces in the previous century. Thus the two peoples lived side by side, each preserving its own laws, its own institutions and its own religion—in the one case Catholic, in the other Arian. They were parasites upon the Roman social organism, and though they weakened its vitality, they did not destroy it. The life of the old Roman landowning aristocracy went on without essential change, as we see from the letters of Sidonius Apollinaris in Gaul and Cassiodorus in Italy, and like the latter, they often held high office under the new rulers.

Hence the East Germanic kingdoms were short lived. They had no roots in the soil and quickly withered away. In Gaul they were absorbed by the Franks, in Italy and Africa they were swept away by the Byzantine revival under Justinian, in Spain they were destroyed by the Moslem conquest at the beginning of the eighth century. In the North, however, the situation was different. The West German peoples swarmed across the frontiers—the Franks in Belgium and on the lower

Rhine, the Allemanni on the Upper Rhine and in Switzerland, the Rugians and the Bavarians on the Upper Danube—and took possession of the whole land. All these peoples were heathens, who still lived their old tribal life and had little contact with the higher Roman culture. They did not live as a parasitic military aristocracy on the conquered population like the Goths; they sought not subsidies, but land for settlement. The Roman landowning class was exterminated, the cities were in many cases destroyed, and a new tribal agrarian society came into existence. In so far as the old population survived, it was as serfs and vinedressers, or as refugees in the mountains and the forests.

In Britain the situation was rather different, for here the movement of invasion was twofold. From the middle of the fourth century the main danger to Roman Britain had come not from the Germans, but from the Celts beyond the frontiers, in Ireland and Scotland. In 367 their combined forces had swept over the whole country, and it was at this time that the majority of the towns and villas had been destroyed. At the same time the Saxon pirates were raiding the eastern and southern coasts of Britain as well as the western coasts of France.

Thus Roman British civilisation was caught between two fires and perished. Its last sign of vitality was the conversion of its Celtic destroyers by men like St. Ninian and St. Patrick, the latter the son of a British decurion who had been carried off to Ireland as a slave in one of the many invasions. The tradition that the Saxons were invited into Britain by the provincials themselves as a protection against the Picts and Scots is in itself very probable. For it is but another instance of the custom of quartering barbarian "allies" on the provinces in return for military services, and the departure of the legions would have left large tracts of land vacant for settlement. But by that time the Roman British civilisation was already moribund, and the subsequent history of the Saxon conquest is that of the struggle between two rival tribal societies—neither of them Roman in culture—the Celtic in Wales and Strathclyde, and the Germanic in Eastern Britain. It is true that the former was now Christian, but it was not the Christianity of the imperial Church with its city bishoprics and strict hierarchical constitution, such as had existed in Roman Britain. It was a new creation due to the grafting of Christianity on to the Celtic tribal culture. Its organisation was based on the local monastery rather than the diocesan bishopric, and it reached its highest development, not in Britain, but in Ireland, which in this age was the seat of a rich and original culture. The work of the Irish monastic schools and the Irish monastic saints was of enormous importance to European society in the age that followed the barbarian invasions, but it is not in them that the chief element of continuity with the civilisation of the ancient world is to be sought. The bridge between the Roman and the mediaeval worlds is to be found in Gaul. In the Mediterranean provinces the traditions of Roman culture were still overwhelmingly strong. In Roman Germany and Britain the barbarian tribal society had carried everything before it. It was only in Gaul that the two societies and the two cultures met on comparatively equal terms, and that the conditions were favourable to a process of fusion and unifica-tion which might supply the basis of a new order.

Before this was possible, however, it was necessary to find some principle of union. It was not enough for the barbarians to tolerate Roman culture and to adopt some of the external forms of Roman government. The true representative of the conquered population was not the Roman bureaucrat or lawyer, but the Christian bishop. When the collapse of the imperial government in the West took place, the bishop remained the natural leader of the Roman population. He organised the defence of his city, like Sidonius Apollinaris at Clermont; he treated with the barbarian leaders, like St. Lupus with Attila and St. Germanus with the king of the Alans; and above all he was at once the representative of the new spiritual society and of the old secular culture.

Through all the disaster of the age of invasion, the leaders of Christian society, men like Sidonius Apollinaris or St. Avitus, kept their faith not only in their religion, but in the imperial destiny of Rome and in the supremacy of the ancient culture.

The Christians felt that so long as the Church survived, the work of the Empire could not be undone. By becoming Christians—or rather Catholics—the barbarians would themselves become Roman, "the barbarian flood would break itself against the rock of Christ." As Paulinus of Nola writes concerning a Christian missionary (Niceta of Remesiana),

Per te
Barbari discunt resonare Christum
Corde romano.

The one great obstacle to the union of Roman and barbarian in a single society was the difference of religion. All the early Germanic kingdoms, in Gaul the Burgundians and Visigoths, the Ostrogoths in Italy, the Visigoths and Suevi in Spain, and above all the Vandals in Africa, were Arians and were thus in a state of permanent opposition to the Church of the Empire and the subject populations. Hence the paradoxical fact that the unification of Gaul proceeded not from the comparatively civilised Roman-Gothic kingdom of the south-west, but from the barbarous Frankish kingdom in the north-east. Yet in spite of their heathenism, the Franks possessed a longer tradition of association with the Empire than any of the other West German peoples. The Salian Franks had been settled on imperial territory in Belgium and on the Lower Rhine since the middle of the fourth century, and in the fifth century they fought as allies of the Roman governors of Gaul against the Saxons, the Visigoths and the Huns. In 486 their king, Clodovech or Clovis, conquered the territory between the Loire and the Somme, which was the last relic of independent Roman Gaul, and thus became ruler of a mixed Roman-Germanic kingdom. But it was his conversion to Catholic Christianity in 493 which was the turning-point in the history of the age, for it inaugurated the alliance between the Frankish kingdom and the Church, which was the foundation of mediaeval history, and which ultimately gave rise to the restored Empire of the West under Charlemagne. Its immediate effect was to facilitate the unification of Gaul by the absorption of the Arian kingdoms, and to cause the recognition of Clovis by the imperial government at Constantinople as the representative of Roman authority.

It was as the representative of Catholicism against Arianism that Clovis undertook his great campaign against the Goths in 507. "Verily it grieves my soul," he is reputed to have said, "that these Arians should hold a part of Gaul; with God's help let us go and conquer them and take their territories." [7] In the pages of Gregory of Tours, the campaign appears as a holy war and the advance of Clovis is marked at every step by miraculous signs of the divine favour. The victory of Vouillé and the conquest of Aquitaine certainly marked the appearance of a new Catholic state in the West, and its importance was recognised by the Emperor Anastasius, who forthwith conferred on Clovis the insignia of a Roman magistrate. In the course of the next thirty years the Frankish monarchy advanced with extraordinary rapidity. Not only was Gaul united once more, but eastward its power extended far beyond the old Roman frontiers. The Allemanni, the Thuringians and the Bavarians were conquered in rapid succession, and a great state arose which was the ancestor not only of France but of me-diaeval Germany as well. And in nothing did the Franks show more clearly their assimilation of the Roman tradition than in this work of conquest and organisation east of the Rhine. To this day Southern Germany and its people bears the mark of their rule.

The new state behaved from the first as the heir of the im-perial tradition. It salvaged what remained of the wreckage of the Roman administrator, and set it to work anew. After the model of the Emperors, the barbarian king had his "Sacred Palace" with its hierarchy of officials. His Chancery, with its Roman-Gallic scribes, preserved the forms and the routine of the old administration. His revenue was derived from the es-tates of the imperial fisc and from the land tax, which was based on the old system of property registers. The administra-tive unit was not the Germanic Hundred as it existed in the old Frankish territories of the north, but the city territory under the authority of the Count. Even the personnel of the administration was as much Roman as Frankish. Protadius and Claudius were mayors of the Palace under Queen Brunihild, and the ablest commander of the Frankish armies in the sixth century was the Patrician Mummolus. In some respects the power of the Frankish monarchy was more absolute than that of the old imperial government, at least in regard to the Church, which now falls more and more under the control of the state, so that the bishop, while losing nothing of his so-cial importance, becomes, along with the count, the leading representative of the royal authority in his diocese.

But, on the other hand, the barbarian element in the new state is no less evident. The Roman unity has disappeared and with it the Roman ideal of a reign of law. Indeed, there is a medley of tribes and peoples, each living its own life accord-ing to its own code of laws. The Frank, the Gallo-Roman and the Burgundian are judged not by the common law of the state, but each by his own national code. Even where institu-tions have been taken over bodily from Rome, the spirit that informs them is no longer the same. For the moving power be-hind the imposing structure of the Frankish state is still the barbarian warrior tribe. The power that keeps society together is not the civil authority of the state and its law courts, but the personal loyalty of the tribesman to his chief and his kinsfolk and of the warrior to his leader. The notion of "fidelity," the relation of the individual who swears allegiance to a powerful lord in return for protection, takes the place of the legal relation of the public magistrate to the free citizen. Crime was considered primarily as an offence against the individual and his kin, and was atoned for by a composition or *wergild* that differed according to a man's rank and nationality.

This intermingling of Germanic and late-Roman elements which we see in the structure of the state runs through the whole culture of the age. At the beginning of the conquest the two elements stand over against one another in sharp contrast, but in the course of time each loses its individuality and finally gives place to a new unity. It is possible to study this process with exceptional clearness in the field of art, owing to the recent work of archaeologists, especially those of Scandinavia. We can trace two distinct currents of art coming into Europe from the fourth century onwards, the Iranian-Gothic and the Syrian-Byzantine. Both of these originated, like so many of the cultural influences of prehistoric times, in Western Asia, and they also follow the two great channels of prehistoric intercourse—on the one hand the way of the Mediterranean, on the other the way of the Russian steppe north of the Black Sea and the valleys of the Danube and the Vistula. It was during their settlement in South Russia that the Germanic peoples acquired from the Sarmatians the art of polychrome jewellery and the fantastic style of animal ornamentation which had already characterised Scythian art. The latter became the characteristic style of the whole Germanic world from the sixth century, even as far north as Scandinavia; but the former is confined to the peoples who migrated from South Russia, such as the Goths and the non-Germanic Alans, and to the peoples whom they influenced. Beautiful examples of this fine jewellers' work have been found as far west as Spain, at Herpes in South-west France, and in Kent and the Isle of Wight, a fact which points to the close connection of Jutish culture with that of the Franks across the Channel rather than with Denmark. On the other hand, the region of Anglian settlement shows signs, in its cruciform and square-headed brooches, of a connection with Scandinavia, while the early Saxon art of Southern Britain differs alike from the rest of England and from the continent in the use of geometric rather than animal ornament and in the preservation of typically Roman designs, such as the "egg and tongue" border and the guilloche.[8] The comparative duration of these schools of Germanic art affords a measure of the degree to which the invading peoples preserved their independent culture or yielded to the influence of their new environment. In this country the Teutonic artistic tradition survived until the close of the seventh century, but in France the Mediterranean influence of Syrian and Byzantine art appeared as early as the middle of the sixth century, and its victory is a sign of what a Scandinavian scholar has termed "the de-Germanization of Frankish culture."

The same problem exists in the case of religion and literature and thought, though here the evidence is much less satisfactory. Except in England, the native German religion hardly survived the conquest of the Empire. In some cases, as with the Goths, Christianity was victorious in the fourth century, and the Gothic translation of the Bible by the Arian bishop Ulfilas is the first beginning of Teutonic literature. From the Goths Christianity quickly spread to the other East German peoples, but the West Germans retained their national religion to a much later date; and the conversion of the Frankish royal house and that of the ruling classes of the other German peoples whom they conquered did not immediately affect the mass of the rural population. Moreover, even when the Germans had nominally accepted Christianity, their manners and ideas remained those of a pagan warrior society. The burial of King Alaric in the bed of the River Busento, surrounded with his treasure and his slaughtered slaves, recalls the funeral of Patroclus rather than that of a Christian king. For this was the Heroic Age of the Germanic peoples, and as Professor Chadwick has shown, it affords a real sociological parallel to the Homeric Age of ancient Greece. In both periods the contact of an ancient settled civilisation with a primitive warlike society had set up a process of change, which broke down the organisation alike of the conquered state and the conquering tribe, and left the individual war-leader and his followers as the dominant social factor. The splendour of these warrior princes, the "sackers of cities," and the dramatic story of their adventures remained a memory and an ideal to the barbarous ages that followed. Theodoric of Verona, Günther of Worms, King Etzel the Hun, Beowulf, Hildebrand and the rest are the figures of an epic cycle that became the common property of the Teutonic peoples, and though they never found their Homer, the story of the Need of the Nibelungs and the destruction of the Burgundian Kingdom by the Huns is not inferior in tragedy to that of the fall of Troy and the fate of the House of Atreus. Compared with these heroic legends the literature of the conquered society seems poor enough. The poetry of Sidonius Apollinaris and Venantius Fortunatus is the expiring effort of a decadent tradition. Nevertheless, it was the Latin tradition that was victorious throughout the conquered lands, and the survival of the classical tradition was of vital importance for the future of Europe and the birth of the mediaeval culture. In spite of their lack of literary quality, writers like Orosius and Isidore of Seville, Cassiodorus and Gregory the Great, did more to shape the minds of later generations than many geniuses of the first order.

The tradition of Latin culture lived on in the Church and the monasteries, and since the barbarians themselves had yielded to Christianity, it was no longer merely the culture of the conquered population, but the dominant power in the new order.

Thus by the sixth century a preliminary fusion had already taken place between the four different elements that went to make up the new European culture. The effect of the invasions was to set up a process of cultural and racial intermixture between the Germanic barbarians on the one hand, and the society of the Roman Empire on the other. The vital centre of the process was in Gaul, where the two societies met on more nearly equal terms than elsewhere, but its influence extended over the whole of Western Europe, so that all the Western peoples became in varying degrees Romano-Germanic in culture. Where the Germanic element was weakest, as in Italy, it was reinforced in the sixth century by new barbarian invasions, and where the tradition of Roman culture seemed to have perished, as in Britain and Germany, it was revived by the work of the Church and the monasteries in the seventh and eighth centuries. In spite of the apparent victory of barbarism, the Church remained as the representative of the old traditions of culture and as a bond of spiritual unity between the descendants of the conquered Romans and their barbarian conquerors. But it was centuries before the constructive elements in Western Europe were strong enough to overcome the forces of disintegration and barbarism. The leadership of culture had passed to the East, and the "Dark Ages" of western civilisation coincide with the golden age of Byzantine and Islamic culture.

PART TWO:

The Ascendancy of the East

VI

THE CHRISTIAN EMPIRE AND THE RISE OF THE BYZANTINE CULTURE

While the Latin West was gradually sinking into chaos and barbarism, in the East the Empire not only survived but became the centre of a new movement of culture. The history of this development has suffered more from depreciation and neglect than that of any other phase of European culture. The modern study of history has taken its departure from two points—from the history of classical antiquity and from that of the modern European nationalities—and anything which failed to fit into this scheme was disregarded or misunderstood. Even the greatest of our historians of the Eastern Empire—Edward Gibbon—shows a complete lack of sympathy for its culture; to him it is simply an appendix to Roman history, while his Victorian successor, Finlay, regards it mainly as an introduction to the history of modern Greece. In reality, the Byzantine culture is not merely a decadent survival from the classical past; it is a new creation, which forms the background of the whole development of mediaeval culture, and to some extent, even of that of Islam. It is true that the greatness of Byzantine culture lies rather in the sphere of religion and art than in its political and social achievements. The great awakening of interest in Byzantine history during recent years is due almost entirely to the new appreciation of Byzantine art, for if we admire the art of a people, we cannot utterly despise its culture. Nevertheless, the very durability of the Eastern Empire shows that it must also have possessed elements of political and social strength.

But if we are to understand Byzantine culture and appreciate its true achievement, it is useless to judge it by the standards of modern Europe or even by those of classical Greece and Rome. We must view it rather in relation to the oriental world and place it in its proper setting side by side with the great contemporary civilisations of the East, such as those of Sassanian Persia and the Khalifate of Damascus of Bagdad.

In the third and fourth centuries after Christ, the ancient oriental civilisations seem to renew their youth and once more show signs of an intense cultural activity. In India it was the period of Samudragupta and Chandragupta II, the classical age of Hindu art and literature. In China, in spite of the political disintegration of the Empire, it was the beginning of a new period in art and religion, owing to the rise of Buddhism, which had a profound effect on Chinese civilisation. Above all, in Persia, it was an age of political and religious revival—the age of the great Sassanian kings who restored the national tradition of Iranian monarchy and made Zoroastrianism the official religion of the new state. For the new Persian monarchy, like that of ancient Egypt and Babylonia, was a sacred monarchy, based on religious conceptions. Its spirit is well shown in the great rock carvings of Shapur and Nakshi Rustam. Here we see Aura Mazda bestowing the emblems of majesty on the King of Kings, each of them seated on a great war-horse and wearing the same dress and royal ornaments, while another relief shows the Emperor Valerian kneeling before his conqueror Sapor, in token of the humbling of the pride of Rome before the triumphant East.

This victorious wave of Oriental influence did not, indeed, destroy the Roman Empire, but it changed its character. Already in the third century Aurelian, the restorer of the Empire, had brought back from his Syrian campaign the oriental ideal of sacred monarchy and had established a kind of solar monotheism—the worship of the Unconquered Sun—as the official cult of the restored Empire. This solar theism was the religion of Constantine's house and prepared the way for his own acceptance of Christianity. The new Christian Empire of Byzantium is a parallel phenomenon to the new Zoroastrian Kingdom of Sassanian Persia.[1] It also was a sacred monarchy, based on the new world religion of Christianity. The Holy Roman Empire—*sancta respublica romana*—was the creation, not of Charlemagne, but of Constantine and Theodosius. By the fifth century it had become a veritable church-state, and the emperor was a kind of priest-king whose rule was regarded as the earthly counterpart and representative of the sovereignty of the Divine Word.[2] Consequently the power of the emperor is no longer disguised, as it had been during the early Empire, under the constitutional forms of republican magistracy: it is surrounded with all the religious prestige and the ceremonial pomp of oriental despotism. The ruler is the Orthodox and Apostolic Emperor. His court is the Sacred Palace; his property is the Divine Household; his edicts are "the celestial commands"; even the annual assessment of the taxes is known as "the Divine Delegation."

The whole government and administration of the Empire was transformed in accordance with this ideal. There was no longer any room for the Senate as an independent constitutional authority collateral with that of the Emperor, as it had been in the days of Augustus, nor for the existence of the city state, as the centre of an autonomous local administration. All authority was in and from the Emperor. He was the apex of a vast official hierarchy which enveloped the whole life of the Empire in its tentacles. Every social and economic activity was subjected to the closest scrutiny and regulation, and every citizen, every slave, every head of cattle and plot of land, was recorded in duplicate or triplicate in the official registers.

The civil service was, apart from the army and the Church, the one path to social advancement. Its higher ranks formed the new aristocracy and the Senate itself was no more than a council of ex-officials. The system centred in the central departments of the five great ministers—the Praetorian Praefect, the Master of the Offices, the Count of the Sacred Largesses, the Count of the Private Estate and the Quaestor of the Sacred Palace—and their departments (*officia*), staffed with hundreds of clerks and notaries, exerted an absolute control over the minutest details of administration in the remotest provinces. This bureaucratic system is the characteristic feature of the later Empire from the fourth to the seventh centuries, and distinguishes it alike from the early Empire, with its unpaid civic magistracies, and from the semi-feudal society of the Sassanian Kingdom. It was not, however, like the theocratic ideal of royalty and court ceremonial, a result of new Oriental influences, but an inheritance from the imperial civil service of the Antonine age and from the bureaucratic organisation of the

Hellenistic monarchies. Ultimately, no doubt, as Professor Rostovtzeff has shown, it has its roots in the administrative traditions of the great oriental monarchies of Persia and Egypt, but if it was oriental in origin, it had been rationalised and systematised by the Western mind. Consequently, in spite of its faults—and they were many—it possessed something of the political spirit of Western civilisation which was lost alike by the feudal barbarism of the Germanic kingdoms and by the theocratic despotism of the East. The Byzantine empire was exposed to both these influences: on the one hand, the great landowners and tenants of the crown were tending to assert their independence and to combine political functions and privileges with the ownership of the land; while, on the other, the imperial authority was in danger of being regarded as the irresponsible fiat of a divinised monarch. Owing to the existence of the civil service, however, neither of these tendencies was completely realised, and the Western conceptions of the State and of a reign of law survived. Indeed, it is to the Byzantine civil service that we owe not only the preservation of Roman law, but also the completion of its development. The study of the Roman law was the regular training of civil servants, and it was as a text-book for them that the *Institutes* of Justinian were compiled. It is to the bureaucracy of Theodosius II and Justinian that we owe the great codes through which the inheritance of Roman jurisprudence was handed on to the mediaeval and modern worlds.

In the same way, the social life of the Eastern Empire, however coloured by Oriental influences, still possessed something of the Hellenistic tradition. Although the institutions of the classical city-state had lost all their vitality and survived only as an empty husk, the city itself did not disappear, as it was destined to do in Western Europe. It remained the centre of social and economic life and imprinted an urban character on Byzantine civilisation. The Byzantine city was not, like the Roman municipality, a community of landowners and rentiers. It derived its importance mainly from trade and industry. Throughout the age of destruction and economic retrogression which accompanied the fall of the Empire in the West, the Eastern provinces retained a large measure of economic prosperity. The workshops of Alexandria and Northern Syria were still flourishing and their products were exported in every direction. Colonies of Byzantine merchants, usually Syrians, were established in every important centre in the West, not only in

Italy and Spain, but throughout Gaul, even as far north as Paris, where a Syrian merchant was actually elected bishop in 591. Eastwards an active trade was carried on with Abyssinia and India, by way of the Red Sea; and with China and Central Asia through Persia, and afterwards by way of the Black Sea and the Caspian. Cherson retained its importance as an *entrepôt* for the trade with Russia in furs and slaves,[3] and the corn-ships of Alexandria sailed northward to the Bosphorus and westward to Spain.[4]

All this network of trade routes had its centre in Constantinople, which, unlike Rome, was the economic as well as the political capital of the Empire. This was one of the chief causes of the prosperity and stability of the Byzantine state. While Western Europe in the early Middle Ages was almost lacking in city life; and powerful states, like the Empire of Charles the Great, possessed no fixed capital, the centre of the Eastern Empire remained a brilliant and populous metropolis. The greatness of its walls and buildings, the splendour of its court and the wealth of its citizens, made an even greater impression on the surrounding peoples than the military power of the Empire.

But it is not possible to understand the Byzantine culture if we look at it only from the economic or the political point of view. For, to a greater extent than that of any other European society, its culture was a religious one and found its essential expression in religious forms; and even to-day it survives to a great extent in the tradition of the Eastern Church. The modern European is accustomed to look on society as essentially concerned with the present life, and with material needs, and on religion as an influence on the moral life of the individual. But to the Byzantine, and indeed to mediaeval man in general, the primary society was the religious one, and economic and secular affairs were a secondary consideration. The greater part of a man's life, especially a poor man's, was lived in a world of religious hopes and fears, and the supernatural figures of this religious world were just as real to him as the authorities of the Empire. This "otherworldly" spirit goes back, of course, to the early centuries of Christianity, but after the adoption of the new religion as the official cult of the Empire, it took on new forms which became characteristic of the Byzantine culture. Above all, there was the institution of monasticism, which arose in Egypt early in the fourth century, and spread with extraordinary rapidity both in the East and the

West. The monks of the desert represented in its most extreme form the victory of the Oriental religious spirit over the civilisation of the classical world. They had cut themselves off utterly from the life of the city and all its material culture. They recognised no political obligation, they neither paid taxes, nor fought, nor reared children. Their whole activity was centred in the spiritual world, and their life was a superhuman effort to transcend the limitations of earthly existence. Nevertheless, these naked fasting ascetics became the popular heroes and ideal types for the whole Byzantine world. Rutilius Namatianus might compare them to Circe's swine, "except that Circe changed only men's bodies, these the soul itself." But Namatian was one of the last survivors of the old guard of Roman conservatism. In the East all orders of society from the emperor downwards vied with one another in honouring the monks. Even great men of the court, like Arsenius, the tutor of Arcadius, gave up their position and their wealth to go into the desert. And even when it was not realised in practice, the monastic ideal became the standard of the religious life of the Empire. The monk was the superman, the ordinary cleric and layman followed the same ideal at a distance. They all accepted the subordination of secular activities to the purely religious life. To them the real forces that ruled the world were not finance and war and politics, but the powers of the spiritual world, the celestial hierarchy of angelic Virtues and Intelligences. And this invisible hierarchy had its counterpart and manifestation in the visible order of the ecclesiastical hierarchy, and in the sacramental order of the Divine Mysteries. It was not hard for a Byzantine to believe in the miraculous interposition of Providence in his daily life, for he saw enacted before his eyes in the liturgy the continual miracle of the Divine Theophany.

This vision of spiritual reality and mystery was the common possession of the Byzantine world. The educated man reached it through the mystical philosophy of the Greek Fathers, above all Dionysius the Areopagite and Maximus Confessor, while the uneducated saw it through the many-coloured imagery of art and legend. But there was no conflict between the two views, since the symbolism of art and the abstractions of thought found their common ground in the liturgy and dogma of the Church.

And so, while the people took no share in the politics of the Empire and the affairs of the secular government, they fol-

lowed with passionate interest the affairs of the Church and
the religious controversies of the age. It is difficult for us to
understand an age in which the clauses of the Athanasian
Creed were matters of passionate debate at street corners, and
abstruse theological terms, like "consubstantial" and "uncon-
substantial," became the battle-cry of rival monks. No less an
authority than St. Gregory Nazianzen has described how, if
you went into a shop in Constantinople to buy a loaf, "the
baker, instead of telling you the price, will argue that the Father is greater than the Son. The money-changer will talk
about the Begotten and the Unbegotten, instead of giving you
your money, and if you want a bath the bath-keeper assures
you that the Son surely proceeds from nothing."

In such a world it was obviously of the greatest importance
that the relations between State and Church should be close;
for if the Empire lost the allegiance of the latter, half its power
would be gone, and it would have not only an ecclesiastical
organisation, but the whole force of popular feeling arrayed
against it. Hence the unity of the Church was one of the leading considerations of the imperial policy, and from the time
when Constantine called together the council of Nicaea the
Emperors did all in their power to preserve ecclesiastical unity
and to enforce conformity on the recalcitrant minorities. The
true founder of the state church of the Eastern Empire was
Constantius II, who was typically Byzantine alike in his passionate interest in theological controversy and in his belief in
his imperial prerogative as the defender of the faith and the
supreme arbitrator in ecclesiastical disputes. His ecclesiastical
policy was carried out through the court bishops headed by
Ursacius and Valens, who formed a kind of Holy Synod in
close relations with the Emperor, and through the general
councils convoked and guided by imperial authority.[5] This
system met with vehement opposition from two quarters: from
Athanasius, the great bishop of Alexandria, and from the
West, where the doctrine of the independence of the Church
was uncompromisingly maintained, above all by St. Hilary and
Hosius, the famous bishop of Cordova.

Hence there arose the long schism between the West and
the state church of the Eastern Empire, which was not termi-
nated until the faith of Nicaea was re-established by an Emperor from the West. At the beginning of his reign Theodosius attempted to restore unity by enforcing the Western
standard of authority. "We will," he wrote, "that all our sub-

jects should hold the faith which the Divine Apostle Peter delivered to the Romans . . . and which is followed by Pope Damasus and Bishop Peter, Bishop of Alexandria, a man of apostolic sanctity." [6] This decree, however, was not sufficient of itself to secure a settlement, and Theodosius had resort to the traditional Eastern method of holding a general council. But though the council—held at Constantinople in 381— marks the victory of Nicene orthodoxy, it was strongly oriental in feeling and sought to secure the independence of the Eastern churches against all interference from without. It decreed that the ecclesiastical organisation was henceforth to follow the lines of the secular dioceses,[7] and that the bishop of Constantinople should have the primacy of honour after the bishop of Rome, "because that city is the New Rome."

Thus the primacy of the new Patriarchate was explicitly based on its connection with the imperial government, as against the principle of apostolic tradition, on which the three great Sees of Rome, Antioch and Alexandria founded their authority. And its subsequent evolution was conditioned by the same principles. It developed as the centre of the state church and the instrument of imperial ecclesiastical policy. While Rome and Alexandria each possessed a distinct and continuous theological tradition, the teaching of Constantinople fluctuated with the vicissitudes of imperial politics. Its tradition was in fact diplomatic rather than theological, since in every dogmatic crisis the primary interest of the government was to preserve the religious unity of the Empire, and the Patriarchate became the instrument of its compromises. The typical representative of the Byzantine ecclesiastical tradition was Eusebius of Nicomedia, the great court prelate of the Constantian house, who himself occupied the see of Constantinople before his death. And as the state church had been semi-Arian in the days of Constantius and Eusebius, so it was semi-Monophysite with Zeno and Acacius, and Monothelite with Heraclius and Sergius.

It is true that this policy of comprehension by compromise failed to attain its object and led to the alienation both of the East and the West. By degrees the church of the Empire itself became a national church, and the Patriarch of Constantinople the spiritual head of the Greek people. But this was a later development: the Christian Empire from the fourth to the sixth centuries was still Roman and international. Latin was still the official language, and the emperors, with the exception of the Spanish Theodosius and Zeno the Isaurian, were all of them natives of the Balkan provinces—Pannonia, Thrace and Illyria—regions which were still largely Latin in culture. The great emperor who, more than anyone else, is the embodiment for us of this tradition and the typical representative of the Byzantine theocratic ideal of a state church and a church state—Justinian—was himself an Illyrian of Latin tongue who regarded himself as the representative and the upholder of the imperial tradition of Rome, and who devoted his life to the task of restoring the lost unity of the Roman Empire.

During the fifth century the forces of disintegration were everywhere victorious, and the Empire seemed about to dissolve itself into a number of separate unities. In the West the Goths were building up independent kingdoms in the Roman provinces, and the Vandals controlled the Mediterranean. In the East the subject oriental peoples were beginning to re-assert their nationality under religious forms, and the Empire itself was rapidly becoming orientalised, especially after Zeno the Isaurian had attempted to re-unite the Monophysites to the imperial church, at the cost of schism with Rome. It seemed as though the Eastern Empire would lose all contact with the West and become a purely oriental power, Graeco-Syrian in culture and Monophysite in religion.

This development was, however, checked by the reign of Justinian, and the sixth century witnessed a general revival of Western influences. The first acts of the new dynasty were to restore the communion with Rome which had been interrupted for thirty-five years and to put an end to the Syrian influences which had dominated the court of Anastasius. And this was the prelude to the work of imperial reorganisation and expansion which was the great achievement of Justinian's reign. One by one Africa, Italy and South-Eastern Spain were recovered by the imperial armies, and the Roman Empire once more dominated the Mediterranean world. These victories were indeed purchased by an expenditure of blood and treasure which the Empire could ill afford, and which seriously overstrained the resources of the Byzantine state. It may even be argued that the conquests of Justinian were fatal to the existence of the Empire, since his military adventures in the West led to the neglect of the essential defences on which the safety of the realm depended—the frontiers of the Danube and the Euphrates. But at least the Christian Empire enjoyed a last hour of triumph before the darkness of the following centuries, and its victorious expansion was accompanied by a remarkable revival of cultural activity, which made the sixth century the classical age of Byzantine culture.

It is true that the creative genius of the age is to be seen only in its architecture and art. In literature and thought it is not an age of new beginnings, but a last autumnal flowering of the old classical tradition. Yet this intellectual conservatism is itself an essential element in Byzantine culture. As the political revival of the sixth century was a return to the tradition of the Roman state and as its legislative achievement was the final culmination of the development of Roman jurisprudence, so the literature of the period is the last expression of twelve centuries of Hellenic culture. For it is a remarkable fact, and one that has never been fully recognised by historians, that in spite of the religious and theocratic spirit which appears to dominate Byzantine civilisation, the literary development of the sixth century shows a reaction towards secular and even pagan standards. Procopius of Caesarea writes of the theological disputes of his age with the cynical detachment of a cultivated sceptic, and in Egypt a whole school of poets was composing elaborate epics on the old themes of heathen mythology.[8] The great age of Greek Christian literature ends in the fifth century with Cyril and Theodoret. In the following age theological literature holds a very subordinate position. The leaders of culture were rhetoricians like Procopius of Gaza and Choricius, who prided themselves on the Attic purity of their style, historians like Agathias and Procopius of Caesarea, whose minds were steeped in Hellenic traditions, and Neoplatonic philosophers and men of science like Damascius and Simplicius. It is true that Justinian closed the schools of Athens and forced the philosophers to take refuge for a time in Persia, but his repressive policy was not altogether harmful, since it induced the philosophers to devote their energies to scientific criticism in place of the theosophy and magic which had influenced Neoplatonism since the days of Iamblichus. There was no attempt on the part of the government to suppress secular learning or the pagan literary and scientific tradition. While infuriated fanatics were hunting the patriarch through the streets of Alexandria, the professors of the university still lectured in the halls of the Museum on physics and mathematics, and as Pierre Duhem has shown,[9] their learning was by no means so sterile and lacking in originality as is usually supposed. It has a permanent importance in the history of human thought, since it was not only the conclusion of the scientific development of the ancient world, but also the foundation of that of the new. It is the source from which the science of the Islamic East, and through it that of the Christian West, has its origin.

This survival of secular culture which distinguishes the culture of the Eastern Empire from that of the West was due in great measure to the influence of the civil service. The Byzantine Empire, at least in the sixth century, was ruled neither by ecclesiastics nor unlettered soldiers, like the West, but after the manner of the Chinese, by an official class of *litterati* who prided themselves on their learning and scholarship. This literary tradition, like that of the Chinese mandarin, sometimes took the form of a pedantic antiquarianism, as we see in John Laurentius, the Lydian, whose writings show a curious mixture of misplaced erudition and bureaucratic traditionalism. But it was also responsible for historical work of genuine value and for the last flowering of Hellenic poetry. The last important contribution to the Greek anthology was made by a group of lawyers and officials who held high office in the reigns of Justinian and Justin II—Agathias the historian and Paul the Silentiary, Julian the Ex-prefect, Macedonius the Consul, Rufinus the Domesticus, and seven or eight others. No doubt it was an artificial hot-house growth, but the graceful love poems of Agathias and Paul are not unworthy of the tradition of Meleager, and even their verses to the extinct divinities of Hellas, Pan, Poseidon and Priapus, are not without a certain charm.[10]

There is nothing in this poetry to remind us of the change which had passed over the ancient world: it belongs altogether to the past, to the purest traditions of the Hellenistic age. If we wish for a literature which expresses the mind of the new age, we must look for it in the rhythmic liturgical poetry of Romanus of Emesa, or in the chronicle of John Malalas of Antioch, who lives in a world of miracle and legend, and who had so completely lost touch with the old culture that he regards Cicero as a Roman poet and Herodotus as a successor of Polybius. Yet it is Malalas rather than Procopius who is the source of the mediaeval Byzantine historical tradition and who became the model of the earliest Slavonic and Armenian chroniclers.[11]

But this popular tradition never gave birth to a new Byzantine literature of high quality. The classical tradition continued to dominate the higher levels of culture, and each revival of Byzantine civilisation is accompanied by a renaissance of classical studies and a return to the ancient models. The loyalty of the Byzantines to the Hellenic inheritance did not admit of the possibility of new creative activity.

In art, however, this was not the case, for the age of the Christian Empire witnessed an artistic revolution of the most far-reaching kind. The decline of the ancient city-state and its religion was accompanied by the decline of its art—the great Hellenic tradition of the portrayal of the human form and of representative naturalism in sculpture and painting. In its place came the nonrepresentational religious and decorative art of the East, with its love of arabesque and its subordination of plant and animal forms to schemes of decoration. So, too, the Greek temple and the civic architecture of the ancients, which looks outwards to the frieze and the peristyle, was replaced by the oriental vaulted and domed architectures, originating in the brick buildings of Mesopotamia and Persia, which concentrates itself on the richness of its internal decoration and the construction of a lofty and spacious interior. The great brick buildings of later Rome, the thermae and the basilica of Constantine and perhaps even the Pantheon, already show the influence of the new spirit. This spirit found its fullest expression in the art of Sassanian Persia, which in this, as well as in its conceptions of monarchy and government, exercised a most powerful influence on the Byzantine culture. Indeed some modern writers regard the new art as a hybrid growth arising from the intermingling of the tradition of imperial Rome with that of Sassanian Persia. But we must not forget that Northern Syria and Asia Minor itself possessed deep-lying native artistic and cultural traditions, and that these provinces were the most active and living members of the New Empire.

Syria was the meeting-place of the two currents of artistic influence, those of the Hellenistic West and the Persian East, and it contributed an element of its own—the use of art for the purpose of religious instruction by the means of figures and scenes which are depicted with a simple emotional realism quite unlike the classical naturalism of Hellenic art. This new religious art, which developed in Syria by the fourth century, was gradually diffused throughout the Empire by monastic influence and also, no doubt, through the colonies of Syrian merchants which were to be found in all the principal ports. But in the great centres of culture, Antioch, Alexandria and Constantinople, the Hellenistic tradition still survived and continued to dominate secular art and decoration. Even in religious art this tradition was still supreme at Rome and Constantinople during the fourth century, and long after the introduction of the new Syrian style it continued to coexist as a constituent element in the mature religious art of the Christian Empire.

Thus Byzantine art is a composite creation, due to the blending of many different influences. It is oriental in its use of ornament and symbolism, in its reliance on colour and light instead of plastic form, in its development of the vault and the dome and in the bareness and simplicity of the exterior of its churches. On the other hand it preserved the Roman-Hellenistic type of the basilica with its range of columns and its porticoes; it carried on to a certain extent the Hellenistic ornamental motifs; and it did not entirely banish the human, naturalistic, and representational element which had been the essence of the classical tradition. Indeed, the use of the image, carved in relief, painted, and above all, inlaid in mosaic, is one of the most characteristic features both of Byzantine art and of Byzantine religion.

By the sixth century the Eastern Empire had evolved its own artistic tradition, in which Eastern and Western elements were brought into organic union with one another. The noblest creation of this art was the Church of the Holy Wisdom at Constantinople, which was the work of architects from Ionia, the motherland of Hellenic culture, but which at the same time grew up under the direct inspiration and supervision of Justinian himself. It is the greatest domed church in the world, the perfect union of oriental plan and decoration with Greek organic structure, and though it has lost something of the splendour of its polychrome decoration, it is possible to supplement this from the contemporary art of the churches of Ravenna, so that we can form a complete idea of the Byzantine art in its greatest age. In the octagonal domed church of San Vitale at Ravenna, we have a perfect example of Byzantine mosaic decoration. In the apse sits the figure of Christ Pantocrator, not the terrific judge of later Byzantine art, but almost Hellenic in youth and beauty. He is aureoled with light, throned on the orb of the world with the four rivers of Paradise at his feet, and saints and angels on either hand,

and he holds forth the diadem of celestial monarchy, like the figure of Aura Mazda on the Sassanian rock reliefs. Below on either side are two solemn lines of figures: the Emperor Justinian with the clergy and the officials of the Sacred Palace, and the Empress Theodora with the ladies of her court. It is the Panathenaic procession of the new civilisation, and if it lacks the naturalism and triumphant humanism of the Parthenon frieze, it is unsurpassed in its impression of solemn majesty. And when we look at the Byzantine church as a whole, with its polychrome adornment of mosaic and coloured marbles, its antique columns, its carved capitals, oriental in richness and variety, yet Hellenic in proportion and grace, above all the crowning miracle of the dome of St. Sophia, in which architecture transcends its limitations and becomes impalpable and immaterial as the vault of the sky itself, we must admit that never has man succeeded more perfectly in moulding matter to become the vehicle and expression of spirit.

And this concentration on interior splendour in the Byzantine church was intimately related to its function in the life of the people. The Greek temple, like the Indian temple to-day, was the dwelling-place of the god, and its dimly lighted cella was entered only by his priests and servants. The Byzantine church was the home of the Christian people, and it was the theatre of the great year-long drama of the liturgical cycle. For the liturgy summed up the art and music and literature of the Byzantine people. Here, as in architecture, the Eastern and the Western spirits met on a common ground. Liturgical poetry was the creation of Christian Syria, and the greatest Byzantine hymnographer, Romanus of Emesa, carried over into the Greek language the poetical and rhythmical forms of the Syriac *Madrasa* and *Sogitha*; but at the same time it was a dramatic mystery in which every external act had a symbolic significance, and the splendour of its ceremonial was the artistic expression of a theological idea. Here also, as in painting and architecture, the Hellenic tendency to externalise—to clothe thought in the vesture of matter—found a new religious expression.

But the perfect synthesis of the different elements in Byzantine culture which was achieved in the art of the sixth century was not realised elsewhere. In religion, above all, the opposition between East and West still endangered the unity of the Empire and of its civilisation. Although at the beginning of his reign Iustinian had done all in his power to conciliate the Papacy and to strengthen the union between Constantinople and the West, the attraction of the East gradually reasserted itself. It was represented in the palace and in his own life by Theodora, the dark and subtle woman who fascinated and subdued the simpler and more hesitant mind of her Illyrian husband. She was a Monophysite both by conviction and policy, and under her protection the palace itself became a refuge for the Monophysite leaders and a centre for their intrigues. It was through her influence that Justinian returned to the old Byzantine policy of reunion by compromise, to which he continued faithful even after her death. In spite of the unexpected resistance of Theodora's protégé, Pope Vigilius, Justinian succeeded in getting his solution endorsed by a General Council in 553 and in imposing his will on the Papacy. But, as on so many other occasions, a compromise imposed by force afforded no real solution. It gave rise to a new schism in the West, which endured long after Justinian's death, and it failed to conciliate the Monophysites, who from this time develop an organised existence outside the Church of the Empire. The tendency towards religious disunion which had been growing since the fifth century had become realised in the permanent alienation of the Eastern provinces from the state church and the religion of the Empire. And this religious disaffection was the symptom of the great social and spiritual changes which were taking place in the oriental world and from which a new civilisation of world-wide importance was soon to emerge.

VII

THE AWAKENING OF THE EAST
AND THE REVOLT OF THE
SUBJECT NATIONALITIES

The coming of Islam is the great fact which dominates the history of the seventh and eighth centuries and affects the whole subsequent development of mediaeval civilisation, in the West as well as in the East. To the mind which regards history from an exclusively secular and occidental standpoint the appearance of Islam must always remain an inexplicable problem, since it seems to mark a complete breach in historical development and to have no relation with anything that has gone before. It is only when we look under the surface of political history and study the subterranean activity of the oriental underworld that the existence of the new forces which were to determine the future of oriental culture becomes visible.

For the ecclesiastical and theological disputes of the fifth century, which have so little meaning for the ordinary secular historian, involve a crisis in the life of the Eastern Empire that was no less far-reaching in its results than the barbarian invasions in the West. They imply the revival of the subject nationalities and the passing of the Hellenistic culture which had dominated the Levant since the age of Alexander. It is true that this culture had been practically confined to the cities, and the great mass of the peasant population had remained unaffected by it. But throughout the Hellenistic and imperial age the citizen class was the ruling element in culture, and the native population had passively accepted its domination. But the coming of Christianity, coinciding, as it did, with a decline in the importance of the city and the urban bourgeoisie, was accompanied with a great revival of cultural activity on the part of the subject peoples. It saw the rise of a vernacular literature and the awakening of a national consciousness among the oriental peoples. In the West Christianity had spread through the cities, and it was assumed that a peasant (*paganus*) would necessarily be a heathen. But in the East this was not the case, and Christianity seems to have spread as rapidly among the peasants as among the townsmen.

This was particularly the case among the Syrians, who formed a solid block of Aramaic-speaking peoples, extending from the Mediterranean to Kurdistan and the Persian highlands and from Mt. Taurus to the Persian Gulf. In the West, Hellenistic influences were dominant and the rich cities of the coast lands, Antioch, Berytus, Caesarea and Gaza, were strongholds of Greek culture; but east of the Euphrates the city of Edessa, on the frontiers of the Roman and the Persian Empires, was the centre of a native Syrian state which became the starting point of oriental Christianity and the cradle of Syriac literature. Long before the conversion of the Roman Empire, as early as the beginning of the third century A.D., Osrhoene became a Christian state, and from there Christianity spread eastward into the Persian Empire and northwards to Armenia, which also became a Christian kingdom at the beginning of the fourth century. To the Syrian people, thus torn asunder by rival empires and dominated by alien culture, Christianity became a vehicle for national traditions and ideals. We see in Syrian literature, for example in the poetry of James of Sarug, how intense was the pride in the antiquity and purity of their national church. While the chosen people had proved faithless and the heathen empires had persecuted the name of Christ, Edessa, "the daughter of the Parthians espoused to the Cross," had always been found faithful. "Edessa sent to Christ by an epistle to come and enlighten her. On behalf of all the peoples did she make intercession to Him that He would leave Zion which hated Him and come to the peoples who loved Him." [1] "Not from common scribes did she learn the faith: her King taught her, her martyrs taught her and she firmly believed them."

"This truth has Edessa held fast from her youth and in her old age she will not barter it away, as a daughter of the poor. Her religious King became to her a scribe and from him she learnt concerning our Lord—that He is the Son of God, yea God. Addaeus, who brought the bridegroom's ring and put it on her finger, betrothed her thus to the Son of God, Who is the Only Begotten." [2]

Syrian Christianity was the religion of a subject people who found in it their justification against the pride of the dominant culture.

"Shamuna, our riches, richer art thou than the rich:
For lo! the rich stand at thy door that thou mayest relieve
*   them.*
Small thy village, poor thy country: who then gave thee
That lords of villages and cities should court thy favour?
Lo! judges in their robes and vestments
Take dust from their threshold, as though it were the
*   medicine of life*
The cross is rich, and to its worshippers increaseth riches;
And its poverty despiseth all the riches of the world.
Shamuna and Guria, sons of the poor, lo! at your doors
Bow down the rich that they may receive from you their
*   wants.*
The Son of God in poverty and want
Showed to the world that all its riches are as nothing.
His disciples, all fishermen, all poor, all weak,
All men of little note, became illustrious through its faith.
One fisherman, whose village was a home of fishermen,
He made chief over the twelve, yea head of the house.
One a tent-maker who was aforetime a persecutor,
He seized upon and made him a chosen vessel for the
*   faith."* [3]

This autochthonous Syrian Christianity, which had its humble beginnings at Edessa in the third century, was the starting-point of a vast oriental expansion which, during the Middle Ages, was destined to extend to India and China and the Turkish peoples of inner Asia. But owing, perhaps, to its geographical remoteness, it did not come into immediate conflict with the Church of the Empire. The great religious crisis of the fifth century had its origin in the very heart of the Hellenistic world, at Alexandria itself.

For in Egypt, no less than in Syria, the ancient traditions of oriental culture were asserting themselves under a Christian form. Throughout the Ptolemaic and the Roman periods the people of Egypt had preserved its ancient religion and culture. While Alexandria was the most brilliant centre of Hel-

lenistic civilisation, in the valley of the Nile the immemorial
routine of Egyptian life still went on unchanged. The two
currents of civilisation ran side by side without mingling with
one another, because the native culture was still confined in
the strict hieratic forms of Egyptian religious tradition. The
conversion of Egypt to Christianity changed all this. It destroyed the religious barriers which kept the native population
artificially segregated in a world of its own and brought them
into contact with the rest of the population of the Empire.
It did not, however, weaken the forces of nationalism or lead
to the assimilation of Egypt by Graeco-Byzantine culture. On
the contrary, from this moment the importance of the Greek
element in Egypt steadily declined and the use of the Greek
language was gradually replaced by Coptic, *i.e.*, the old Egyptian tongue written in Greek characters. The Church naturally
took the place of the old state religion as the organ of Egyptian nationality, but, whereas the head of the old hierarchy
had been the foreign rulers who had usurped the place of
Pharaoh, the head of the new Church was the Egyptian Patriarch. As, in the days of the decline of ancient Egypt, the
High Priest of Amon Ra at Thebes had become the leader
of the nation, so now all the forces of Egyptian nationalism
rallied round the Patriarch. He was "the most Divine and all
Holy Lord, Pope and Patriarch of the great city of Alexandria, of Lybia, Pentapolis, Ethiopia, and all the land of Egypt,
Father of Fathers, Bishop of Bishops, Thirteenth Apostle and
Judge of the World." His control over the Egyptian Church
was absolute—far greater, in fact, than that of the Pope over
the churches of the West, since all the bishops of Egypt were
consecrated by him and were directly dependent on his will.
The only power to be compared with his was that of the monks,
who were, to a far greater extent than the bishops, the natural
leaders of the people.

Egyptian monasticism was the supreme achievement of oriental Christianity, and it expresses all that is best and worst
in the national temperament, from the wisdom and spirituality
of a Macarius or a Pachomius to the fanaticism of the mobs
who murdered Hypatia and filled the streets of Alexandria
with tumult and bloodshed. But even this fanaticism was a
further source of strength to the Patriarchate, which found in
the monks an army of fearless and passionate partisans. When
the Patriarch of Alexandria attended a general council he was
accompanied by a bodyguard of monks and *parabolani*,[4] who

sometimes terrorised the whole assembly by their clamour and violence. So great was the power of the Egyptian Patriarch that he aspired to be the religious dictator of the whole Eastern Empire. Athanasius had stood alone against Constantius II and the whole Eastern episcopate,[5] and his successors were not prepared to accept the superiority of the upstart Patriarchate of Constantinople. During the first half of the fifth century Alexandria, led by her great Patriarchs, Theophilus and Cyril, was uniformly victorious, and on three occasions she succeeded in humbling her rivals of Constantinople and Antioch. But the third occasion—the condemnation of Flavian at Ephesus in 449—was her undoing, for it led to a breach with Rome and the West, on whose co-operation she had hitherto depended. At Chalcedon, in 451, the combined forces of Rome and Constantinople, of Pope Leo and the Emperor Marcian, succeeded in defeating the great See which had so long dominated the churches of the East.

Of all the councils that of Chalcedon is the most remarkable for its dramatic interest and its historical results. For in the church of St. Euphemia at Chalcedon there were gathered all the forces which were henceforward to divide the Christian world. The rival forces of Egypt and the East shouted defiance and abuse at one another from either side of the nave, while the great officers of the Empire, seated in front of the chancel rails, with the Roman legates by their side, impassively dominated the turbulent assembly and guided it with inflexible persistence towards a final decision in accordance with the wishes of the Emperor and the Pope. This decision was not reached without a struggle. In fact, it was not until the Roman legates had demanded that they should be given their passports and that a new council should be summoned in the West, and the Emperor had supported their ultimatum, that the majority were brought to accept the Western definition of the two natures of Christ in one person. The decision thus reached was, however, of incalculable importance for the history of Christendom, both Eastern and Western. If the issue of the Council of Chalcedon had been different, the schisms between the East and the West would have taken place in the fifth century instead of the eleventh, and the alliance between the Empire and the Western Church, which was an essential element in the formation of Western Christendom, would have been impossible.

But, on the other hand, this *rapprochement* with the West

widened the breach between the Empire and its oriental subjects. The solution which had been imposed by the imperious will of a great Pope and a strong Emperor could not remove the underlying causes of national disunion. Already, in the presence of the Council, the Egyptian bishops had declared that they dared not return home with the news that the Patriarch had been deposed, lest they should be murdered by their infuriated countrymen. And their fears were not imaginary, for when the news reached Alexandria the populace rose in revolt and massacred the imperial garrison. The vigorous measures of the government succeeded for a time in imposing a Chalcedonian Patriarch on Alexandria, but as soon as the strong hand of Marcian was removed, he too, fell a victim to the fury of the mob, and was torn to pieces on Good Friday in his own church. Henceforward Monophysitism became the national religion of Egypt, and the minority, which remained faithful to orthodoxy and the Church of the Empire, were contemptuously named Melchites or Basilici, "the King's Men." The real power in Egypt lay in the hands, not of the imperial governor, but of the schismatic Patriarch, and Justinian seems to have recognised this by his reputed offer to unite the prefecture and the Patriarchate in a single office, on condition that the schismatics should return to orthodoxy.

Thus it is impossible to deny the importance of the political element in the rise of the great oriental heresies of the fifth century. If the Church of the Eastern Empire had not become identified with the imperial government the whole history of Monophysitism and the other oriental sects would have been different. Nevertheless, there were deeper causes at work than any nationalist or local separatism. Underlying everything there was the fundamental opposition between the two spiritual elements in the Byzantine world. As the Empire lay on the frontiers of Asia and Europe, so, too, its culture embodied an eastern and a western tradition. To us the oriental element may seem to predominate, but to the native oriental the Empire still appeared Greek. It still represented the old Hellenistic tradition. Indeed, it was the last stage of that mutual interpenetration of East and West which had begun in the days of Alexander. The last expansion of Hellenism took place in the Byzantine age, for it was only then, through the influence of the Orthodox Church, that the native peoples and languages of Asia Minor were absorbed in the unity of Hellenic speech. Although Christianity itself was of oriental origin, it had increasingly incorporated itself into large elements of Greek culture, just as Greek religion and philosophy were, at the same time, assimilating oriental elements; so that by the fourth century the struggle between Christianity and paganism was no longer a struggle between East and West, but one between two rival syntheses of Hellenism and orientalism. The pure oriental spirit, as represented by Gnosticism, was no less opposed to the theology of Origen than to the philosophy of Plotinus, and, in the same way, the Fathers of the Latin Church carried on a double warfare with Roman paganism and with oriental Montanism and Manichaeanism. The religion of the Emperor Julian and his Neoplatonist teachers, in spite of their devotion to the Hellenistic past, was, on the whole, more impregnated with oriental elements than that of the great Cappadocians, Basil and the two Gregories, who were the Fathers of the Byzantine Church. Moreover, the Greeks had carried over into the new religion their traditional love of disputation and logical definition, and it was here that they aroused the strongest resistance in the mind of the oriental world. The poetry of the great leader of the native Syrian Church, Ephrem of Nisibis, is one long diatribe against the Disputers, "the children of strife," the men who seek "to taste fire, to see the air, to handle the light." "The hateful sight of the image of four faces" (Gnosticism or Manichaeanism), says he, "is from the Hittites. Accursed disputation, that hidden moth, is from the Greeks." To him faith is not a thing to be reasoned about or investigated, it is the hidden mystery which he calls the pearl, translucent, but incomprehensible, "whose wall is its own beauty." "The daughter of the sea am I, the illimitable sea. And from the sea whence I came up it is that there is a mighty treasury of mysteries in my bosom. Search thou out the sea, but search not out the Lord of the sea." [6]

The same spirit characterises the greatest of the Byzantine mystics, the fifth-century Syrian, who wrote under the name of Dionysius the Areopagite, and whose influence is so important in the whole history of mediaeval thought. In spite of his debt to the Neoplatonists, above all to Proclus, his essential teaching is the oriental idea of the absolute inaccessibility of the Godhead to human thought and reasoning. It is "the Divine Darkness that is beyond light," the super-essential Something, which has neither mind nor virtue nor personality nor existence, which is neither deity nor goodness nor unity, which is beyond being and eternity, and transcends every con-

ceivable category of human thought. These two writers are
orthodox, but it is easy to see how the same temper of mind
would naturally tend to lose itself in the religion of pure
spirit and to deny the reality of the body and the material
world. This explains the success of Manichaeanism and Gnosticism, but it also found a less radical expression in Monophysitism, which saw in the Incarnation the appearance upon
earth of the divinity in bodily form, and denied the orthodox
doctrine of the human nature of Christ. Thus it was not
mere national sentiment which caused the Eastern provinces
to revolt from the Church of the Empire on this question,
while the West followed the doctrine of the co-existence of
the two natures and the full humanity of Jesus.

Under the influence of these forces the Eastern peoples in
the course of the fifth and sixth centuries all fell away from
union with the Church of the Empire: Egypt, Western Syria
and Armenia became Monophysite, while the East Syrians of
Mesopotamia and the Persian Empire, who remained faithful
to the theological traditions which they had received from
Antioch, became Nestorian. Both parties agreed in their rejec-
tion of Chalcedon and in their alienation from the religious
policy of the imperial government. The sixth century saw the
conversion of the Monophysites from a party into an organised Church and the development of Monophysite monasticism and literature. It was the classical age of Monophysite
culture—the age of the Fathers and Doctors of the Monophysite Church. Two of the greatest of these—Severus of Antioch and Julian of Halicarnassus—were Greeks from Asia
Minor, but the majority—Philoxenus of Mabug, James of
Sarug and the historian, John of Asia, wrote in Syriac, while
the great physician and scholar, Sergius of Reschaina, used
his mastery of both languages in order to translate Aristotle
and Galen into the vernacular. Thus the foundations were
laid of the great work of transmitting Greek science to the oriental world, which had so far-reaching an influence on the
history of mediaeval thought.

Both Nestorians and Monophysites did all in their power to
spread their teachings among foreign peoples, and the expansion of Christianity in Asia and Africa from the fifth century
onwards was almost entirely due to their activity. By the sixth
century the Nestorian missions had reached Ceylon and the
Turks of Central Asia, and in the following century they
penetrated as far as China. Abyssinia, in which the origins of

Christianity go back to the fourth century, adopted Mono-physitism through the influence of Alexandria, and in the sixth century the Nubians and the neighbouring tribes of the desert were converted to Christianity by Monophysite missionaries. At the same time Christianity was penetrating into Arabia by many different channels. In the far south of Arabia, the coun-try of the Himyarites, there was a native Arab church in rela-tions with Abyssinia, which had been founded in the fourth century, and which in the sixth century passed through a ter-rible persecution. From Mesopotamia the Nestorians founded churches among the Arabs of the Persian Gulf and in the in-dependent state of Hira, while the Monophysites and the Church of the Empire were in relation with the tribes of the Syrian Desert and North Arabia, and found powerful protec-tors in the Ghassanid princes, Harith ibn Jabalah and al Mundhir. The contact between the new religion and the old pagan society had a profound effect on Arabic culture. Its in-fluence is seen in the rise of Arabian literature, which sud-denly sprang into vigorous life in the sixth century. Several of the earliest poets were Christians, such as, an Nabigha, Adi ibn Zaid of Hira, and, above all, the greatest of the pre-Is-lamic poets, Imru'ul-Qays, the son of the ruler of Nejd, who entered the Byzantine service under Justinian.

But this is a comparatively superficial manifestation of the deep movement of spiritual fermentation and social change that was passing over the Arab world. A spiritual crisis was imminent which was to transform the scattered warring barba-rous tribes of the Arabian peninsula into a united power that in the seventh century swept over the East in an irresistible wave of religious enthusiasm.

VIII

THE RISE OF ISLAM

The Arabic conquest of the East in the seventh century is in many respects a counterpart to the Germanic invasions of the West two centuries earlier. Like the latter, it marks the end of the centuries of the predominance of the Graeco-Roman civilisation and the formation of a new mixed culture which was to characterise the following mediaeval period. The coming of Islam was the last act of the thousand years of interaction between East and West, the complete victory of the oriental spirit which had been gradually encroaching on the Hellenistic world since the downfall of the Seleucid monarchy. Mohammed was the answer of the East to the challenge of Alexander.

But the Arabic conquest differs profoundly from that of the Germans in the West, in that it owed its origin to the work of a great historic personality. It is true that, as we have seen in dealing with the Byzantine culture, the East was ripe for revolt, and a cataclysm of some kind was probably inevitable. It is true also that the tribes of Arabia, like those of Northern Europe, were on the move, perhaps owing to the pressure o climatic conditions and the progressive desiccation of Arabia But without the work of Mohammed the Arabs could never have attained the unity and the religious impulse which rendered them irresistible. To the Byzantine government the Arabs were a frontier problem, rather than a great menace, like the power of Persia, which was always looked upon as the real eastern peril. For centuries the Empire had been in relations with the Arabian states—the Nabathaeans, Palmyra, and latterly the kingdom of Ghassan, which was a client state of the Byzantine Empire. Any danger from the interior of the peninsula was hardly to be thought of. The wandering Beduin tribes of the desert were in a perpetual state of fluctuation and internecine war, and the settled communities of the west and south owed their prosperity to their trade with the Byzantine world. Nevertheless a process of cultural fermentation and change was taking place in Arabia in the sixth century, and the situation was ripe for the rise of a new power.

For ages the centre of Arabian civilisation had lain in the far south—in the land of Saba, the modern Yemen. Here there had arisen in prehistoric times a settled culture of the archaic type, derived from Mesopotamia, perhaps even as far back as Sumerian times; indeed their later portrait sculpture suggests a Sumerian rather than a Semitic physical type. The Babylonian divinities—Ishtar and Sin and Shamash (with their sexes reversed, however)—were worshipped, and the Sumerian type of temple state existed. In Saba the earliest rulers bore a priestly title—Mukarrib (the blesser)—and in Ma'in the king stood in close relation to the priestly corporation. The god was conceived as the ruler of the land, he possessed rich revenues and numerous priests and dependents. Existing Sabaean inscriptions frequently record the dedication of individuals or families as slaves of the deity, or temple servants, while rulers and priests were, so to speak, adopted into the family of the god as his children or nephews. Unlike the nomadic tribes of the north, the southern peoples were peaceful agriculturalists who constructed extensive irrigation works, notably the great dam of Marib. They were no dwellers in tents; on the contrary they were great builders, and the Yemen is full of the ruins of their castles and temples. Their inscriptions are numerous and are beautifully carved in a fine symmetrical alphabetic script, which probably goes back to the ninth or tenth century B.C.[1]

The prosperity of the land of Saba, however, rested above all on trade. It was a land of gold and precious spices—the frankincense and myrrh that were in such request in the temples of Egypt and Asia; and it was from very early times the half-way house for trade between India and the West, and the starting point of the great caravan route which passed northwards through Mecca and Medina to Sinai and Palestine. Sabaean influence extended along this road, and the state of Ma'an, in Northern Arabia and the land of Midian, seems to have been an early offshoot of the kingdom of Ma'in in the South.

From the time of the foundation of the Roman Empire the prosperity of Saba declined, owing to the rise of new trade routes to India and the establishment of direct contact between Egypt and Abyssinia by sea. Arabic tradition ascribes the fall of Saba to the breaking of the great dam of Marib, which did actually occur both in the year 450, when 20,000 men were employed in its repair, and again in 542, but this no doubt was the result, rather than the cause, of the decline of prosperity. From the third century onwards, Southern Arabia fell more and more under the influence of the kingdom of Abyssinia, and in the sixth century, after the defeat of the Jewish king, Dhu Nuwas, it was ruled for fifty years by an Abyssinian viceroy, who made Christianity the religion of the land. Finally in 570 it was conquered by a Persian expedition, and remained under Persian suzerainty until the victory of Islam.

Nothing could be in more complete contrast to this settled civilisation of the South than the life of the wild nomad tribes of the North, which we are accustomed to think of as characteristically Arab. Their whole existence was devoted to warfare, to raiding the flocks and herds of their neighbours and levying tribute on the caravans of the traders.

While the social organisation of the sedentary peoples possessed a strong matriarchal element, as we see from the legendary Queen Bilkis of Saba, and the historic Zenobia of Palmyra, that of the nomads was purely patriarchal—indeed it is the purest example of the patriarchal type that exists, and it has endured with little change from the days of Abraham to our own. Religion played a far smaller part in their lives than in that of the settled peoples, but it was of the same type, and in this and other respects the ancient Sabaean culture exercised a considerable influence on the nomad peoples.

Moreover from the north they were exposed to the influence of the higher cultures of Syria and Mesopotamia. Here there had arisen first the trading state of the Nabathaeans with its centre at Petra, then that of Palmyra, which during the third century controlled the great trade route between the Roman Empire and the Persian Gulf, and finally the border states of Ghassan and Hira, which stood in immediate relations, the one with the Byzantine Empire, the other with Persia. In the age that immediately preceded the rise of Islam, the latter were the chief centres of Arab culture, and it was at their courts that the early Arabic poets flourished and that the classical form of the language was developed.

Thus Mohammed was born at a critical moment in Arabian history. The ancient civilisation of the South was in full decline, and alike from the North and the South the land was being invaded by foreign civilisation and foreign religions. Mecca, the city of his birth, was one of the last strongholds of Arabian heathenism. It lay upon the great prehistoric trade route from the Yemen to the north, and it probably owed its foundation, like Al Ala and Teima further north, to the Sabaean colonising movement, but we have no knowledge of its early history before its conquest by the Quraysh, a tribe of North Arabian origin about the fourth century A.D.

It was a Temple City of a rudimentary type and owed its importance to the great sanctuary of the Kaaba, the shrine of the god Hobal and his oracle, and to the famous annual pilgrimage which took place at Mount Arafa some miles away. As in the case of the Sabaean temples, the god of the Kaaba was the lord of the city territory, and the Meccans were his clients and subjects, paying to him the tithe of their crops and the first-born of their herd, and the power of the Quraysh rested on their position as priests and guardians of the shrine. On the other hand, the pilgrimage was a ceremony of independent origin, perhaps characteristic of the nomad peoples, and it was accompanied by an inter-tribal truce, a kind of sacred fair, such as is common among peoples of tribal culture.

Thus the Meccan culture had a double character. It occupied an intermediate position between two different types of society—the ancient sacred city of Southern Arabia and the warlike nomad tribes of the desert. And in the same way the age was a transitional one between the old world of Arabian paganism and the advance of the new world religions. These influences played a great part in the development of Mohammed's character and teaching. It is important to remember that he was a townsman, dominated by the tradition of the temple-city-state and the trading community, and with a considerable contempt for the Arabs of the desert,[2] though no doubt he derived from his desert ancestry the warlike and daring spirit which comes out increasingly in the second part of his career. His mind was deeply impressed by the anarchy and barbarism of the warring pagan tribes, and by the vestiges of the vanished greatness of an earlier civilisation. He felt the need for a moral reform of Arabian society—for some new principle of order to replace the primitive tribal law of kinship and of the blood feud—and at the same time he was conscious of the absolute helplessness of man to accomplish anything of his own strength; for like all Semites he possessed that conception of human unimportance before the absolute and irresponsible divine power, which is perhaps the natural psychological result of the harsh conditions of a desert environment. But the all-powerful divinity of Mohammed was not like the deified powers of nature of the old Arabian religion, it was the Gods of the new religions—Jewish and Christian—which were making their power felt in Arabia. No doubt Mohammed came into contact with these new influences during the trading journeys that he undertook on behalf of his wife—the rich and elderly widow Kadijah. The Jewish communities in Southern Arabia, and even as near as Medina, were numerous and active in proselytising—so likewise were the Christians—and though we know little of the flourishing church of Southern Arabia, there is much in the code of laws ascribed to the apostle of the Himyarites—St. Gregentius—which recalls the severe puritan spirit of early Islam. Moreover there was also a class of native ascetics—the so-called Hanifa—who, like Mohammed, were preachers of monotheism and a strict moral law, and one of the most celebrated of them, Zaid ibn 'Amr, was a citizen of Mecca, and died when Mohammed was a youth. Nevertheless it would be a great mistake to look on Mohammed as one who was an apostle of the ideas of others rather than an original force. He was profoundly convinced of his own direct inspiration. Like so many religious mystics, he used to fall into a kind of trance in which he heard a voice—always the same voice—whose utterances he was powerless to control or resist. These utterances took the form of a kind of rhythmic and rhyming prose, similar no doubt to the oracular verses of the heathen poetry, for Mohammed constantly has to defend himself against the accusation of being "a poet" or one possessed by a spirit.

These brief ecstatic utterances gave place, as Mohammed became the leader of a party and the founder of a sect, to a more prosaic and didactic tone, to regulations for the guidance of the young community, to controversies with opponents and

legendary histories drawn from the most diverse sources—
the Talmud, the apocryphal gospels, the stories of pagan Arabia, even the tale of the two-horned Alexander and his expedition to the bounds of the earth. Yet, in spite of its crudities
and its motley character, the Koran has exercised a greater influence on the history of the world than any other single book.
Even to-day it is the supreme authority for the social life and
thought of 200 millions of the human race and is regarded
as divinely inspired in every line and syllable.

The power of the religion of Mohammed rests above all on
its absolute simplicity. It is the new type of world-religion reduced to its simplest elements. It rests on the principle of the
absolute unity and omnipotence of God and of the all-impor-
tance of the life to come. But in spite of its simplicity it is
far from being a rational Deism, as some of its modern apologists have conceived it. It is based not on Reason, but on prophetic Revelation in the strict sense of the word, and on the
belief in the miraculous interposition of the supernatural powers. The life to come is portrayed in vivid material imagery:
the fire of hell in which the unbelievers shall burn eternally,
feeding upon the hellish fruit of the tree Zakkoum, and the
shady gardens of Paradise, in which the faithful shall recline
for ever on high couches, with linings of brocade, drinking
of the waters of the fount Es Selsebil, and accompanied by
their brides, the maidens of Paradise, "the large-eyed ones,
with modest refraining glances, fair like the sheltered egg."

The moral and social teaching of Mohammed is as simple
and straightforward as his theology. To the Unity of God corresponds the fellowship of believers, which abolishes all dis-
tinctions of race and tribe and social rank. The primary duty
is almsgiving: "To ransom the captive, to feed the orphan and
the poor that lieth in the dust." Polygamy and slavery are
permitted, but otherwise the moral code is puritanical in its
strictness and was enforced by corporal punishment.

On the other hand, the moral and doctrinal simplicity of
Islam is balanced by an elaborate ceremonial code; the five
daily times of prayer with the due number of prostrations,
the recitations of the Koran, the severe annual fast of Rama-
dan, the strict rules concerning ceremonial purity and ablu-
tions; above all the ceremonies of the pilgrimage to Mecca
make the Moslem a race apart from other men, like the Jews,
with its centre at Mecca instead of Jerusalem. For Mohammed, in spite of his abandonment of the old Arabian pagan-

ism, remained faithful to his sacred city. The Kaaba remained the House of God, and even the traditional ceremonies of kissing the sacred black stone and performing the sevenfold circumambulation of the Kaaba were preserved, as well as the primitive rites of the pilgrimage to Mount Arafat with the sacrifice of sheep and the cutting of the hair and the nails at Mina. All these practices were justified as part of the "Religion of Abraham," who was the founder of the Kaaba and the ancestor of the Arab race.

The full development of Mohammed's teaching and the organisation of the Moslem community was of course a gradual process. The crisis of Mohammed's career came when he was driven out by the heathen Quraysh of Mecca and took refuge with his followers in the neighbouring city of Yathrib—the modern Medina. This was the Hegira of the year 622 A.D., which became the starting-point of all Moslem chronology. It was at Medina that the new community took form as a political society which was to supersede the old tribal unity, and it was thence that Mohammed sent out the raiding parties against the caravans of the Meccans, which were the beginnings of the secular power of Islam and of the institution of the Holy War. In the desert skirmishes of the next few years, from the Battle of Badr in the year 2 to the taking of Mecca and the Battle of Hunain in the year 8, the whole future of Western Asia and North Africa was decided.

From this point Islam becomes a conquering power that absorbs and unites all the tribal communities of Arabia. It was one of the fundamental principles of Mohammed's teaching that the true believers should live in peace with one another, and the cessation of tribal warfare liberated a great wave of warlike energy, which flooded the surrounding countries. Within two years of the death of the Prophet, the attack on Syria and Persia had begun. But the extraordinary success and rapidity of the Moslem expansion was not merely due to the warlike spirit of the Arab; it was far more a result of the intense religious enthusiasm which makes the Holy War a supreme act of consecration and self-sacrifice, so that to die in "the Path of God" is the Moslem's highest ideal.

This fighting puritanism, which is of the essence of Islam, found its highest expression in the Moslem state under the first Khalifs, and it is this period, and not the great age of culture and philosophy under the Abbasids, which has always been regarded as the Golden Age of Islam by the Moslems themselves. It is described by the writer of *Al Fakhri* in a celebrated passage as follows: "Know that this was not a state after the fashion of the states of this world, but rather resembling the conditions of the world to come. And the truth concerning it is that its fashion was after the fashion of the Prophets, and its conduct after the model of the Saints, while its victims were as those of mighty kings. Now as to its fashion, this was hardness in life and simplicity in food and raiment; one of them (the Khalif Omar) would walk through the streets on foot, wearing but a tattered shirt reaching halfway down his leg, and sandals on his feet, and carrying in his hand a whip wherewith he inflicted punishment on such as deserved it. And their food was of the humblest of the poor. The commander of the Faithful, 'Ali (on whom be peace), had from his properties an abundant revenue all of which he spent on the poor and needy, while he and his family contented themselves with coarse cotton garments and a loaf of barley bread.

"As for their victories and their battles, verily their cavalry reached Africa and the uttermost parts of Khurasan and crossed the Oxus." [3]

It is easy to understand how the professional army of the Byzantine Empire or the feudal levies of Persia were no match for men animated by such a spirit as this, especially as the military strength of the two empires was exhausted by the great struggle with one another that was just concluded. Alike in Syria and Iraq the native population was alienated from its Greek and Persian nobles by fiscal oppression and religious persecution. The Aramaean peasantry had more in common with the democratic simplicity of primitive Islam than with the orthodoxy of the imperial Church or the Zoroastrian state religion, and if they were still in a subject position, the Monophysite and Nestorian Christians were at least on a level with their hated oppressors. But the conquest was an unmitigated disaster to the national Persian culture, and to the flourishing Greek cities of North Syria and the coast region, which latter never recovered from the blow.

Thus the brief years of Omar's Khalifate, 634-643, had converted Islam into a vast empire which embraced Syria, Iraq and Egypt, as well as the Arabian peninsula, but this expansion was fatal to the primitive theocracy. The Arabs had become the rulers of a vast subject population, who retained their old religion, but were bound to pay a poll-tax and were not allowed to carry arms. Society was thus divided into two classes, the Moslem warriors and the tax-paying Christian or Zoroastrian peasants and townsfolk, and to these there was soon added a third class of non-Arab Moslem converts—the *Mawwali* or Clients. Omar attempted to preserve the simplicity and equality of Mohammed's ideal, by forbidding the warriors to acquire conquered lands, and by giving them a regular salary from the state treasury. The main garrisons were established in the camp cities of Kufa near Ctesiphon and Fostat near Cairo, to guard the newly conquered territories, but it was difficult to control these turbulent armies of fanatics from distant Medina, and the old tribal jealousies began to reappear. On the one hand there was the party of the old tribal aristocracy headed by the House of Umayya; on the other the party that was faithful to the original ideals of Islam, the Helpers of the Prophet and the Companions of his Exile—and these, again, were divided between those who supported the claims of his next-of-kin, his cousin and son-in-law 'Ali ibn Talib, and the strict puritans whose principles were as democratic as they were theocratic, and who recognised no man as having any personal claim to the Khalifate. These were the *Kharijites* or the Seceders, but they named themselves the Sellers, *Shurat*—the sellers of their own lives in the cause of God, in allusion to the passage of the Koran, "Verily of the faithful has God bought their powers and their substance, on condition of Paradise for them in return. On the Path of God shall they fight, and slay and be slain—a promise, for this is pledged in the Law and in the Gospel and in the Koran, and who more faithful to his engagement than God? Rejoice therefore in the contract that ye have contracted for this shall be the great bliss." [4] Their position is represented to-day, not only by their lineal descendants, the Ibadites of Southern Arabia, but even better by the modern Wahabite movement, which attempts to restore the primitive simplicity of Islam and has once more almost united Arabia and has driven the King of the Hejaz from the Holy Cities of Mecca and Medina.

From these three parties sprang all the civil wars and dissensions which rent asunder the primitive unity of Islam and left a deep mark on future history. The Khalif Othman, the successor of Omar, and the leader of the Umayyads and the Meccan aristocracy, was slain by the partisans of the strict Moslem tradition. Of his successors, 'Ali abandoned Medina

for Kufa, while Moawwiya, the representative of the House of
Umayya, held Damascus and Syria. In 681 'Ali was murdered by a puritan fanatic, and the Khalifate fell to the
Umayyads, by whom 'Ali's son, Husain, the grandson of Mohammed himself, was defeated and slain at Kerbela in 681—
an event which is still commemorated throughout the Shiah
world on the feast of Ashura with the most passionate grief
and extravagant acts of mortification. Thus the secular principle in Islam was victorious, and Damascus became the capital of a great oriental state under the hereditary rule of the
Umayyad Dynasty. Its frontiers were extended eastwards
to meet those of the Chinese Empire, and westwards to the
shores of the Atlantic: in one year (711) Sind and Spain
were added to the Khalif's domains.

This expansion was accompanied by the rapid transformation of Moslem culture. The Khalifs took over the old Byzantine and Persian methods of government. The lower officials
were almost entirely natives, and Greek and Persian were at
first the languages of the administration. The court of Damascus was the centre of a brilliant culture, and great buildings
like the Mosque of Omar at Jerusalem and the Great Mosque
of Damascus mark the rise of Islamic architecture and art on
the foundation of the Syro-Byzantine tradition.

Thus the Umayyad period (661-750) marks the final triumph of the oriental reaction, the progress of which we have
been tracing. Syria, Egypt and Mesopotamia had been wrested
from their Greek and Iranian rulers and had become the centre of a homogeneous Semitic Empire possessing its own religion and culture, whose power extended from the Atlantic to
the Oxus. The Roman Empire was brought to the verge of destruction and the whole civilised world seemed about to become Moslem. Even in the Christian world, oriental influences
were everywhere in the ascendant. The age of the Syrian Khalifs also saw the Eastern Empire governed by a Syrian dynasty[5]
and the Western Church led by a Syrian Pope,[6] while the
leader of Christian thought and the last of the Greek Fathers
was the Syrian, John Mansur, who had been head of the
revenue department under Walid I and his successors. It is in
the seventh century, and not in the fifth, that we must place
the end of the last phase of ancient Mediterranean civilisation
—the age of the Christian Empire—and the beginnings of the
Middle Ages.

IX

THE EXPANSION
OF MOSLEM CULTURE

During the ninth and tenth centuries Moslem civilisation attained its full development and the whole world of Islam from Spain to Turkestan witnessed the most brilliant efflorescence of culture that it has ever known. But this culture was not purely Moslem, and still less Arabic, in origin. It was a cosmopolitan product, in the creation of which all the subject peoples and cultures, Syrian, Persian, Spanish, Berber and Turk, contributed their share. The foundations of the whole structure had been laid by conquests of the first four Khalifs and by the political organisation of the Umayyads at Damascus, but it was not until the fall of the house of Umayya, in 747, that the great age of cosmopolitan culture began.

The movement which installed the new dynasty of the House of Abbas was to a great extent due to the discontent of the eastern provinces with the purely Arab domination of the Syrian Khalifate. It was in the eastern provinces of the empire, in Khorasan, that the revolt against the Umayyads began, and its success marks the end of the purely Arabic period of Islamic culture. The Khalifate was transferred from Syria to Mesopotamia, which had been from time immemorial the centre of oriental civilisation and empire. Here the new capital of Bagdad was built by al Mansur in 752, and it inherited the prestige, and to a certain extent also the traditions of the Sassanian monarchy.[1] The government was often in the hands of the viziers of Persian blood, such as the great family of

137

the Barmecides under Harun ar Rashid, and Fadl ibn Sahl
under Mamun, and the social life of the court and the capital during the whole period was profoundly affected by Persian influences. Persian or semi-Persian men of letters took a
leading share in Moslem culture, as, for instance, Abu Nuwas
(d. 810), the court poet of Harun ar Rashid, and al Kisai,
the tutor of the Khalif al Mamun. The latter was himself
the son of a Persian woman, and it was during his reign
(813-33) that the predominance of Persian influence at court
was most complete. Nevertheless this was only one element in
the new cosmopolitan civilisation. Mesopotamia was essentially the meeting ground of different cultures, Syrian, Persian,
Arab and Byzantine, and still more of different religions. Not
only was it the centre of Judaism and of Nestorian Christianity; every kind of sect and heresy was represented there,
from Monophysitism and Manichaeanism to such strange relics
of the Gnostic and pagan tradition as the Mandaeans of Babylonia and the star-worshippers of Harran.

The country was a palimpsest on which every civilisation
from the time of the Sumerians had left its trace.

In such an atmosphere it was difficult for the dominant
people to retain the uncompromising orthodoxy and the puritan ethics of primitive Islam. The luxurious and sophisticated
society of the Abbasid capital indulged not only in wine and
music but in the pleasures of unbridled intellectual curiosity
and free religious discussion. Al Mamun was called in jest
"the commander of the Unbelievers," and according to the
amusing epigram that von Kremer has cited, a man could not
be in the fashion unless he professed himself a heretic.

> "O Ibn Ziyad, father of Ja'far!
> Thou professest outwardly another creed than that which
>   thou hidest in thy heart.
> Outwardly according to thy words thou art a Zindiq
>   (Manichaean),
> But inwardly thou are a respectable Moslem.
> Thou art no Zindiq, but thou desirest to be regarded as
>   in the fashion." [2]

These conditions explain the peculiar character of the new
civilisation of the Abbasid period. Although it was Arabic in
language and Mohammedan in religion, its intellectual con-
tent was derived from the older civilisations which had been
absorbed in the world-empire of the Khalifs. This is true above
all in the case of the new Arabic philosophy and science

which arose in this period, and which were to exert so great an influence on the whole mediaeval world. For more than four centuries the intellectual leadership of the world passed to the Islamic peoples, and it was from the Arabs that the scientific tradition in Western Europe derived its origin. Nevertheless, in spite of this, the scientific and philosophical achievements of Islamic culture owe little either to the Arabs or to Islam. It was not an original creation but a development of the Hellenistic tradition which was incorporated in Islamic culture by the work of men of Aramaean and Persian blood. With the single important exception of al Kindi, "the philosopher of the Arabs," the Arabs took little share in the movement. It produced its richest fruits on the very frontiers of Islam—in Central Asia with al Farabi and Avicenna and al Biruni, and in Spain and Morocco with Averroes and Ibn Tufayl.

The origins of the movement are to be found among the Syriac-speaking Christians of Babylonia and the "Sabaean" pagans of Harran, who acted as the intermediaries between Greek and Islamic culture. The Nestorian school of Jundi-Shapur, near Ctesiphon, which was an offshoot of the school of Nisibis, had inherited the traditions of the Syriac scholars and translators of the sixth century and was a centre of scientific as well as theological studies. It was from here that the Arabic philologists of Basra first derived some knowledge of Aristotelian logic, and it was also renowned as a school of medicine. From the time of the foundation of Bagdad the position of court physician was held by Nestorian Christians, and these men were the authors of the first translations of Greek scientific works into Arabic. Al Mamun gave official support to their work by the foundation of the school and observatory known as "The House of Wisdom" at Bagdad in 832 under the direction of the Nestorian physician Yahyah ibn Masawaih. The activity of the school reached its greatest development under the pupil of Yahyah, Hunayn ibn Ishak (809-877), who was not only the greatest of the Syrian translators but also the author of many original works.[3] Through him and his school a large part of Greek scientific literature, including Galen, Euclid and much of Plato and Aristotle and his Neoplatonic commentators was made accessible to the Islamic world. During the same period the foundations of Arabic mathematics and astronomy were being laid by the writings of al Khwarizmi and the three brothers of the Banu

Musa family.[4] Here, however, the dependence on the Hellenic tradition was less complete owing to the knowledge of Indian science which had reached Bagdad in the latter part of the eighth century. Al Khwarizmi, who wrote under the patronage of al Mamun, used this new knowledge in his works, above all the supremely important decimal system of numeration and the use of the zero; and it was from him that the mediaeval Europeans derived their name for the new numerical system (Algorismus) as well as their first knowledge of the science of Algebra.[5] Nevertheless, Arabic astronomy and mathematics were essentially based on the Greek tradition, and here also its transmission was mainly due to the labours of the Syrian translators, especially the Christians Hunayn ibn Ishak and Qusta ibn Luqa (c. 835), and the "Sabaean" pagans, Thabit ibn Qurra (835-900) and at Battani (Albategnius) (c. 850-928), who was one of the greatest astronomers of the Islamic world.[6]

This incorporation and reconstitution of the Hellenic tradition was of course one-sided and incomplete. It took no account of Greek poetry and drama. Its literary influence was limited to prose, and even so was not of the first importance, though it is easy to see traces of the Greek rhetorical tradition in Arabic literature, for example, in al Jahiz, the one-eyed mulatto, who was the greatest stylist and scholar of the ninth century.[7] But from the point of view of science and philosophy, the recovery of the legacy of Greek culture was almost complete. Here the Moslems took up the tradition where it had been dropped by the schools of Athens and Alexandria in the sixth century, and they pursued the same ideal of a reconciliation or conflation of Aristotelianism and Neoplatonism which had been the aim of the last Greek thinkers. But though the main elements of this synthesis were already provided, they carried it out with a vigour of thought and an intellectual ingenuity which render their work one of the most complete and symmetrical philosophical structures that have ever been created. The modern European mind is so accustomed to regard religion and metaphysics and the various natural sciences as independent and autonomous fields of knowledge that it is difficult for us to comprehend a system in which physics and metaphysics, cosmology and epistemology were all combined in a single organic unity. Nevertheless this was the ideal of the Arabic philosopher, and he succeeded to such a degree that the reconstitution of the Hellenic tradition resulted

THE NEW PEOPLE

Ultima Cumæi venit iam carminis ætas ;
Magnus ab integro sæclorum nascitur ordo.
Iam redit et Virgo ; redeunt Saturnia regna ;
Iam nova progenies caelo demittitur alto.

JULIUS CÆSAR

CHRISTUS RHETOR

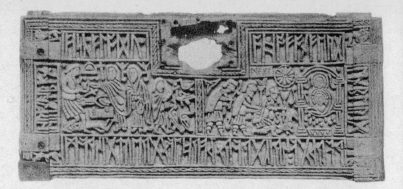

CHRISTIAN-BARBARIAN ART : THE FRANKS CASKET

THE KING AND THE GOD

THE BYZANTINE CHRIST

THE HOMAGE OF THE EAST

IRISH CHRISTIAN ART : THE ST. GALL GOSPELS

ANGLIAN CHRISTIAN ART : THE LINDISFARNE GOSPELS

THE CAROLINGIAN EMPEROR : CHARLES THE BALD

THE CAROLINGIAN BISHOP

THE CONVERSION OF THE NORTH: KING CANUTE

LEWIS THE PIOUS

THE HOLY ROMAN EMPIRE: OTTO III RECEIVING

THE HOMAGE OF THE PEOPLES OF THE EMPIRE

CONSTANTINE THE GREAT

not in a mass of miscellaneous fragments of information, but in a complete system of knowledge, each element of which was inseparable from the whole.

But the universality and consistency of this synthesis rendered it impossible to avoid a conflict with the orthodox doctrine of Islam. The stern simplicity of the religion of the Koran, which taught that the duty of man was not to discuss the nature of God but to obey His Law, had nothing in common with the thorough-going intellectualism of the philosophers. The Hellenic vision of a universal cosmic law, intelligible to the human intellect, left no room for the Semitic belief in a personal God who governed the world and the fates of men with the arbitrary despotism of an oriental monarch. The latter ultimately led to the denial of the principle of causality and of the existence of any necessary order in the state of the universe, the former to the scientific determinism which found its classical expression in the Aristotelian cosmology. As Duhem writes: "Aristotle and his most exact commentators, such as Alexander of Aphrodisias and Averroes, taught that every god is an eternally unmoving intelligence, the simple mover of a First Matter as eternal as itself, and the first and final cause of the necessary and perpetual celestial revolutions; they taught that these revolutions determine in unending cyclical recurrence all the events of the sublunary world; that man, inserted in the chain of this absolute determinism, has only the illusion of liberty; and that he has no immortal soul, or rather that he is momentarily animated by an intelligence that is indestructible, but at the same time is impersonal and common to the whole human race." [8]

But although this theory was irreconcilable alike with Christianity and with Islam, it was not without its partisans in the Islamic world. The astral paganism of Western Asia was still a living tradition in the ninth century A.D., and its adherents were still proud of their ancient culture, as we see from the bold words of Thabit ibn Qurra: "We are the heirs and offspring of paganism which has spread gloriously over the world. Happy is he who for the sake of paganism bears his burden without growing weary. Who has civilised the world and built its cities, but the chieftains and kings of paganism? Who has made the ports and dug the canals? The glorious pagans have founded all these things. It is they who have discovered the art of healing souls, and they too have made known the art of curing the body and have filled the world with civil institutions and with wisdom which is the greatest of goods. Without paganism the world would be empty and plunged in poverty." [9]

It was indeed the pagans who were the founders of science as it was known to the Arabs, and now they had brought back the tradition of ancient wisdom from its long sojourn among the Greeks to the sacred cities of Babylonia, from which it had first sprung. For Thabit was a man of Harran, the daughter of Ur of the Chaldees, and her temples still kept alive the tradition that reached back unbroken to the remote Sumerian past. It is impossible to understand the civilisation of the Abbasid period without recognising that it was not a purely Islamic creation, but that it was the culminating phase of a process of cultural evolution that stretched over more than three thousand years. Empire after empire had risen and fallen, but again and again the ancient Mesopotamian culture had reasserted its power and had imposed its tradition on the minds of its conquerors.

It is true that orthodox Islam realised the danger with which it was faced and did all in its power to check the influence of this alien tradition. For the new philosophy was even more dangerous to mediaeval Islam than was Averroism to mediaeval Christendom, and in the East there was no Aquinas to reconcile the Aristotelian and the theological orthodoxies. For a time the liberal theologians of the Mutazilite school did indeed attempt to bridge the gulf between traditional orthodoxy and the philosophic thought. But this movement owed its origin to the influence of Christian theology rather than to Greek science, and it was the attempt of thinkers like an Nazzam to come to terms with Greek thought that did more than anything else to discredit the movement. The orthodox reaction under the Khalif al Mutawakkil in 834 led to the downfall of the Mutazilites, who had enjoyed the favour of Mamun and his immediate successors, and to the persecution of philosophers like al Kindi. Henceforth Islamic orthodoxy fell back on a strict traditionalism that refused to accommodate itself to philosophy and met all the objections of the rationalist with the formula—Bila kayf—"Believe without asking how."

Nevertheless the victory of the theologians was purely a theological victory. It was powerless to check the cosmopolitan tendency in Islamic culture that had destroyed the supremacy of the Arab element and had liberated the alien and centrifugal forces of the oriental world. In the ninth century all these submerged forces of the older cultures—the Hellenism and paganism of the philosophers, the illuminism of the Gnostic sects, and the revolutionary socialism of the Mazdakites—came to the surface and threatened to subvert the very foundations of Islam that were already shaken by the internal divisions of the Moslem community.

Ever since the seventh century, the question of the rightful law of succession to the Khalifate had not ceased to be a source of strife and schism in Islam. A large part had always remained faithful to the claims of 'Ali, the cousin and son-in-law of Mohammed. They believed that he had been appointed by the Prophet himself at the Pool of Quum, in the last year of his life, to be his Trustee and successor, and consequently that all the Khalifs who were not descended from him and who did not belong to the Holy House of the Prophet were impostors who had no legitimate claim to the obedience of Moslems. This is the origin of the Shi'at 'Ali—the party of 'Ali—that still numbers some 70 million adherents in Persia and India and Iraq, who recognise only the descendants of 'Ali—the Twelve Imams—as true Khalifs. This Shiah party found support above all among the descendants of the conquered peoples, who had brought with them into Islam the old oriental belief in the sacred character of royalty and its inalienable rights—the idea of the Divine Right of Kings as against that of the derivation of authority from the community which was the primitive Islamic theory. Moreover, this idea became blended with traditions and beliefs of a more transcendental character, such as the Gnostic or Manichaean doctrine of the manifestation in human form of the Divine Aeons and with the Iranian belief in the coming of a Saviour King—the Saoshyant. Under the influence of these ideas the somewhat prosaic figure of 'Ali became surrounded with a halo of religious emotion. He was transformed into a semi-divine saint and hero, the holiest and wisest of mankind and the light of God. Thus the house of 'Ali became the object of a devotion which blended the romantic loyalty of the Jacobite with the Messianic faith of the religious fanatic.

Nevertheless their history is an unbroken record of undeserved misfortunes. Every attempt to assert their claims was a forlorn hope which ended in disaster, and even when they lived in obscurity they fell victims to poison and assassination. The Abbasids used them as catspaws to overthrow the Umay-

yads and then thrust them aside in the moment of victory.
Finally, in 873, the main line of the Alids came to an end
with the disappearance of the twelfth Imam Mohammed ibn
Hassan, a boy of ten years of age, whom the Khalif al Mu-
tamid sought to slay.

But even this did not extinguish the hopes of the Shiah.
They refused to believe that the Imam had really perished, for
if there were no true Imam they held that the "world could
not endure for the twinkling of an eye." He was not dead, but
only "hidden," and from his concealment he still watches over
the world and guides the affairs of the faithful until the day
when he will return in triumph to restore the state of Islam
and to fill the earth with justice as now it is filled with injustice. Thus the unfortunate child who vanished so mysteri-
ously more than a thousand years ago has become one of the
most famous figures in the history of the world. In the eyes of
more than seventy millions to-day he is the Mahdi, the Master of the Age, the Rightful Lord, the Plea, the Expected to
Arise, and the Salvation of God. The rulers of Persia since
the sixteenth century have held their power as his vicegerents
and subordinates, and in token of their dependence they were
accustomed to keep a horse always saddled and bridled in
readiness for his expected return.

But though this is the faith of the vast majority of modern
Shiah, it was by no means the only form which the movement
took. There have been numberless other claimants to the succession of 'Ali, and many of the Moslem dynasties, including
the Idrisids of Morocco and the Zaydite Imams of the
Yemen to-day, trace their origin to this source. But the
greatest of all these movements and the one which produced
the most profound effects on the Islamic world was that of
the Ismailia, "the sect of the Seven," which based itself on
the claims of the descendants of the seventh Imam—Jafar as
Sadiq.

The founder of this sect, Abdullah ibn Mamun, seems to
have conceived the idea of combining all the forces of intellectual and social disaffection in a vast subterranean conspir-
acy against the Abbasid Khalifate and orthodox Islam. Its doctrines and its methods of propaganda are known chiefly from
the reports of its adversaries, but it is clear that the movement
was essentially syncretistic, and united the Neoplatonic ideas
of the philosophers with the Gnostic traditions which had
been preserved by the Manichaeans and lesser sects such as

the Mandaeans and the Bardesanians. Like the Gnostics, the Ismailians taught the evolution of the universe from the un·known and inaccessible Godhead through a hierarchy of successive emanations. These are seven in number and correspond to the seven aeons or cycles of the temporal process in each of which the Universal Intelligence manifests itself anew in human form. These seven manifestations are the seven Speakers (Natiq), Adam, Noah, Abraham, Moses, Jesus, Mohammed and the Ismaili Messiah—the Master of the Age. Corresponding to these are seven manifestations of the Universal Soul—the Helpers or Bases—whose function it is to reveal to the elect the esoteric meaning of the Speakers' teaching; thus Aaron supplements Moses, Peter Jesus, and 'Ali Mohammed.

All these revelations, embodied successively in the different world religions, are summed up and fulfilled in the Ismailian teaching in which all veils are removed. But this teaching was essentially esoteric and was imparted in full only to those who had passed through the seven degrees of initiation which made up the Ismailian hierarchy. Only when the disciple had given himself up body and soul to the Imam and to his representative—the da'i or missionary—was the secret doctrine, the Ta'·lim, revealed. The adept was then emancipated from all posi·tive doctrines and all moral and religious laws, for he had learnt the inner meaning that lies hidden under the veils of dogma and ritual in all the positive religions. For all religions are equally true and equally false to the "Gnostic"—the Ismailian initiate who alone understands the supreme secret of the Divine Unity: that God is One because God is All and that every form of reality is but an aspect of the Divine Being.

But this esoteric theosophy is only one side of the Ismailian movement. It also embodied a revolutionary social tendency similar to that which had inspired the earlier movements of Mazdak in the seventh century, and Babak the Khurramite, the famous leader of "the Reds" (al Muhammira) in the ninth century. It was, in fact, the reappearance in a new form of that mysterious "white religion" which had already caused so much bloodshed and social disturbance. On this occasion, however, the movement was directed not by ignorant fanatics like Babak and Al Muqanna, "the Veiled Prophet of Khorasan," but by far-sighted and subtle minds. From their hiding place in an obscure Syrian town,[10] the Grand Masters of the Ismailians controlled the workings of an immense secret organisation and sent out their emissaries in every direction.

During the last thirty years of the ninth century the movement spread far and wide through the Islamic world. One branch of the sect, under the name of the Carmathians, established a remarkable semi-communistic robber state in Bahrein, on the Arabian shore of the Persian Gulf, which exercised a reign of terror throughout Arabia during the tenth century. Basra was sacked by them in 924, Kufa in 930, and finally they horrified the Islamic world by capturing Mecca, massacring its inhabitants and carrying off a vast booty, including the sacred Black Stone of the Kaaba itself.

Meanwhile the Grand Master, on the discovery of his headquarters, had transferred his activities in 907 to Tunisia, where he proclaimed himself Mahdi, and established the Fatimid Khalifate which gradually came to include the whole of North Africa. In 967, after the conquest of Egypt and the transference of the capital to Cairo, the Fatimid Empire had become the richest and most powerful state in the Moslem world. Its dependencies included Syria and Sicily, and owing to the Ismailian propaganda it possessed adherents and secret agents in every part of the Islamic world. The first two Fatimid rulers in Egypt, al Mo'izz (953-975) and al'Aziz (976-996) were wise and far-sighted rulers who made Egypt the most prosperous country in the East. But the most famous member of the dynasty was the sinister al Hakim (990-1021), at once a monster of cruelty and an enlightened patron of learning. In spite of his atrocities, al Hakim espoused the extreme Ismailian doctrine more whole-heartedly than any other member of the dynasty. He proclaimed his own divinity and his followers paid him divine honours. Even to-day he is still worshipped by the Druse of Mount Lebanon as the supreme manifestation of the Divine Intelligence and the final sum of revelation.[11]

After al Hakim the history of the Fatimid dynasty is one of misgovernment and decline. Nevertheless, its external prestige was never higher than in the reign of the weak al Mustansir (1030-1094), who was recognised as Khalif in the Holy Cities of Arabia, and for a time even at Bagdad, the Abbasid capital itself. The devotion which the dynasty inspired amongst many of the Shiah is shown by the lines of the great Persian poet Nasir i Khusraw, who spent a life of labour and hardship in the service of the Fatimid cause:

"God, to Whose Name be Glory! me hath exempted and
    freed
 In this troubled life of transit from the things that most
    men need.
 I thank the Lord Almighty Who plainly for me did trace
 The way to Faith and Wisdom, and opened the Door of
    Grace,
 And Who in His boundless mercy in this world hath made
    me one
 Whose love for the Holy Household [the Fatimids] is clear
    as the noonday sun." [12]

No less devoted to the Fatimid cause was the famous
Hasan-i-Sabbah, who captured the rock fortress of Alamut in
Persia in 1090, and organised the "New Propaganda" of
methodical assassination in the name of al Mustansir's eldest
son Nizar. This branch of the Ismailians attained considerable
notoriety owing to the terrorism which the Old Man of the
Mountain and his emissaries, the Fidais, exercised in Syria
during the crusading period. It outlived the main branch of
the Fatimids and still exists as the Khoja sect whose head,
the Aga Khan, a well-known figure in English society, is a
lineal descendant of the last of the Grand Masters of Alamut and of the Fatimid dynasty itself.

Meanwhile the Abbasid Khalifate was undergoing a process of political dissolution. Since the middle of the ninth century the Khalifs had become more and more dependent on
the Turkish slaves and mercenaries who formed their bodyguard, while the outlying provinces were asserting their independence under the rule of local dynasties. Spain had declared
its independence under a survivor of the Umayyads as early as
755, and the same process took place by degrees in every region
of Islam, until the Khalifate had lost all real power and retained only a kind of religious primacy as the representative
of the unity of orthodox Sunni Islam. In the tenth century,
however, even this nominal hegemony was endangered by the
growth of the Shi'ites who included the most important of the
Eastern dynasties—the Samanids who ruled Khorasan (including modern Turkestan) from their capital at Bokhara, the Zai-
dites and Ziyarids of the Caspian provinces and the Buwayids
of Western Persia and Mosul. In 945 the Buwayids even
made themselves masters of Bagdad, and for more than a century the Khalifs were little more than puppets in the hands of
a Persian and Shiah dynasty. The same century saw not only

the establishment of the Fatimid power in North Africa, but the rise of yet a third Khalifate in Spain, which was founded in 929 by the greatest of the Western Umayyads, 'Abdurahman III of Cordova.

Nevertheless, this loss of political unity did not affect the progress of Moslem culture, and the period of the decline of the Khalifate was also the golden age of literature and science. The rise of the new dynasties favoured the development of local centres of culture, and the tenth century saw the beginnings of the Persian renaissance at the Samanid court of Bokhara and the rise of the new Spanish-Arabic culture in the West, while the court of the Hamdanids at Aleppo was the centre of a still more brilliant development of Arabic culture in Syria. Philosophy and science, which had been discouraged by the orthodox reaction in the Abbasid Khalifate, flourished under the liberal patronage of the Shiah princes. It was the age of al Farabi (d. 950) and Ibn Sina (Avicenna) (980-1037), the greatest of all the oriental philosophers, of al Razi (Rhazes) (865-925), the physician, and al Biruni (973-1048), the astronomer and chronologist, whose works on Indian culture and on the Chronology of Ancient Nations are the most remarkable scientific achievements of the age. It is a curious fact that the mediaeval revival of Hellenistic thought should have had its centre in the ancient Greek kingdom of Bactria, for, with the exception of al Razi, all the writers that we have mentioned were natives of the lands about the Oxus, the region of Bokhara and Khiva and Samarkand. It was here too that the union of the Neoplatonic tradition with the religion of Islam produced its noblest expression in the great Persian poets of the late Middle Ages, Jalalu'ddin of Balkh and Jami' of Herat.

Nevertheless, the tenth and eleventh centuries were, above all, a cosmopolitan age, in which the rivalry of the local dynasties in their patronage of literature and learning, the number of schools and libraries, the activities of trade, and the rise of the great Sufi confraternities, like the religious orders of mediaeval Christendom, contributed to the inter-communion and the variety in unity of Islamic culture. Scholars and men of letters travelled through every part of the oriental world, like al Biruni, who was the first to make a scientific study of Indian religion and culture, and Mas'udi, whose thirst for knowledge led him from the Caspian to Zanzibar and from Ceylon to the Mediterranean.

The encyclopaedic character of the culture of the age can be realised not only from the great world histories of Tabari (838-923) and Mas'udi (d. 956), but best of all from the *Fihrist* of Ibnu'l Nadim (d. 955), "an index of the books of all nations on every branch of knowledge with biographical particulars concerning their authors and compilers, since the beginning of every science that has been invented down to the present epoch." This is a striking proof, not only of the literary riches of Arabic culture during its highest development, but also of the impoverishment and degeneration which it has since undergone.

Even more interesting from the historical point of view is the encyclopaedic collection of some fifty treatises on philosophy and science known as the *Tracts of the Brethren of Purity*, which were composed at Basra about the end of the tenth century; for they seem to represent the esoteric teachings of the higher grades of the Ismailian sect which are otherwise known to us chiefly from the reports of their opponents. Although from the scientific point of view they are very inferior to the writings of Avicenna and the other great philosophers, they show an even more complete fusion of Hellenistic thought and oriental religion. It was their deliberate aim to purify Islam from superstition and irrationality and to unveil the esoteric meaning which lies hidden behind the veil of orthodox dogma. According to their teaching all things are due to the action of the Universal Soul, which through the agency of the celestial spheres exercises its power on all earthly beings. "This power is named Nature by the philosophers, but Religion gives it the name of 'Angel.' The Universal Soul is one, but it possesses many powers which are diffused in every planet, in every animal, in every plant, in every mineral, in the four elements and in everything which exists in the universe." What we call the individual soul is simply the power of the Universal Soul which informs and directs the individual, and consequently the Resurrection of which the theologians speak is nothing but the separation of the Universal Soul from its temporary connection with a material body: in other words, the death of that body; and in the same way the General Resurrection is the separation of the Universal Soul from its connection with the material universe, *i.e.*, the death of the world. And with these doctrines they combined the belief in the cyclical movement by which the world follows the circular movement of the heavens, and returns in 36,000

years to the point from which it started. Only for the wise
there is no return, save for the Brethren, whose mission it is to
guide men to this final deliverance. "Know," they write, "that
we are the society of the Brethren of Purity, sincere, pure
and generous; we have been aforetime in the cavern of our
Father; then the times have changed, the periods have re-
volved, and the time of the promise has come. We have
awakened after the sleepers have finished their cycle, and after
having been dispersed in the lands we have reassembled together according to the promise in the kingdom of the Great
Master of the Law. And we have seen our spiritual city, hanging in the air, whence our parents and their descendants were
driven out by the deceit of the ancient enemy." And they
quote the words of Pythagoras, "If thou accomplish that which
I counsel then when thou art separated from thy body, thou
shall subsist in the air, seeking no more to return to humanity
nor to undergo death once more." [13]

These ideas were widely diffused in the Islamic world in
the tenth and eleventh centuries and form the esoteric or religious background of the higher philosophical and scientific culture. They occur in Avicenna's noble *Ode on the Soul*, and in
the *Diwan* of Nasir-i-Khusraw, and there are even traces of
them to be found in the work of the blind poet Abu'l-'Ala al
Ma'arri (973-1057), who combined the Pythagorean ideas and
the scientific fatalism of the Brethren of Purity with a profound pessimism and scepticism that have no parallel in Arabic literature.

In the West the school of Ibn Masarra (883-931), the mystic of Cordova, represents a similar tendency of thought, while
the treatises of the Brethren of Purity themselves reached
Spain at a very early period through the medium of the Spanish traveller and astronomer Maslama of Madrid (d. 1004)
and al Kirmani of Saragossa, thanks to whom they had a considerable influence on mediaeval Spanish thought.

But this brilliant and sophisticated civilisation already contained the germs of decay. Its luxury and scepticism were
fatal to the spirit of militant puritanism that had been the
strength of the early Moslems, and its centrifugal tendencies
weakened the political solidarity of Islam. The leaders of Islamic culture, the Arabs and the Persians, were relinquishing
their power to ruder and more virile peoples, such as the
Turks, who founded the kingdom of Ghazna in Afghanistan
at the close of the tenth century and the great Seljuk sul-

tanate of Persia and Asia Minor in the following century. This was not altogether a misfortune, since the new peoples infused fresh vigour into the failing forces of Islam and set in motion a new wave of conquest which spread eastward over Northern India and westward to Asia Minor. But this external expansion was accompanied by a lowering and narrowing of Islamic culture. The jealous despotism and rigid orthodoxy of barbarian potentates like Mahmud, "the Idol-Breaker" of Ghazna, consorted ill with the free thought and cosmopolitan culture of the Persian scholars, such as Avicenna and al Biruni, who were their dependents. Thus the coming of Turkish hegemony in Islam was followed by the victory of Sunni orthodoxy over the religious syncretism of the Shiah and by the gradual decline of the scientific and philosophic movement. Persian culture still flourished for a time under the Seljuk sultans owing to the enlightened policy of their Persian vizirs, such as the famous Nizam-ul-Mulk (1017-1092), the founder of the Nizamiyya College at Bagdad, and the patron of the poet and astronomer Omar Khayyam. But the creative period of oriental thought was over. Only in the far West, in Spain and Morocco, did Moslem philosophy and science enjoy a brief period of brilliant expansion before its final eclipse in the thirteenth century.

Nevertheless, Islamic culture retained its pre-eminence throughout the early Middle Ages, and not only in the East, but in Western Europe also. At the very moment when Christendom seemed about to succumb to the simultaneous attacks of Saracens, Vikings and Magyars, the Moslem culture of the Western Mediterranean was entering on the most brilliant phase of its development. In the tenth century, under the Khalifate of Cordova, Southern Spain was the richest and most populous region of Western Europe. Its cities, with their palaces and colleges and public baths, resembled the towns of the Roman Empire rather than the miserable groups of wooden hovels that were growing up in France and Germany under the shelter of an abbey or a feudal stronghold. Cordova itself was the largest city in Europe after Constantinople, and is said to have contained 200,000 houses, 700 public baths, and workshops that employed 13,000 weavers, as well as armourers and leather workers whose skill was famous throughout the civilised world. And the intellectual culture of Moslem Spain was no less advanced. Moslem princes and governors rivalled one another in their patronage of scholars, poets and musicians, and the Khalif's library at Cordova is said to have contained 400,000 manuscripts.

We are so accustomed to regard our culture as essentially that of the West that it is difficult for us to realise that there was an age when the most civilised region of Western Europe was the province of an alien culture, and when the Mediterranean, the cradle of our civilisation, was in danger of becoming an Arabic sea. It is, in fact, hardly accurate to identify Christendom with the West and Islam with the East, at a time when Asia Minor was still a Christian land and Spain and Portugal and Sicily were the home of a flourishing Moslem culture. This, however, was the situation in the tenth century, and it had a profound effect on the development of the mediaeval world. Western culture grew up under the shadow of the more advanced civilisation of Islam, and it was from the latter rather than from the Byzantine world that mediaeval Christendom recovered its share in the inheritance of Greek science and philosophy. It was not until the thirteenth century, after the age of the Crusades and the great catastrophe of the Mongol invasions, that the civilisation of Western Christendom began to attain a position of relative equality with that of Islam, and even then it remained permeated with oriental influences. Only in the fifteenth century, with the Renaissance and the great maritime expansion of the European states, did the Christian West acquire that leadership of civilisation which we regard to-day as a kind of law of nature.

X

THE BYZANTINE RENAISSANCE
AND THE REVIVAL OF
THE EASTERN EMPIRE

While the Islamic world was producing the brilliant civilisation of the ninth and tenth centuries, the Byzantine culture was neither decadent nor stationary. Although for a time there had been a real danger that the Empire might succumb to the victorious forces of the oriental revival, its traditions of discipline and civilised order and the strength of its religious foundation enabled it to survive the crisis. By degrees the Byzantine Empire recovered the position that it had lost in the seventh century, until it became once more the foremost military and economic power in the Eastern Mediterranean.

But it was in many respects a new empire. Both its culture and its political and social organisation had been profoundly affected by the crises through which it had passed. The bureaucratic state founded by Diocletian and Constantine perished in the century that followed Justinian, and much of the older tradition of culture disappeared with it. It was in this period, rather than in the age of the German invasions or at the time of the Turkish conquest, that so much of the intellectual heritage of the ancient world was lost. While the contemporaries of Justinian still retained much of the intellectual traditions of the Alexandrian age, the men of the ninth century possessed little more of the classical literature of Greece, apart from some historians and encylopaedists, than we have to-day. This was partly due to the loss of Alexandria and the Syrian coast towns, such as Gaza, which were the chief centres of classical studies, but the fundamental cause of the change was that orientalisation of Byzantine culture, the development of which has been already described. This process reached its climax in the seventh century, when the eastern and southern provinces were overrun by the Arabs, and the Balkans by the Bulgarians and the Slavs. When the Empire was reconstituted in the eighth century, it was as a predominantly Asiatic state based upon the soldiers and peasants of the Anatolian and Armenian provinces. The old provincial organisation had disappeared and its place was taken by the new military *themes*, whose commanders combined civil and military authority. Under the Isaurian and Armenian soldier emperors, especially Leo III, 717-740, Constantine V, 740-775, and Leo the Armenian, 813-820, both the military and the oriental elements in Byzantine culture attained complete predominance; the tradition of learning and Hellenism, which had been maintained by the old civil service, almost completely disappeared, and the Church became, as in the West, the chief representative of literary culture.

Moreover, the same tendencies showed themselves also in the religious life of the Empire. The loss of the Eastern provinces had freed the Empire from its long struggle with the Monophysites, and it was now more than ever a unitary Church-State of which the secular and religious aspects were almost indistinguishable. But there still remained a latent opposition between the oriental and Hellenic elements in the religious life of the Empire, and the attempt of the new oriental dynasty to enforce its religious policy on the Byzantine Church led to a bitter and far-reaching strife. To Western historians the Iconoclastic controversy, even more than the Christological heresies which preceded it, has always appeared a meaningless strife about ecclesiastical trifles, and it seems absurd that such a question should have the power to shake Byzantine society to its depths. But underlying the superficial issue there was the same deep-seated opposition between two cultures and two spiritual traditions that we have already described in dealing with the Monophysite movement. Indeed the Dispute of the Images involved even more fundamental principles than the earlier controversies. It had behind it not the explicit doctrines of a theological school, but the vague and formless spirit of an oriental sectarianism which rejected the whole system of Hellenic dogma.

From very early times there had existed in the oriental borderland a type of sectarian Christianity which had nothing in common with Western orthodoxy. Instead of the Nicene doctrine of the Incarnation, it regarded Christ as a creature who had received the divine adoption by the descent of the Holy Spirit. It rejected the sacramental teaching of the Church and the use of external forms and ceremonies in favour of a purely spiritual and interior religious ideal. Matter was evil, and all reverence paid to material objects was essentially idolatrous. The water of baptism was "mere bathwater," the material cross was an accursed instrument, and the only true Church was invisible and spiritual. All this current of ideas was not derived from Manichaeanism, though no doubt the Manichaeans themselves were influenced by it. It was derived from a yet older tradition, represented by Bardesanes and some of the Gnostic and Encratite sects, and also by Messalianism.

At a later date it was to appear in the West in the form of the mediaeval Catharist movement, and even to-day it still survives in the strange doctrines of obscure Russian sects, such as the Molokhani, the Dukhobors and the Khlysty.

The link between the earlier and later phases of this great religious movement is to be found in the Paulician heresy, which made its appearance in Byzantine Armenia about the middle of the seventh century and remained for more than two centuries a vigorous and militant power on the Eastern frontiers of the Empire. It was in this region that the new dynasty originated, and it is possible that Leo III himself had been affected by the influence of their ideas. Moreover, his struggle with the Moslem and his attempt to complete the religious unity of the Empire by the forcible conversion of the Jews and the Montanists had made him realise the strength of the oriental aversion to the cult of images which played so large a part in the orthodox worship.

Consequently, in 725, the Emperor inaugurated his iconoclastic policy of ecclesiastical reform and embarked on the struggle with the Church which was to last for more than a century (725-843). On the one side were the Emperor, the army and the eastern provinces, and on the other the monks, the Papacy and the West; indeed, so strong was the hostility of the European provinces to the imperial policy that it led to disaffection and revolt both in Italy and in Greece. Thus the controversy involved on the one hand a struggle between the oriental and Western elements in Byzantine culture and, on the other, a struggle between the secular and ecclesiastical powers which Professor Diehl has compared to the Investitures controversy of the eleventh century in the West. The religious opposition saw in the Iconoclast movement the same spirit which lay behind the Monophysite heresy—the oriental refusal to admit the dignity of the material creation and its capacity for becoming the vehicle of the Spirit, above all in the Incarnation—the visible manifestation of the Divine Logos in human flesh. For was not Christ, in the words of St. Paul, the *image* of the invisible Deity? And did not the visible manifestation of the Divine Logos in the flesh involve the sanctification of material things and the visible representation of spiritual realities? This principle lay at the very heart of Hellenic Christianity, and the last forces of Hellenic culture rallied in defence of the holy images. Their leaders were monks, but they were also artists and poets and men of letters; in fact, the champions of the anti-Iconoclastic party such as John of Damascus, Theophanes the historian, George Syncellos, Nicephorus the Patriarch, and, above all, Theodore of Studium, were practically the only representatives of Byzantine literature in this dark age.[1]

Consequently it is not merely a coincidence that the final triumph of the image-worshippers was followed by a revival of art and scholarship, for their victory was the religious side of a general renaissance of Greek culture and of the waning of the oriental influences which had been in the ascendant for nearly three centuries. Learning was no longer confined to the monasteries, for the civil service recovered its old position as the representative of the classical tradition and of secular learning. The university of Constantinople was refounded by Bardas in 863 and became the centre of the Hellenic revival. From the ninth to the twelfth centuries a series of great scholars devoted themselves ardently to the study of the classics and the recovery of ancient learning—Photius and Arethas in the ninth century, Suidas, the encyclopaedist, and Constantine Cephalas, the editor of the Greek Anthology, in the tenth, and Michael Psellus, John Mauropus, John Italus, Christopher of Mytilene, and many more, in the eleventh. This was the culminating point of the Byzantine Renaissance, and its greatest representative, Psellus, has all the characteristics of the Italian humanists—their romantic cult of antiquity, above all of ancient Athens, their devotion to Homer and Plato, their sedulous imitation of the classical modes of style, and not least, their literary vanity and quarrelsomeness. But it was not an age of creative genius. Its typical products were the great lexicons and encyclopaedias, such as the "Library" of Photius, the Lexicon of Suidas and the compilations of Constantine Porphyrogenitus, works which resemble the literary encylopaedias of China rather than anything in modern literature. Nevertheless, in spite of its lack of originality, it was an age of refined and sophisticated culture, and it is easy to understand the contempt of a scholar like Photius in the ninth century, or a learned princess like Anna Comena in the twelfth, for the crudity and barbarism of the contemporary civilisation of Western Europe.

The same tendency towards a return to the Hellenic tradition which inspired the renaissance of Byzantine scholarship is no less strongly marked in the region of art. There was a reaction from the abstract symbolism of oriental art towards the naturalistic and representational ideal of the Hellenistic tradition. Both painting and ivory carving show strong traces of classical influence, and the illustrations of such manuscripts as the famous Paris Psalter are purely Hellenistic in style. Still more curious is the tendency shown in some eleventh- and twelfth-century manuscripts to illustrate the writings of the Fathers with scenes from pagan mythology, such as the legend of Artemis and Actaeon, or Zeus and Semele, or the dance of the Curetes. And apart from these instances of the direct imitation of ancient subjects and models, there is no lack of classical inspiration in the art of the new age. Even the religious art of the Church, which since the defeat of the Iconoclasts was dominated by theological ideals and subordinated to a strict liturgical and dogmatic scheme, was not immune from this influence, and the finest mosaics of the period—those of the Church of Daphni, near Eleusis—are thoroughly Hellenic in the symmetry of their composition and their statuesque dignity of attitude and gesture.

In architecture, on the other hand, the influence of the East was still supreme, and the new style of church that remained typical of the later Byzantine development was a cruciform structure with five domes, which may have had its origin in Armenia. But even here we can trace the influence of the Hellenic spirit in that the decoration is no longer confined to the interior of the building after the oriental fashion, but flows outwards to the portico and the façade, as we see in St. Mark's at Venice, perhaps the finest remaining example of a Byzantine building of this period. And the fact that so magnificent a specimen of Byzantine art should be found in the West is a proof of the renewed vitality of the imperial culture. In fact there is no other age, not even excluding that of Justinian, in which the influence of Byzantine art was so widely diffused. It reached Europe in many different forms and through many different channels, extending from the Black Sea to Kiev and the interior of Russia, through the Adriatic to Eastern and Northern Italy, and from the Greek monasteries of Calabria to Monte Cassino and Rome.

This renaissance of Byzantine culture was accompanied by a corresponding political revival. The Empire once more turned its face to the West and became a great European power. The Isaurian emperors had already checked the advance of Islam and restored the military power of Byzantium, but the recovery of its European provinces had been prevented by the rise of the Carolingian Empire in the West and by the appearance of a formidable barbarian power in the Balkans. The Bulgarians were, like the Magyars, a people of mixed Finnish and Hun origin, who had formed part of the confederation of Hunnish tribes in South Russia during the fifth and sixth centuries. During the decline of the Empire in the sixth century, they had established themselves as overlords of a subject Slavonic population south of the Danube in the old province of Moesia. The Isaurian Emperors had checked their advance and had planted military colonies of Paulician heretics from Armenia to guard the frontiers. At the beginning of the ninth century, however, Krum, the Khan of the Bulgarians, had taken advantage of Charlemagne's destruction of the Avar power to found a new empire in its place, which extended from the Black Sea to Belgrade, and from the Danube to Macedonia. Henceforward for two centuries the Bulgarians were the most serious menace which the Empire had to face. Again and again they defeated the Byzantine armies and threatened Constantinople itself. Nevertheless they could not avoid the influence of the higher culture with which they were brought into contact by their conquests, and in 864 Boris, the Tsar of the Bulgarians, accepted the Christian faith.

The foundation of Slavonic Christianity was due to the SS. Cyril and Methodius, "the Apostles of the Slavs," who had devoted themselves to the conversion of Moravia; but in spite of the support of the Papacy, they were unable to overcome the opposition of the Carolingian Church and state, and it was in the Balkans, above all in Bulgaria, that their work bore its real fruit. It was here, especially during the reign of the greatest of the Bulgarian rulers, Tsar Simeon, 893-927, that a Slavonic literature was formed by translations from the Greek, and a new Christian Slavonic culture was created which was subsequently transmitted to Russia as well as to the other Balkan peoples.[2] But the new Christian Bulgarian state was not strong enough to maintain itself against the growing power of the Macedonian emperors. Eastern Bulgaria was conquered in 963-72 by Nicephorus Phocas and John Zimisces, and their work was completed by their great successor, Basil, "the Bulgarcide," who extinguished the last remains of Bulgarian independence in 1018 by the annexation of the Western or Macedonian Kingdom.

Thus the Byzantine Empire had once more recovered its old European frontiers which it had lost since the time of Justinian, but this extension of territory brought it again into contact with the warlike peoples across the Danube, who continued to raid the Balkan provinces as they had done in the fifth and sixth centuries. The Magyars, who had taken the place of the Avars in Hungary, were indeed rapidly becoming a settled Christian state, but the nomad Patzinaks who occupied the Russian steppe were a perpetual scourge to the Balkan lands as the Huns had been in the past. The menace of these nomads was, however, lessened by the growth of a new power in their rear in Western Russia. This Russian state owed its origin to the companies of Scandinavian adventurers (Ros) who had settled among the Slavonic tribes and had gained control of the trade route from the Baltic to the Black Sea. Every summer their boats descended the Dnieper from Kiev with cargoes of slaves and furs and wax to the markets of Byzantium or to those of the Khazar kingdom which controlled the oriental trade route from the Volga to the Sea of Azov. Like the western Vikings, they were pirates as well as traders, and throughout the tenth century they made repeated raids on the coasts of the Black Sea and on Constantinople itself. The most formidable of these were the great expeditions of Igor, the prince of Kiev, in 941 and

944, which were followed by the conclusion of a new treaty and by a resumption of friendly relations between the Russians and the Byzantine Empire. Throughout the second half of the tenth century, under the wife of Igor, the Christian Princess Olga, her son, Svyatoslav, and Vladimir the Great (980-1015) the Russian power was advancing at the expense of its neighbours, until it came to replace the Khazar Empire of the Volga as the greatest political and commercial power of the North. The Byzantine Empire succeeded in checking the attempt of Svyatoslav, in 967-71, to conquer Bulgaria and establish his capital south of the Danube, and thenceforward relations between the two powers became steadily closer and more friendly. Finally, in 988, Vladimir, the son of Svyatoslav, made a treaty with the Emperor, Basil II, by which he agreed to receive baptism and to furnish the Empire with a body of 6,000 auxiliary troops, the origin of the famous "Varangian" guard, on condition that he received the hand of Boris' sister Anna in marriage. But it was not until the Russians had brought pressure to bear on the Empire by capturing Cherson, the last survivor of the ancient Greek settlements north of the Black Sea, that Basil fulfilled his part of the treaty. Thus the way was opened for the conversion of the Northern Slavs, and Russia became a part of the Orthodox world.

During the following century Byzantine influence had a profound effect upon Russian society. The bishops and teachers of the new church were all of them Greeks (many of them natives of Cherson), and they brought with them into the north the religious and artistic traditions of the Byzantine Church and the Christian Slavonic script and literature that were to be basic elements in the Russian culture. The churches and monasteries of Kiev with their purely Byzantine frescoes and mosaics bear witness to the strength of this movement in the eleventh and twelfth centuries, and it extended its influence not only to the old Russian centres in the north, such as Novgorod and Pskov, but also, in the course of the twelfth century, to the newly-settled lands in the north east—the region of Suzdal and Moscow that was later to be the centre of Russian national life.

This external expansion of Byzantine influence was the outstanding achievement of the Middle Byzantine period. Unfortunately the spiritual conquest of the Slavonic world was counterbalanced by the decline of Byzantine influence in the West and by a growing alienation between the Eastern and the Western Churches. The close of the Macedonian period saw the consummation of the schism between the Byzantine Empire and the Papacy. The seeds of this process lie deep in Byzantine history. The real cause of the schism was not the dispute between Michael Cerularius and Leo IX, or even the theological controversy concerning the Procession of the Holy Spirit which had arisen in the time of Photius; it was the growing cultural divergence between East and West. The new Hellenic patriotism of the Byzantine revival caused the ruling classes in the Eastern Empire to regard the Romans and the Franks as mere barbarians, and the gradual emancipation of Rome and the Exarchate from their political dependence on the Empire gave fresh grounds for this attitude. Already, in the eighth century, the Emperor, Leo III, had deprived the Papacy of its jurisdiction over the sees of Illyricum and Southern Italy, and had confiscated the patrimonies of the Roman Church in the East. Thus the Byzantine Patriarchate became identified with the Church of the Empire, and the rivalry between the Œcumenical Patriarch at Constantinople and the Pope of Old Rome was more sharply defined than ever.

This rivalry was no new thing. It goes back to the very origins of the Byzantine Patriarchate. St. Gregory Nazianzen satirised the patriotic ardour with which the Eastern bishops vindicated the religious superiority of the Orient over the West at Constantinople in 381,[3] and both at that council and at Chalcedon the attempt was made to assimilate the ecclesiastical position of the new Rome to that of the old. Throughout the preceding centuries Rome and Constantinople were constantly divided on dogmatic questions; indeed, from the fourth to the ninth centuries the years in which they were in schism were hardly less than those in which they were in communion with one another.[4]

Nevertheless these schisms themselves contributed to preserve the prestige of Rome in the East, since the defenders of orthodoxy from the days of Athanasius to those of Theodore of Studium regarded the Papacy as the bulwark of their cause against the attempts of the imperial government to enforce its theological ideals on the Church. It was only after the close of the age of theological controversy and the definite establishment of orthodoxy that this bond of union was relaxed, and the divergence of culture and ecclesiastical usage became more acutely felt. And it was just at this period that Rome lost its political connection with the Byzantine Empire and became closely associated with the rival power of the Franks. The Byzantines were ready to accept the Papacy as the supreme arbiter in matters of faith and the representative of apostolic authority *within* the imperial church, but they were not prepared to admit the superiority of a foreign and "barbarous" church to the Church of the Empire. The acceptance of Frankish rule in Italy and the coronation of Charles as Roman Emperor were in Byzantine eyes an act of secular schism which found its natural fulfillment in a religious one. And while Rome, in the eighth century, was still almost Byzantine in culture and thought, the Frankish Church already possessed a different tradition. The distinctive Western usages that provoked Byzantine hostility, such as the addition of the Filioque clause to the creed, and the use of unleavened bread in the Eucharist, were of Frankish origin and had made their first appearance in the far West in Spain and Britain.

Apart from the question of the Procession of the Holy Spirit, which only by degrees assumed the significance that it was to hold in subsequent controversy, all the matters at issue were points of ritual which to the modern mind appear of infinitesimal importance.[5] But Byzantine religion was so largely bound up with liturgical piety and ritual mysticism that uniformity of rite was of primary importance. While the Western Church was a church of many rites and a single jurisdiction, the unity of the Eastern Church was before all things a unity of rite. Even as early as the seventh century the Council in Trullo had attempted to enforce the observance of its canons on the Western Church, and this claim was never altogether abandoned. Indeed, Michael Cerularius, in 1054, looks back to the Council in Trullo of 692 as marking the beginning of the schism between the Churches.

The Franks on their side were equally uncompromising, and Charlemagne and his bishops adopted a very aggressive attitude towards the Byzantine Church. Rome, on the other hand, occupied an intermediate position between the old Byzantine culture and that of the new Western world, and the Papacy at first attempted to act as a mediator between them; but as Rome was increasingly drawn into the orbit of the Carolingian Empire and its culture, this position became no longer possible.

In the second half of the ninth century the first serious breach occurred when Nicholas I, the forerunner of the great mediaeval popes, came into conflict with Photius, the typical representative of the Byzantine Renaissance, and though the resultant schism was comparatively brief, the restoration of unity was superficial and insecure. It no longer rested on the ideal of spiritual unity, but on the fragile basis of imperial policy. The monastic party in the Eastern Church, who had in the eighth century looked to Rome as their chief support in their struggle for the freedom of the Church against the Caesaropapism of the Iconoclast emperors, could no longer hope for anything from the Papacy of the tenth century, which had become the puppet of local factions or of German emperors.[6] It was now able to rely on its own resources, and Byzantine monasticism flourished anew, not only at Constantinople, at Mount Olympus in Bithynia and at Mount Athos, but in Italy itself, where St. Nilus founded the Basilian monastery of Grotta-ferrata only a few miles from Rome. And if the monastic element no longer preserved its old sympathy for the Papacy, the secular bureaucratic element from which so many of the leaders of the Byzantine Church were drawn[7] was positively hostile. It was only the desire of the emperors to remain in friendly relations with the Papacy for political reasons that preserved the unity of the Church. The decline of the Carolingian Empire had revived Byzantine ambitions in Italy, and ever since the time of Pope John VIII the Papacy had assumed considerable importance in Byzantine diplomacy. Consequently the relations between the Churches fluctuated with the changes of the political situation, and a complete breach between Rome and the East, such as threatened to occur in 1009, was discountenanced by the Emperor, who required the support of the Papacy in his plans for the restoration of Byzantine power in Italy.

Under such conditions, however, schism was eventually inevitable, and it was precipitated in 1054 by the action of Cerularius, whose personal prestige and ambition were strong enough to override the wishes of the emperor. Nevertheless, even this breach might not have been final had it not coincided with the rise of the Norman power and the loss of the Byzantine possessions in South Italy. Henceforward the East had to face the growing menace of Western aggression, and the religious controversy between the Byzantine and the

Latin Churches became identified with the cause of Byzantine patriotism and political survival.

At the beginning of the eleventh century, however, no one could have foreseen the fate that was to overtake the Byzantine world. The Eastern Empire had never appeared stronger or more prosperous than in the last years of the Emperor Basil II. It far surpassed Western Europe in wealth and civilisation, and the conquest of Bulgaria and the conversion of Russia offered fresh opportunities of cultural expansion. The foundations had been laid for the development of a new Byzantine-Slavonic culture in Eastern Europe which seemed to contain no less promise for the future than the corresponding Roman-Germanic development in the West. Actually, however, the former was prematurely checked and stunted while the latter was destined to give birth to the world-embracing movement of modern Western civilisation.

This contrast is due in part to external causes. After the end of the tenth century the culture of Western Europe in spite of its backwardness was free to pursue its own course of development, while that of Eastern Europe was constantly exposed to violent interruptions from without. Within fifty years of the death of Basil II the Byzantine Empire had lost its eastern provinces to the Seljuk Turks, and its communications with Russia were being endangered by the renewed incursions of the Patzinaks and Kuman Tartars from the Northern steppes. In the following century these invasions almost destroyed the promising Christian Russian culture of Kiev, and shifted the centre of gravity of Slavonic Russia to the north-east—the region of Vladimir and Moscow—while a century later these territories also were overwhelmed by the Mongol conquest. And, finally, in the fourteenth century the Ottoman Turks entered Europe, and after putting an end to the short-lived career of mediaeval Serbia, completely destroyed the last remnants of the Byzantine power that had escaped the assaults of the Norman and Angevin rulers of South Italy, and the conquests of French crusaders and the Italian merchant adventurers.

But these external causes, important as they were, are not sufficient to explain the premature arrest and decline of Eastern European culture. The Byzantine culture had preserved the traditions of classical civilisation far more completely than the Latin West, but they failed to propagate them or to hand them on to the new peoples. The higher culture remained the possession of a small and highly-educated class, connected with the court and the capital, and the Slavonic peoples inherited only the religious and artistic elements in Byzantine culture. Consequently, when the end came, the intellectual heritage of Greek thought and letters was taken up not by the daughter cultures of Eastern Europe, but by their old enemies and rivals in the Latin West.

The Byzantine culture faithfully preserved its original tradition, but it was powerless to create new social forms and new cultural ideals. Its spiritual and social life was cast in the fixed mould of the Byzantine church-state and when that fell there was no basis for a new social effort. In the West, on the other hand, no such fixed political framework of culture existed during the early Middle Ages. Society was reduced to its bare elements, and the state was so poor and barbarous that it was incapable of maintaining the higher forms of civilised life. It was to the Church rather than the State that men looked for cultural leadership, and thanks to its spiritual independence the Church possessed a power of social and moral initiative that was lacking in the East. And thus, although civilisation of Western Europe was far lower than that of the Byzantine Empire, it was a dynamic and not a static force, which exerted a transforming influence on the social life of the new peoples. In the East there was one all-embracing organ of culture, the Empire; but in the West every country or almost every region had its own centres of cultural life in the local churches and monasteries, which were not, as in the East, entirely dedicated to asceticism and contemplation, but were also organs of social activity. The Byzantine ideal is typified by the sublime isolation of Mount Athos, a world by itself apart from the common life of men; that of Western Europe by the great Benedictine abbeys which were, like St. Gall, the chief centres of Western culture, or, like Cluny, the source of the new movements that had so profound an influence on mediaeval society.

PART THREE:

The Formation of Western Christendom

XI

THE WESTERN CHURCH AND THE CONVERSION OF THE BARBARIANS

The fall of the Western Empire in the fifth century did not result in the immediate formation of an independent cultural unity in Western Europe. In the sixth century Western Christendom was still dependent on the Eastern Empire, and Western culture was a chaotic mixture of barbarian and Roman elements which as yet possessed no spiritual unity and no internal principle of social order. The temporary revival of civilisation in the sixth century was followed by a second period of decline and barbarian invasion which reduced European culture to a far lower level than it had reached in the fifth century. Once again it was on the Danube that the crisis developed. The second half of the reign of Justinian had seen a progressive weakening of the frontier defences and the Balkan provinces were exposed to a series of destructive invasions. The Gepids, an East German people allied to the Goths, had taken the place of the Ostrogoths in Pannonia, while the Kotrigur Huns held the lower Danube and carried their raids to the very gates of Constantinople. In their wake came the Slavs, who now for the first time emerge from the prehistoric obscurity that envelops their origins. Faced by so many dangers, the imperial government found itself unabl to defend its frontiers by military means and fell back upo diplomacy. It egged on the Utigurs of the Kuban steppe to attack the Kotrigurs, the Herules and the Lombards against

the Gepids, and the Avars against the Gepids and the Slavs.
Thus in 567, after the death of Justinian, the Avars united
with the Lombards to destroy the Gepid kingdom, and the
government of Justin II, hoping to recover Sirmium for the
Empire, left the Gepids to their fate. But here the Byzantines overreached themselves, for Bayan, the great Khan of
the Avars, was no petty chieftain to be made the catspaw of
imperial diplomacy, but a ruthless Asiatic conqueror of the
type of Attila and Genghis Khan. In place of a relatively
stable Germanic state, the Empire now had to deal with a
people of warlike nomads whose empire extended from the
Adriatic to the Baltic. Under its pressure the Danube frontier
finally gave way, and the Illyrian provinces, which had been
for nearly four hundred years the foundation of the military
strength of the Empire and the cradle of its soldiers and
rulers, were occupied by Slavonic peoples who were dependent on the Avars.

But the Empire was not the only power to suffer. All Central Europe fell a prey to the Asiatic conquerors. Their raids
extended as far as the frontiers of the Frankish kingdom. The
Northern Sueves were forced to evacuate the lands between
the Elbe and the Oder, and Eastern Germany was colonised
by the Slavonic subjects of the Avars. Thus of the East German peoples who had formerly ruled Eastern Europe from the
Baltic to the Black Sea, there remained only the Lombards,
and they were too wise to try conclusions with their Asiatic
allies. Immediately after the fall of the Gepid Kingdom
they evacuated their lands on the Danube and marched on
Italy. Here again the Empire was powerless to protect its
subjects. Lombardy and the whole of the interior of the peninsula was occupied by the invaders, and the Byzantines only
preserved their hold upon the coastal districts—the Venetian
Islands, Ravenna and the Pentapolis, the Duchy of Rome,
and Genoa, Amalfi and Naples.

This was the last blow to the declining civilisation of Italy,
and we cannot wonder that to the men of that age the end of
all things seemed at hand. The writings of St. Gregory the
Great reflect the appalling sufferings and the profound pessimism of the age. He even welcomes the pestilence that was
devastating the West as a refuge from the horrors that surrounded him. "When we consider the way in which other
men have died we find a solace in reflecting on the form
of death that threatens us. What mutilations, what cruelties

have we seen inflicted upon men, for which death is the only
cure and in the midst of which life was a torture!" [1] He sees
Ezekiel's prophecy of the seething pot fulfilled in the fate of
Rome: "Of this city it is well said 'The meat is boiled
away and the bones in the midst thereof.' . . . For where is
the Senate? Where is the People? The bones are all
dissolved, the flesh is consumed, all the pomp of the digni-
ties of this world is gone. The whole mass is boiled away."

"Yet even we who remain, few as we are, still are daily
smitten with the sword, still are daily crushed by innumerable
afflictions. Therefore let it be said, 'Set the pot also empty
upon the coals.' For the Senate is no more, and the People
has perished, yet sorrow and sighing are multiplied daily
among the few that are left. Rome is, as it were, already
empty and burning. But what need is there to speak of men
when, as the work of ruin spreads, we see the very buildings
perishing. Wherefore it is fitly added concerning the city
already empty, 'Let the brass thereof be hot and melt.' Already the pot itself is being consumed in which were first
consumed the flesh and the bones. . . ." [2]

But the worst had not yet come. In the seventh century the
Arabs conquered Byzantine Africa, the most civilised province of the West, and the great African Church, the glory of
Latin Christianity, disappears from history. Early in the eighth
century the tide of Moslem invasion swept over Christian
Spain and threatened Gaul itself. Christendom had become
an island isolated between the Moslem south and the Barbarian north.

Yet it was in this age of universal ruin and destruction
that the foundations of the new Europe were being laid by
men like St. Gregory, who had no idea of building up a new
social order but who laboured for the salvation of men in a
dying world because the time was short. And it was just this
indifference to temporal results which gave the Papacy the
power to become a rallying-point for the forces of life in the
general decadence of European civilisation. In the words of
the inscription which Pope John III set up in the Church
of the Most Holy Apostles: "In a straitened age, the Pope
showed himself more generous and disdained to be cast down
though the world failed." [3]

At the very moment of the fall of the Empire in the West,
St. Augustine, in his great book *Of the City of God*, had set
forth the programme which was to inspire the ideals of the

new age. He viewed all history as the evolution of two opposite principles embodied in two hostile societies, the heavenly and the earthly cities, Sion and Babylon, the Church and
the World. The one had no final realisation on earth, it was
"in via," its *patria* was heavenly and eternal; the other found
its realisation in earthly prosperity, in the wisdom and glory
of man; it was its own end and its own justification. The
State, it is true, was not condemned as such. In so far as it
was Christian, it subserved the ends of the heavenly city. But
it was a subordinate society, the servant and not the master:
it was the spiritual society that was supreme. The moment that
the state came into conflict with the higher power, the moment that it set itself up as an end in itself, it became identified with the earthly city and lost all claims to a higher sanction than the law of force and self-interest. Without justice,
what is a great kingdom but a great robbery—*magnum latro-
cinium?* Conquering or being conquered does no one either
good or harm. It is pure waste of energy, the game of fools
for an empty prize. The terrestrial world is unsubstantial and
transitory, the only reality worth striving for is that which is
eternal—the heavenly Jerusalem—"the vision of peace."

This ideal of the supremacy and independence of the spiritual power found its organ of expression above all in the
Papacy.[4] Already before the fall of the Empire the Roman
bishop possessed a unique position as the successor and representative of St. Peter. Rome was the "Apostolic See" *par
excellence*, and in virtue of this authority it had intervened
decisively against both Constantinople and Alexandria in the
doctrinal struggles of the fourth and fifth centuries. The decline of the Empire in the West naturally enhanced its
prestige, for the process by which the bishop became the
representative of the Roman tradition in the conquered provinces was far more accentuated in the case of the ancient
capital. The old imperial tradition was carried over into the
sphere of religion. In the fifth century St. Leo the Great,
addressing his people on the Feast of SS. Peter and Paul,
could say, "These are they, who have brought thee to such
glory as a holy nation, a chosen people, a royal and priestly
city that thou mightest be made the head of the world by the
Holy See of St. Peter, and mightest bear rule more widely
by divine religion than by earthly dominion." [5]

The Pope was still a loyal subject of the Emperor and regarded the cause of the Empire as inseparable from that of

the Christian religion. The Liturgy couples together "the foes of the Roman name and the enemies of the Catholic Faith," and the Roman Missal still contains a prayer for the Roman Empire "that God may subdue to the Emperor all the barbarous nations, to our perpetual peace." But after the Lombard invasion and the age of St. Gregory, the actual authority of the imperial government in Italy was reduced to a shadow, and it was on the Pope that the responsibility fell for the safety of Rome and the feeding of its inhabitants. Rome became, like Venice or Cherson, a kind of semi-independent member of the Byzantine state. It remained an open door between the civilised East and the barbarised West; it was a common meeting-ground to both, without exactly belonging to either.

This anomalous position was very favourable to the exercise of papal influence in the barbaric kingdoms of the West, since the Papacy enjoyed the prestige of its connection with the Eastern Empire without any danger of being considered an instrument of imperial policy, and thus the Frankish kings raised no objection to the Bishop of Arles receiving the office of Apostolic Vicar for the Church in Gaul. Nevertheless, the power of the Papacy, and with it that of the Universal Church, was greatly limited by the inherent weakness of the local churches. The Church of the Frankish kingdom, especially, suffered from the same process of barbarisation and cultural decadence that affected the whole society.

The bishop became a territorial magnate, like the count, and the greater was his wealth and power, the greater was the danger of the secularisation of the office. The monarchy had no direct intention of interfering with the prerogatives of the Church, but it naturally claimed the right of appointing to an office which took such an important share in the administration of the kingdom, and its candidates were often of very dubious character, like the "robber bishops," Salonius and Sagittarius, whose exploits are described by Gregory of Tours (*Lib. IV, cap.* 42; V, *cap.* 20). Moreover, the transformation of the state into an agrarian society and the progressive decline of the city had a most deleterious effect on the Church, since the influence of the barbarous and half pagan countryside came to predominate over that of the cities. For while in the East Christianity had penetrated the countryside from the first, and the peasantry was, if anything, more Christian than the townspeople, in Western Europe the Church had grown up in the towns and so had failed to make a deep impression on the peasants and countryfolk. They were *pagani*, the "pagans," who clung after the manner of peasants to their immemorial customs and beliefs, to the rites of seedtime and harvest, and to the venerations of their sacred trees and springs.

Yet the fundamental ethos of the new religion was in no way alien to the peasant life. Its first beginning had been amongst the fishermen and peasants of Galilee, and the Gospel teaching is full of the imagery of the field and the fold and the vineyard. Christianity only needed a new organ besides the city episcopate in order to permeate the countryside. Now at the very moment when the conversion of the Empire was binding the Church closer to the urban polity, a new movement was drawing men away from the city. The heroes of the second age of Christianity, the successors of the martyrs, were the ascetics—the men who deliberately cut themselves off from the whole inheritance of city culture in order to live a life of labour and prayer under the simplest possible conditions.

In the fourth century the deserts of Egypt and Syria were peopled with colonies of monks and hermits which became schools of the religious life for all the provinces of the Empire, and the neighbouring peoples of the East. But in the West, though its fundamental ideals were the same, the difference of social conditions forced the monasteries to take up a different attitude towards the society that surrounded them.

In the rural districts of the West the monastery was the only centre of Christian life and teaching, and it was upon the monks rather than upon the bishops and their clergy that the task of converting the heathen or semi-heathen peasant population ultimately fell. This is evident even as early as the fourth century in the life of the founder of Gallic monasticism, the great Martin of Tours, but its great development was due to the work of John Cassian, who brought Gaul into direct contact with the tradition of the monks of the Egyptian desert, and to St. Honoratus, the founder of Lerins, which became the greatest monastic centre of Western Europe in the fifth century and the source of a far-reaching influence.

But it was in the newly-converted Celtic lands of the far West that the influence of monasticism became all-important. The beginnings of the monastic movement in this region dates from the fifth century, and probably owes its origins to the influence of Lerins, where St. Patrick had studied in the years before his apostolate and where in 433 a British monk, Faustus, had held the position of abbot. But though St. Patrick had introduced the monastic life into Ireland, his organisation of the Church followed the traditional lines of episcopal organisation, as did that of the British Church in Wales. Since, however, the Roman bishop was always the bishop of a city, the normal system of ecclesiastical organisation possessed no natural social basis in the Celtic lands, where the social unit was not the city but the tribe. Consequently, the great extension of monastic influence and culture in the sixth century led to the monastery's taking the place of the bishopric as the centre of ecclesiastical life and organisation. The movement started in South Wales, where the monastery of St. Illtyd on Caldey Island became a great school of the monastic life after the model of Lerins early in the sixth century. From this centre the monastic revival was diffused throughout western Britain and Brittany by the work of St. Samson, St. Cadoc of Llancarvan, St. Gildas and St. David. Moreover, the great development of Irish monasticism that took place in the sixth century under the "Saints of the Second Order" was closely related to this movement.[6] St. Finnian of Clonard (d. 549), the chief inaugurator of the new type of monasticism, was in close relations with St. Cadoc of Llancarvan and with St. Gildas, and it was through him and his disciples, above all St. Ciaran of Clonmacnoise (d. 549), St. Brendan of Clonfert, and St. Columba of Derry and Iona, that the monastic tradition of St. Illtyd and his school was diffused in Ireland. The importance of this movement was literary as well as ascetic, for the school of St. Illtyd and St. Cadoc cultivated the traditions of the old schools of rhetoric, as well as those of purely ecclesiastical learning, and encouraged the study of classical literature.

This is the origin of the movement of culture which produced the great monastic schools of Clonard and Clonmacnoise and Bangor, and made Ireland the leader of Western culture from the close of the sixth century. It is, however, probable that its development also owes something to native traditions, for the Irish, unlike the other barbaric peoples, possessed a native tradition of learning, represented by the schools of the poets or *Filid*, which enjoyed considerable wealth and social prestige. The new monastic schools entered in a sense into the inheritance of this native tradition, and were able to replace the old druidic and bardic schools as the intellectual organs of Irish society. By degrees the imported classical culture of the Christian monasteries was blended with the native literary tradition, and there arose a new vernacular literature inspired in part by Christian influence but founded in part on native pagan traditions. Although this literature has come down to us mainly through Middle Irish versions of mediaeval date, there can be no doubt that its original creation goes back to the seventh and eighth centuries—the Golden Age of Irish Christian culture —and that the literary tradition of mediaeval Ireland has its roots deep in the prehistoric past. The most striking example of this is the great prose epic or saga—the *Tain Bo Cualgne*—which takes us back behind the Middle Age and behind the classical tradition to the heroic age of Celtic culture, and preserves the memory of a stage of society resembling that of the Homeric world. Thus there was no sudden break between the old barbaric tradition and that of the Church, such as occurred elsewhere, and a unique fusion took place between the Church and the Celtic tribal society entirely unlike anything else in Western Europe. The hierarchic episcopal organisation of the Church, which was common to the rest of Christendom, was here completely subordinated to the monastic system. Bishops of course continued to exist and to confer orders, but they were no longer the rulers of the Church. The monasteries were not only the great centres of religious and intellectual life; they were also centres of ecclesiastical jurisdiction. The abbot was the ruler of a diocese or *paroechia*, and usually kept one or more bishops in his community to perform the necessary episcopal functions, except in those cases in which he was a bishop himself. Still more extraordinary is the fact that this kind of quasi-episcopal jurisdiction was sometimes exercised by women, for the see of Kildare was a dependency of St. Bridget's great monastery and was ruled jointly by bishop and abbess, so that it was in the phrase of her biographer "a see at once episcopal and virginal." [7]

The monasteries were closely connected with the tribal society, for it was the prevailing if not the universal custom for the abbot to be chosen from the clan to which the founder belonged. Thus the *Book of Armagh* records in the ninth century that the Church of Trim had been ruled for nine generations by the descendants of the chieftain who endowed the see in the days of St. Patrick. In the same way the early abbots of Iona belonged to the family of St. Columba, the royal race of the northern Ui Niall.[8]

In organisation and way of life the Irish monks closely resembled their Egyptian prototypes. They rivalled the monks of the desert in the rigour of their discipline and the asceticism of their life. Their monasteries were not great buildings like the later Benedictine abbeys, but consisted of groups of huts and small oratories, like the Egyptian laura, and were surrounded by a *rath* or earthwork. Moreover, they preserved the oriental idea of the eremitical life as the culmination and goal of the monastic state. In Ireland, however, this ideal assumed a peculiar form that is not found elsewhere. It was common for monks to devote themselves to a life of voluntary exile and pilgrimage. The case recorded in the Anglo-Saxon Chronicle (*s.a.* 891) of the three monks "who stole away from Ireland in a boat without any oars because they would live in a state of pilgrimage for the love of God, they recked not where," is typical of this development. It led to a movement of travel and exploration which is reflected in a legendary form in the adventures of St. Brendan the Navigator. When the Vikings first discovered Iceland they found that the Irish "papas" had been there before them, and every island of the northern seas had its colony of ascetics. The informants of Dicuil, the Carolingian geographer, had even sailed beyond Iceland and reached the frozen Arctic seas.

But the real importance of this movement lies in the impulse that it gave to missionary activity, and it was as missionaries that the Celtic monks made their most important contribution to European culture. The monastic colonies of St. Columba at Iona, and of his namesake Columbanus at Luxeuil, were the starting points of a great expansion of Christianity. To the one was due the conversion of Scotland and of the Northumbrian kingdom, to the other the revival of monasticism and the conversion of the remaining pagan elements in the Frankish kingdom. Luxeuil, with its six hundred monks, became the monastic metropolis of Western Europe, and the centre of a great colonising and missionary activity. Very many of the great mediaeval monasteries not only of France, but of Flanders and Germany, owe their foundation to its work—for example, Jumièges, St. Vandrille, Solignac and Corbie in France, Stavelot and Malmedy in Belgium, St.

Gall and Dissentis in Switzerland, and Bobbio, the last foundation of Columbanus himself, in Italy. All through Central
Europe the wandering Irish monks have left their traces, and
the German Church still honours the names of St. Kilian, St.
Gall, St. Fridolin and St. Corbinian among its founders.

It is easy to understand what an influence this movement
must have exercised on the peasants. It was essentially rural,
avoiding the towns, and seeking the wildest regions of forest
and mountain. Far more than the preaching of bishop and
priest from the distant city, the presence of these colonies of
black-robed ascetics must have impressed the peasant mind
with the sense of a new power that was stronger than the
nature spirits of the old peasant religion. Moreover, the Irish
monks were themselves countrymen with a deep feeling for
nature and for the wild things. The biographer of Columban
relates how, as he went through the forest, the squirrels and
the birds would come to be caressed by him, and "would frisk
about and gambol in great delight, like puppies fawning on
their master." [9] Indeed, the legends of the monastic saints are
full of an almost Franciscan feeling for nature. It is true
that the Celtic monastic ideal was that of the desert; they
loved the forest or, better still, uninhabited and inaccessible
islands, like Skellig Michael, one of the most impressive of
monastic sites, just as the Eastern monks to-day still choose
Mount Athos or the Meteora. Nevertheless, the monastic
settlements were forced by necessity to take up the peasants'
task, to clear the forest and to till the ground. The lives of
the monastic saints of the Merovingian period, whether Gallic
or Celtic, are full of references to their agricultural labours
—their work of clearing the forest and of bringing back to
cultivation the lands that had been abandoned during the
period of the invasions. Many of them, like St. Walaric, the
founder of St. Valery-sur-Somme, were themselves of peasant
origin. Others, though noble by birth, spent their whole lives
working as peasants, like St. Theodulph, the abbot of St.
Thierry near Rheims, who would never cease from labour and
whose plough was hung up in the church as a relic by the
peasants.

These were the men to whom the conversion of the peasants was really due, for they stood so near to the peasant culture that they were able to infuse it with the spirit of the
new religion. It was through them that the cultus that had
been paid to the spirits of nature was transferred to the

Saints. The sacred wells, the sacred trees and the sacred stones retained the devotion of the people, but they were consecrated to new powers, and acquired new associations. The peasants near Rheims paid honour to a holy tree, which was said to have sprung miraculously from the ox-goad which that same St. Theodulph thrust into the earth. In the West the stone crosses of the saints replaced the menhirs of the heathen cult,[10] just as the great tumulus of Carnac has been crowned by a chapel of St. Michael, and a dolmen at Ploucret has been turned into a chapel of the Seven Saints. It was only with difficulty that the Church succeeded in putting down the old pagan customs, and it was usually done by providing a Christian ceremony to take the place of the heathen one. The statement in the *Liber Pontificalis* that St. Leo instituted the ceremonies of Candlemas in order to put an end to the Lupercalia is perhaps erroneous, but the Great Litanies and processions of April 25th seem to have taken the place of the Robigalia, and the feast of the Collection or *Oblatio* that of the opening of the Ludi Apollinares. Still more remarkable is the correspondence between the Ember Days and the seasonal pagan Feriae of the harvest, the vintage and the seedtime. The liturgy for the Advent Ember Days, especially, is full of references to the seedtime, which it associates with the mystery of the Divine Birth. "The Divine seed descends, and whereas the fruits of the field support our earthly life, this seed from on high gives our soul the Food of Immortality. The earth has yielded its corn, wine and oil, and now the ineffable Birth approaches of Him who through His mercy bestows the Bread of Life upon the Sons of God." [11]

But this liturgical transfiguration of the spirit of the Vegetation Religion was too spiritual to reach the mind of the peasant. In spite of all the efforts of the Church the old pagan rites still survived and all through Europe the peasants continued to light the midsummer fires on St. John's Eve and to practise the magic ritual of fertility in spring.[12] Even to-day, as Maurice Barrès has shown in *La Colline Inspirée*, the sinister powers of the old nature religion are still latent in the European countryside and are apt to reassert themselves whenever the control of the new order is relaxed. Nevertheless it is remarkable that it is just in those regions where the external survivals of pagan customs are most noticeable, as in Brittany and the Tirol, that the Christian ethos has affected the life of the peasant most deeply. For Christianity did succeed in remoulding the peasant culture. The old gods disappeared and their holy places were reconsecrated to the saints of the new religion. It is true that the cult of the local sanctuaries and their pilgrimages gave occasion to all kinds of strange survivals, as we see in the Breton Pardons to this day. But it was this very continuity of culture —this association of the old with the new—which opened the peasant mind to Christian influences that it could not receive in any other way. And the disappearance of the old peasant customs in later times has often been accompanied by a relapse into paganism of a far deeper kind than the paganism of archaeological survivals.

But the evangelisation of rural Europe during the Merovingian period is only one among the services which monasticism rendered to European civilisation. It was also destined to be the chief agent of the Papacy in its task of ecclesiastical reform and to exert a vital influence on the political and cultural restoration of European society. The same period that saw the rise of Celtic monasticism in Ireland was also marked by a new development of monasticism in Italy which was to have an even greater historical importance. This was due to the work of St. Benedict "the Patriarch of the Monks of the West," who founded the monastery of Monte Cassino about the year 520. It was he who first applied the Latin genius for order and law to the monastic institution and who completed that socialisation of the monastic life which had been begun by St. Pachomius and St. Basil. The ideal of the monks of the desert was that of individual asceticism and their monasteries were communities of hermits. That of the Benedictine was essentially co-operative and social: its aim was not to produce heroic feats of asceticism, but the cultivation of the common life, "the school of the service of the Lord." In comparison with the rules of Pachomius and St. Columban, that of St. Benedict appears moderate and easy, but it involved a much higher degree of organisation and stability. The Benedictine monastery was a state in miniature with a settled hierarchy and constitution and an organised economic life. From the first it was a landowning corporation which possessed villas and serfs and vineyards, and the monastic economy occupies a larger place in the rule of St. Benedict than in any of the earlier rules. Hence the importance of co-operative labour which filled so large a part of the life of the Benedictine monk, for St. Benedict was inspired by the ideals which St. Augustine had set forth in his treatise *De opere monachorum* and had an equal detestation of the idle and "gyrovagous" monks who had done so much to bring monasticism into disrepute in the West.

But the primary duty of the monk was not manual labour, but prayer, above all the common recitation of the Divine Office, which St. Benedict terms "the work of God." Nor was study neglected. It was the monasteries which kept alive the classical tradition after the fall of the Empire. In fact the last representative in the West of the learned tradition of the Roman civil service—Cassiodorus—was also a founder of monasteries and the author of the first programme of monastic studies. It is true that the ostentatious literary culture of the old rhetorician at Vivarium was alien from the stern simplicity and spirituality which inspired the Benedictine rule, but Western monasticism was to inherit both traditions. Under the influence of the Papacy the rule of St. Benedict became the Roman standard of the monastic life and finally the universal type of Western monasticism.[13] After the Celtic expansion came the Latin organisation.

The beginning of this Benedictine world mission was due to the action of St. Gregory, himself a Benedictine monk. It was from the Benedictine monastery on the Caelian that St. Augustine and his monks set out on their mission for the conversion of England, and the Benedictine monastery at Canterbury, probably the earliest Benedictine foundation outside Italy, became the starting point of a movement of religious organisation and unification which created a new centre of Christian civilisation in the West.

The appearance of the new Anglo-Saxon culture of the seventh century is perhaps the most important event between the age of Justinian and that of Charlemagne, for it reacted with profound effect on the whole continental development. In its origins it was equally indebted to the two forces that we have described—the Celtic monastic movement and the Roman Benedictine mission. Northern England was common ground to them both, and it was here that the new Christian culture arose in the years between 650 and 680 owing to the interaction and fusion of the two different elements. Christianity had been introduced into Northumbria by the Roman Paulinus who baptised King Edwin in 627 and established the metropolitan see at the old Roman city of York, but the defeat of Edwin by the heathen Penda and the Welsh Cadwallon led to the temporary ruin of the Anglian Church. It was re-established by King Oswald in 634 with the help of St. Aidan and the Celtic missionaries whom he brought from Iona to Lindisfarne, and throughout his reign Celtic influence reigned supreme. It was not until the synod of Whitby in 664 that the Roman party finally triumphed, owing to the intervention of St. Wilfrid, who dedicated his long and stormy life to the service of the Roman unity. It is to him and to his friend and fellow-worker, St. Benedict Biscop, that the establishment of Benedictine monasticism in Northern England is due. Nor was their activity solely of ecclesiastical importance; for they were the missionaries of culture as well as of religion, and they were responsible for the rise of the new Anglian art. They brought back from their many journeys to Rome and Gaul skilled craftsmen and architects, as well as books, pictures, vestments and musicians, and their abbeys of Ripon and Hexham, Wearmouth and Jarrow, were the great centres of the new culture. At the same time in the South, a similar work was being carried out by the Greek-Syrian archbishop, Theodore, and the African abbot, Hadrian, who were sent from Rome in 668. In them we can trace the appearance of a new wave of higher culture from the East, which does much to explain the rise of Anglo-Saxon scholarship and the superiority of the Latin of Bede and Alcuin to the barbarous style of Gregory of Tours or the Celtic author of the *Hisperica Famina*. The higher culture had survived far more in the Byzantine provinces of Africa and the East, and the storm of Arab invasion had brought an influx of refugees to the West, who played somewhat the same part in the seventh century as the Greek refugees from Constantinople in the fifteenth. From 685 to 752 the Roman see was occupied by a succession of Greeks and Syrians, many of them men of considerable character, and the oriental influence was at its height, not only at Rome but throughout the West. In the Anglian art of this period, the oriental influence is especially well marked. From about the year 670—probably as a result of the activity of Benedict Biscop—we find in place of the old Germanic art, a new school of sculpture and decoration, purely oriental in inspiration, and based on the Syrian motive of a vinescroll interwoven with the figures of birds or beasts, as we see it in the great series of Anglian crosses, especially the famous ones at Ruthwell and Bewcastle, which probably date from the beginning of the eighth century. That an Irish school of art also existed in Northumbria is proved by the magnificent Lindisfarne Book of Gospels, but there is no trace of its influence on architecture or sculpture.[14] On the other hand the art of Saxon England is much more composite and shows the influence not only of the oriental style both in its Northumbrian and its Frankish Merovingian forms, but also that of Irish art.

Nevertheless, behind all these foreign influences there lies a foundation of native culture. The same age and district that produced the Anglian crosses also saw the rise of Anglo-Saxon literature. It was the age in which the old pagan story of Beowulf received its literary form, and even more characteristic of the time were the Christian poets, Caedmon, the shepherd of Whitby Abbey, whose romantic story is preserved by Bede, and Cynewulf, the author of several surviving poems, including *Andreas, Elene, Juliana* and, perhaps, also of the noble *Dream of the Rood,* a quotation from which is sculptured on the Ruthwell cross.

The rise of this vernacular literature no doubt owes something to the influence of Ireland where, as we have seen, a remarkable development of vernacular Christian culture was taking place at this time. But Anglo-Saxon literature has a very distinctive character which is neither Celtic nor Teutonic but all its own. It is marked by a characteristic melancholy which has nothing in common with the "Celtic melancholy" of literary tradition. It is the melancholy of a people living among the ruins of a dead civilisation whose thoughts dwell on the glories of the past and the vanity of human achievement.[15]

But this native tradition is not necessarily Anglo-Saxon: it may go back further than that. Mr. Collingwood has explained the sudden flowering of Anglian art as due to a renaissance of the genius of the conquered people,[16] and this seems even more probable in the case of the leaders of religion and culture. The almost entire absence of any remains of heathen Anglian settlements north of the Tees in Bernicia, the centre of Northumbrian power in the days of St. Oswald, is specially noteworthy. It suggests the probability of the survival of native elements in the very region that played so large a part in the history of the Anglian culture, *i.e.*, Tyneside and the east end of the Roman wall.[17]

And the same holds good to a lesser degree of Wessex, both Aldhelm and Boniface being natives of regions not occupied by the Saxons in early, times. The enthusiasm of the newly converted Anglo-Saxons for the Latin culture and the Roman order cannot have been merely fortuitous. A man like Bede, who represents the highest level of culture in the West between the fall of the Empire and the ninth century, cannot have been an artificial product of an Italian mission to Germanic barbarians; the appearance of such a type in Denmark, for example, even after its conversion, is inconceivable. The conversion of the Anglo-Saxons produced such a vital change in England because it meant the reassertion of the old cultural tradition after the temporary victory of barbarism. It was the return of Britain to Europe and to her past.

This was the reason why the Christian and monastic culture attained in England an independence and autonomy such as it did not possess on the continent except for a time in Spain. In the Frankish dominions the kingdom still kept some of the prestige of the ancient state, and exercised, as we have seen, considerable control over the Church. In England, the Church embodied the whole inheritance of Roman culture as compared with the weak and barbarous tribal states. It was the Church rather than the state that led the way to national unity through its common organisation, its annual synods and its tradition of administration. In the political sphere the Anglo-Saxon culture was singularly barren of achievement. The Northumbrian state fell into weakness and anarchy long before the fall of the Anglian art and culture. The popular conception of the Anglo-Saxon as a kind of mediaeval John Bull is singularly at variance with history. On the material side Anglo-Saxon civilisation was a failure; its chief industry seems to have been the manufacture and export of saints, and even Bede was moved to protest against the excessive multiplication of monastic foundations which seriously weakened the military resources of the state.[18]

But, on the other hand, there has never been an age in which England had a greater influence on continental culture. In art and religion, in scholarship and literature, the Anglo-Saxons of the eighth century were the leaders of their age. At the time when continental civilisation was at its lowest ebb, the conversion of the Anglo-Saxons marked the turn of the tide. The Saxon pilgrims flocked to Rome as the centre of the Christian world and the Papacy found its most devoted allies and servants in the Anglo-Saxon monks and missionaries. The foundations of the new age were laid by the greatest of them all, St. Boniface of Crediton, "the Apostle of Germany," a man who had a deeper influence on the history of Europe than any Englishman who has ever lived. Unlike his Celtic predecessors, he was not an individual missionary, but a statesman and organiser, who was, above all, a servant of the Roman order. To him is due the foundation of the mediaeval German Church and the final conversion of Hesse and Thuringia, the heart of the German land. With the help of his Anglo-Saxon monks and nuns he destroyed the last strongholds of Germanic heathenism and planted abbeys and bishoprics on the site of the old Folkburgs and heathen sanctuaries, such as Buraburg, Amoneburg and Fulda. On his return from Rome in 739 he used his authority as Papal Vicar in Germany to reorganise the Bavarian Church and to establish the new dioceses which had so great an impor tance in German history. For Germany beyond the Rhine was still a land without cities, and the foundation of the new bishoprics meant the creation of new centres of cultural life. It was through the work of St. Boniface that Germany first became a living member of the European society.

This Anglo-Saxon influence is responsible for the first beginnings of vernacular culture in Germany.[19] It is not merely that the Anglo-Saxon missionaries brought with them their custom of providing Latin texts with vernacular glosses, nor even that the earliest monuments of German literature —the old Saxon *Genesis* and the religious epic *Heliand*— seem to derive from the Anglo-Saxon literary tradition. It is that the very idea of a vernacular culture was alien to the traditions of the continental Church and was the characteristic product of the new Christian cultures of Ireland and England, whence it was transmitted to the continent by the missionary movement of the eighth century.

But in addition to this, Boniface was the reformer of the whole Frankish church. The decadent Merovingian dynasty had already given up the substance of its power to the mayors of the palace, but in spite of their military prowess, which saved France from conquest by the Arabs in 735, they had done nothing for culture and had only furthered the degradation of the Frankish Church. Charles Martel had used the abbeys and bishoprics to reward his lay partisans, and had carried out a wholesale secularisation of Church property. As Boniface wrote to the Pope, "Religion is trodden under foot. Benefices are given to greedy laymen or unchaste and publican clerics. All their crimes do not prevent their attaining the priesthood; at last rising in rank as they increase in sin they become bishops, and those of them who can boast that they are not adulterers or fornicators, are drunkards, given up to the chase, and soldiers, who do not shrink from shedding Christian blood." [20] Nevertheless, the successors of Charles Martel, Pepin and Carloman, were favourable to Boniface's reforms. Armed with his special powers as Legate of the Holy See and personal representative of the Pope, he undertook the desecularisation of the Frankish Church.

In a series of great councils held between 742 and 747, he restored the discipline of the Frankish Church and brought it into close relations with the Roman see. It is true that Boniface failed to realise his full programme for the establishment of a regular system of appeals from the local authorities to Rome and for the recognition of the rights of the Papacy in the investure of the bishops. But, though Pepin was unwilling to surrender his control over the Frankish Church, he assisted St. Boniface in the reform of the Church and accepted his ideal of co-operation and harmony between the Frankish state and the Papacy. Henceforward the Carolingian dynasty was to be the patron of the movement of ecclesiastical reform, and found in the Church and the monastic culture the force that it needed for its work of political reorganisation. For it was the Anglo-Saxon monks and, above all, St. Boniface who first realised that union of Teutonic initiative and Latin order which is the source of the whole mediaeval development of culture.

XII

THE RESTORATION
OF THE WESTERN EMPIRE
AND CAROLINGIAN RENAISSANCE

The historical importance of the Carolingian age far transcends its material achievement. The unwieldy Empire of Charles the Great did not long survive the death of its founder, and it never really attained the economic and social organisation of a civilised state. But, for all that, it marks the first emergence of the European culture from the twilight of pre-natal existence into the consciousness of active life. Hitherto the barbarians had lived passively on the capital which they had inherited from the civilisation which they had plundered; now they began to co-operate with it in a creative social activity. The centre of mediaeval civilisation was not to be on the shores of the Mediterranean, but in the northern lands between the Loire and the Weser which were the heart of the Frankish dominions. This was the formative centre of the new culture, and it was there that the new conditions which were to govern the history of mediaeval culture find their origin. The ideal of the mediaeval Empire, the political position of the Papacy, the German hegemony in Italy and the expansion of Germany towards the East, the fundamental institutions of mediaeval society both in Church and State, and the incorporation of the classical tradition in mediaeval culture—all have their basis in the history of the Carolingian period.

The essential feature of the new culture was its religious

character. While the Merovingian state had been pre-dominantly secular, the Carolingian Empire was a theocratic power—the political expression of a religious unity. This change in the character of the monarchy is shown by the actual circumstances of the installation of the new dynasty; for Pepin obtained Papal authority for the setting aside of the old royal house and was anointed king in the year 752 by St. Boniface according to the religious coronation rite which had grown up under ecclesiastical influence in Anglo-Saxon England and Visigothic Spain, but which had hitherto been unknown among the Franks. Thus the legitimation of the rule of the Carolingian house sealed the alliance between the Frankish monarchy and the Papacy which St. Boniface had done so much to bring about, and henceforward the Frankish monarchy was the recognised champion and protec-tor of the Holy See. The Papacy had already been alienated from the Byzantine Empire by the Iconoclastic policy of the Isaurian emperors, and the extinction of the last survival of the Byzantine power at Ravenna by the Lombards in 751 forced the Pope to look for support elsewhere. In 754 Ste-phen II visited Pepin in his own dominions, and obtained from him a treaty which secured to the Papacy the Ex-archate of Ravenna and the former Byzantine possessions in Italy, together with the duchies of Spoleto and Benevento. In return the Pope reconsecrated Pepin as King of the Franks, and also conferred on him the dignity of Patrician of the Romans. This was an epoch-making event, for it marked not only the foundation of the Papal State which was to en-dure until 1870, but also the protectorate of the Carolingians in Italy, and the beginning of their imperial mission as the leaders and organisers of Western Christendom.

The Carolingians were naturally fitted to undertake this mission since they were themselves the representatives of both sides of the European tradition. They traced their de-scent from Gallo-Roman bishops and saints as well as from Frankish warriors, and they combined the warlike prowess of a Charles Martel with a vein of religious idealism, which shows itself in Carloman's renunciation of his kingdom in order to enter the cloister, and Pepin's sincere devotion to the cause of the Church. But it is in Pepin's successor, Charles the Great, that both these elements find simultaneous expression. He was above all a soldier with a talent for war and military enterprise which made him the greatest conqueror of his

time. But in spite of his ruthlessness and unscrupulous ambition he was no mere barbaric warrior; his policy was inspired by ideals and universal aims. His conquests were not
only the fulfillment of the traditional Frankish policy of military expansion; they were also crusades for the protection
and unity of Christendom. By his destruction of the Lombard
Kingdom he freed the Papacy from the menace which had
threatened its independence for two hundred years and
brought Italy into the Frankish Empire. The long drawn out
struggle with the Saxons was due to his determination to
put an end to the last remains of Germanic heathenism as
well as of Saxon independence. His conquest of the Avars
in 793-794 destroyed the Asiatic robber state which had
terrorised the whole of Eastern Europe, and at the same time
restored Christianity in the Danube provinces, while his war
with the Saracens and his establishment of the Spanish March
were the beginning of the Christian reaction to the victorious
expansion of Islam. In the course of thirty years of incessant
warfare he had extended the frontiers of the Frankish monarchy as far as the Elbe, the Mediterranean and the Lower
Danube, and had united Western Christendom in a great imperial state.

The coronation of Charles as Roman Emperor and the restoration of the Western Empire in the year 800 marked the
final stage in the reorganisation of Western Christendom
and completed the union between the Frankish monarchy
and the Roman Church which had been begun by the work
of Boniface and Pepin. It would, however, be a mistake to
suppose that the theocratic element in Charles' rule was based
upon his imperial title or that he derived the universal character of his authority from the tradition of Roman imperialism.

Under the influence of his Anglo-Saxon adviser Alcuin,
which was no less decisive than that of Boniface had been
during the previous period, he had already acquired an exalted view of his authority as the divinely appointed leader
of the Christian people. But this ideal was based on the teaching of the Bible and St. Augustine rather than on the classical tradition of imperial Rome. For to Alcuin and the authors of the *Libri Carolini*, Rome—even in its Byzantine form,
was still the last of the heathen empires of prophecy and the
representative of the Earthly Kingdom, whereas the Frankish
monarch possessed the higher dignity of ruler and guide of

the people of God. Charles was the new David and the second Josias, and as the latter had restored the law of God, so too Charles was the lawgiver of the Church and held the two swords of spiritual and temporal authority.[1]

This theocratic ideal dominates every aspect of Carolingian government. The new Frankish state was to an even greater extent than the Byzantine Empire a *church-state*, the secular and religious aspects of which were inextricably intermingled.

The King is the governor of the Church as well as of the State, and his legislation lays down the strictest and most minute rules for the conduct of the clergy and the regulation of doctrine and ritual. The observance of Sunday, the performance of the ecclesiastical chant and the conditions for the reception of novices into the monasteries are all dealt with in the Capitularies, no less than the defence of the frontiers and the economic administration of the royal estate. On one occasion Charles even required a written answer from every parish priest as to the mode in which he administered baptism, the replies being forwarded by the bishops to Charles' palace for his personal inspection.

The government of the whole Empire was largely ecclesiastical, for the bishop shared equally with the count in the local administration of the 300 counties into which the Empire was divided, while the central government was mainly in the hands of the ecclesiastics of the chancery and of the royal chapel[2]; the archchaplain being the King's chief adviser and one of the highest dignitaries of the Empire. The control and supervision of the local administration was ensured by the characteristic Carolingian institution of the *Missi Dominici*, who went on circuit through the counties of the Empire, like English judges of assize, and here too, the most important missions were entrusted to bishops and abbots.

The theocratic spirit which inspired the Carolingian government is well shown by the curious address of one of Charles' Missi which has been preserved. "We have been sent here," he begins, "by our Lord, the Emperor Charles, for your eternal salvation, and we charge you to live virtuously according to the law of God, and justly according to the law of the world. We would have you know first of all that you must believe in one God, the Father, the Son, and the Holy Ghost, ... Love God with all your hearts. Love your neighbours as yourselves. Give alms to the poor according to your means," and after recounting the duties of every class and state of life from wives and sons to monks and counts and public officials he concludes: "Nothing is hidden from God. Life is short and the moment of death is unknown. Be ye therefore always ready." [3]

This address is more in the style of a Moslem Kadi than of a Roman official: indeed the Augustinian ideal of the City of God has become transformed by a crude simplification into something dangerously similar to a Christian version of Islam with Charles as the Commander of the Faithful. There was the same identification of religion and polity, the same attempt to enforce morality by legal means and to spread the faith by war. As Alcuin complained, the faith of the Saxons had been destroyed by tithes, and Charles' missionaries were plunderers (*praedones*) rather than preachers (*praedicatores*). The religion of Charles was like that of Islam, a religion of the sword, and his private life, in spite of his sincere piety, resembled that of a Moslem ruler. Yet for all that, he claimed direct authority over the Church and intervened even in matters of dogma. In the words of his first letter to Leo III, he was "the representative of God who has to protect and govern all the members of God," he is "Lord and Father, King and Priest, the Leader and Guide of all Christians."

It is obvious that these claims were hardly reconcilable with the traditional authority of the Papacy. For Charles regarded the Pope as his chaplain, and plainly tells Leo III that it is the King's business to govern and defend the Church and that it is the Pope's duty to pray for it. Thus the destruction of the Lombard Kingdom seemed only to have increased the difficulties of the Papacy. It left Rome isolated between the two imperial powers of the Frankish monarchy and the Byzantine Empire, neither of which respected its independence. The dangers inherent in the situation soon became evident in the disputes that followed the Second Council of Nicaea in 787. The latter was a victory of the allied forces of Rome and Hellenism over the oriental heresy of the Iconoclasts. But Charles, whose religion had something in common with the militant simplicity of the Isaurian emperors, refused to accept the conciliar decisions. The Franks could hardly appreciate the importance of the question of image-worship for the peoples of Hellenic tradition. For as Strzygowski has shown (though not without exaggeration), the art of the Northern peoples was essentially at one with that of the East in its abstract aniconic character. Moreover, the influence of the Old Testament which was so strong in the Caroline circle led to a Puritanical attitude in the question of image-worship no less than in that of the observance of Sunday. Consequently, Charles in person entered the theological lists against Byzantium and Rome. He caused his theologians to compile a series of treatises against the council which were published in his name as the *Libri Carolini*. He sent a Missus to Rome with a capitulary of eighty-five *reprehensions* for the Pope's instruction, and finally, in 794, he called a great council of all the Western bishops at Frankfurt in which the Council of Nicaea was condemned and the doctrines of the image-worshippers refuted.[4]

The position of Pope Hadrian was one of intense difficulty, and he was forced to temporise. He found himself in agreement with the Byzantine Empire against the Frankish kingdom and the Western Church, and yet the Byzantines had robbed him of his patrimonies in the East and regarded him as no better than an alien. In the event of a schism between East and West he would have been left isolated and powerless. Politically he was entirely dependent on the Frankish power, and on the death of Hadrian in 795, his successor did homage to Charles as his overlord.

This anomalous state of things was ended by the Pope's recognition of Charles as Roman Emperor and his coronation at Rome on Christmas Day in the year 800. It is difficult to say how far the Pope acted on his own initiative or whether he was the instrument of Charles and his Frankish advisers. The testimony of Charles' biographer, Einhard, is in favour of the former alternative, but it has met with little favour from modern historians, at least in France and England. Certainly Charles was the gainer, for his universal authority in the West now received the sanction of Roman law and tradition. For the Papacy, however, the advantage was no less clear. The supremacy of the Frankish monarchy which had threatened to overshadow that of Rome was now associated with Rome, and consequently also with the Papacy. The political allegiance of the Pope was no longer divided between the *de jure* authority of the Emperor at Constantinople and the *de facto* power of the Frankish King. As King, Charles had stood outside the Roman tradition; as Emperor, he entered into a definite juridical relationship with the head of the Church. His power was still as formidable as ever, but it was no longer indefinite and incalculable. Moreover, the idea of the Roman Empire was still indispensable to the Church. It was synonymous with Christian civilisation, while the rule of the barbarians was so identified with heathenism and war that the Liturgy couples together, "the enemies of the Roman name and the foes of the Catholic Faith." Consequently, it is by no means improbable that the Papacy as the representation of Roman universalism should have taken the initiative in the restoration of the Empire in 800, as it did once more seventy five years later in the case of Charles the Bald.

However this may be, it is certain that the restoration of the Roman Empire, or rather the foundation of the new mediaeval Empire, had a religious and symbolic value which far outweighed its immediate importance from a political point of view. Charles used it, no doubt, as a diplomatic counter in his negotiations with the Eastern Empire, but his coronation made no difference in his life or government. He never attempted to ape the ways of a Roman or Byzantine Caesar, as did Otto III and other mediaeval emperors, but remained a thorough Frank, in dress and manners as well as in his political ideals. He even imperilled his whole work of imperial unification by dividing his dominions among his heirs in 806 according to the old Frankish custom, instead of following the Roman principle of indivisible political sovereignty; and the same tradition reasserted itself among his successors and proved fatal to the unity and continuity of the Carolingian Empire.

It was the churchmen and the men of letters, rather than the princes and statesmen, who cherished the ideal of the Holy Roman Empire. To them it meant the end of the centuries of barbarism and a return to civilised order. To Einhard, Charles is a new Augustus, and he views his achievement in the light of the Augustan ideal; while Modoin, the Bishop of Auxerre, writes of his age as the Renaissance of classical antiquity:

> "rursus in antiquos mutataque saecula mores;
> aurea Roma iterum renovata renascitur orbe."

In fact, though the learning of the Carolingian age may seem a poor thing to set by the side of that of the great Italian humanists, it was none the less a genuine Renaissance which had no less importance for the development of European culture than the more brilliant movement of the fifteenth

century. The gathering together of the scattered elements of
the classical and patristic traditions and their reorganisation as
the basis of a new culture was the greatest of all the achievements of the Carolingian age. The movement was due to the
co-operation of the two forces that we have already described—
the monastic culture of the Anglo-Saxon and Irish missionaries
and the organising genius of the Frankish monarchy. At the
beginning of the eighth century continental culture had
reached its lowest ebb, and the turn of the tide was due to
the coming of the Anglo-Saxon missionaries. Boniface himself
was a scholar and poet of the type of Aldhelm, and his reforming activity extended to the education as well as the discipline of the clergy. He was the author of a treatise on grammar founded on Donatus, Charisius and Diomedes, and his
great foundation at Fulda was the centre of a revival of literary culture and calligraphy that had a wide influence
throughout the Eastern part of the Frankish dominions.[5]

But it was the personal influence of Charles the Great
which gave the movement a wider scope, and nothing shows
the real greatness of his character more clearly than the zeal
with which this almost unlettered warrior prince threw himself into the work of restoring learning and raising the standard of education in his dominions. The Carolingian Renaissance, both in letters and art, found its centre in the school
of the Palace and was thence diffused throughout the Empire
by means of the monastic and episcopal centres, such as Fulda,
Tours, the two Corbies, St. Gall, Reichenau, Lorsch, St.
Wandrille, Ferrières, Orleans, Auxerre and Pavia. From all
parts of his realm Charles gathered together scholars and theologians—from Southern Gaul, Theodulf and Agobard; from
Italy, Paul the Deacon, Peter of Pisa, and Paulinus of Aquileia;
from Ireland, Clement and Dungal; and from his own land
of the Franks, Angilbert and Einhard. But as with the earlier
movement of ecclesiastical reform, it was above all from the
Anglo-Saxon tradition of culture that the new movement derived its character. In France and Italy, where Latin was a living language, it had become contaminated by contact with the
barbarised vernacular. In England it was a learned language,
founded upon the study of classical models, and its cultivation
was encouraged by that enthusiasm for the Roman tradition
which had inspired Anglo-Saxon culture since the days of St.
Wilfred and Benedict Biscop.

It was the chief representative of this Anglian culture, Alcuin, the head of the school of York, who became the link between what M. Halphen has termed the Anglo-Saxon "pre-Renaissance" and the new Carolingian movement. He entered Charles' service in 782 as the director of the Palace school, and thenceforward exercised a decisive influence on Charles' educational policy and on the whole literary movement. Alcuin was no literary genius; he was essentially a schoolmaster and grammarian who based his teaching on the old classical curriculum of the seven liberal arts, according to the tradition of Boethius and Cassiodorus and Isidore and Bede. But it was just such a schoolmaster that the age required, and thanks to the support of his royal pupil, he was able to realise his educational ideas on an imperial scale and to make the school of the Palace the standard of culture for the greater part of Western Europe. It was to him, apparently, that Charles entrusted the work of revising the Bible and the service books, and thus of initiating the Carolingian liturgical reform which is the foundation of the liturgy of the mediaeval church. The Roman rite had already been adopted by the Anglo-Saxon Church under Benedictine influence, and it now became the universal rite of the Carolingian Empire, displacing the old Gallican use, which together with the allied Ambrosian and Mozarabic rites had obtained throughout the West, save in Rome and its suburbicarian jurisdiction. But the new Carolingian liturgy still retained traces of Gallican influence, and in this way a considerable Gallican element has entered the Roman liturgy itself.

The influence of Alcuin and the Anglo-Saxon culture is also to be seen in the reform of the script, which is one of the characteristic achievements of the Carolingian age. The new Christian culture of England and Ireland owed its existence to the transmission and multiplication of manuscripts, and had attained a high level of calligraphy. Consequently it was to England, even more than to Italy, that the Carolingian scholars turned for more correct texts, not only of the Bible and the Roman liturgy, but also of the works of classical writers; and both Anglo-Saxon and Irish scholars and copyists flocked to the palace school and the great continental abbeys.[6]

Charlemagne himself took especial pains to secure the multiplication of manuscripts and the use of correct texts. Among the instructions to his Missi is a capitulary *de Scribis, ut non vitiose scribant,* and he frequently complains of the confusion introduced into the services of the Church by the use of cor-

rupt manuscripts. It was largely owing to his efforts and those
of Alcuin that the various and illegible cursive scripts of the
Merovingian Age were replaced by a new style of writing
which became the standard for the whole of Western Europe
outside Spain and Ireland and Southern Italy. This was the
so-called "Caroline Minuscule" which seems to have originated
in the abbey of Corbie in the second half of the eighth cen-
ury, and reached its highest developments in the famous
scriptorium at Alcuin's abbey at Tours. Its general diffusion
was no doubt due to its employment by Alcuin and his fellow
workers in the revised copies of the liturgical books which
were issued under imperial authority.

In this respect the Carolingian Renaissance was a worthy
precursor of that of the fifteenth century. In fact it had a
direct influence upon the achievement of the latter, for the
"humanist script" of the Italian Renaissance is nothing but a
revival of the Caroline minuscule hand, which thus became
the direct source of the modern printed Latin type. Moreover,
it is to the Carolingian copyists that we owe the preservation
of a large part of Latin literature, and the modern textual criticism of the classics is still largely based on the manuscripts that
have been handed down from this period.

The influence of the Carolingian revival was equally felt in
the region of art and architecture. Here again the influence of
the imperial tradition was predominant, and it has been said
that Charlemagne was the founder of a "Holy Roman" architecture as well as a Holy Roman Empire. But the classical
tradition was even more moribund in art than it was in letters. The Carolingian artists were subject both to the ori-
ental-Byzantine and even the oriental-Moslem influences on
the one hand, and to that of the mixed Anglo-Celtic art with
its passion for geometrical ornament and elaborate spiral and
fretted designs on the other. Even Charlemagne's famous Palace Church at Aix-la-Chapelle was built on the thoroughly
oriental octagonal plan, whether it was derived directly from
the East, or through the medium of the Church of S. Vitale
at Ravenna; and this central plan became a favourite model for
Carolingian architects in Germany. Nevertheless, even this
building shows classical features in its architecture, its columns, and its bronze fountain and doors, and there are other
churches, like the one built by Einhard at Steinbach, which
preserve the traditional Roman plan of the basilica with apse

and timbered roof.[7] It was from these that the later German Romanesque type of church, with its apse at each end and four towers, which became typical of the Rhineland and Lombardy, was derived.

But it is in miniature-painting and illumination that the mixed art of the Carolingian period is seen to best advantage. The numerous schools of painting which radiate outwards from the Rhineland to the German monasteries on the one hand, and to Metz and Tours and Reims and Corbie on the other, embody in varied proportions the oriental and Anglo-Irish elements that we have mentioned. But their most characteristic feature is their tendency to return to the classical tradition, both in their treatment of the human figure and in their use of the acanthus-leaf ornament. This neo-classical tendency is most fully represented by the manuscripts of the so-called Palace School, such as the famous Vienna Gospels, on which the later German Emperors used to take their coronation oath. It is clearly inspired by the influence of the Byzantine Renaissance and was probably introduced into the north by scribes from Southern Italy.[8] Carolingian art was the direct ancestor of the fine schools of painting which developed in Germany, especially in the Rhineland, in the tenth and eleventh centuries, and was thus one of the leading influences in the formation of the artistic style of the early Middle Ages.

The Carolingian Renaissance attained its full development in the generation that followed the death of Charlemagne among the pupils and successors of Alcuin; men such as Einhard, the biographer of the great emperor, Rabanus Maurus of Fulda, and his pupils Walafrid Strabo, Abbot of Reichenau, and Servatus Lupus, Abbot of Ferrières. All of these men were great scholars and students of classical literature, and it was through them and their like that the monastic libraries and copying schools attained their full development. The successors of Charlemagne, especially Charles the Bald, carried on his patronage of learning, and under the latter the Palace School of the Western Frankish realm was under the direction of the Irish scholar, Johannes Scotus, or Erigena, who was one of the most original thinkers of the Middle Ages. His philosophy, which was inspired by the writings of Dionysius the Areopagite and through him of the Neoplatonists, resembles that of the Arabic and Jewish philosophers of the tenth and eleventh centuries rather than that of the schools of the West. Indeed a French scholar—the late Pierre Duhem—has traced a direct influence from him on the philosophy of the Spanish Jew —Ibn Gebirol.

Johannes Scotus was also remarkable for his knowledge of Greek, though in this he does not stand alone. It was shared to some extent by several of his fellow-countrymen, above all by Sedulius Scotus, one of the most attractive scholars and poets of the age, who taught at Liège in the middle decades of the ninth century. Moreover, the contact with the culture of the Byzantine world still kept alive a certain amount of Greek scholarship in Italy, as we see from the translations and historical work of Anastasius Bibliothecarius, the author of the later parts of the *Liber Pontificalis*, who was the central figure of that short-lived revival of culture and literary activity which took place at Rome in the age of Nicholas I and John VIII (858-882). The other leading representative of this movement was Anastasius' friend, John the Deacon, surnamed Hymonides, who brought to the service of the Papacy an enthusiastic devotion to classical culture and to Rome as the heir of the Latin tradition. His life of St. Gregory, which he dedicated to Pope John VIII as the representative of "the people of Romulus," is inspired by these ideals to such an extent that he transforms St. Gregory himself into a humanist Pope of the type of Leo X! "In Gregory's time," he writes, "wisdom, as it were, visibly built herself a temple in Rome and the Seven Liberal Arts, like seven columns of precious stone, supported the vestibule of the Apostolic See. Not one of those who attended the Pope, from the greatest to the least, showed the slightest trace of barbarism either in speech or dress, and the Latin genius in its classic toga made its home in the Latin palace." [9]

As a description of the Rome of St. Gregory nothing could be more inept, but it is none the less interesting as foreshadowing the humanist ideal of the Papacy as the patron of classical culture, which was to find its realisation six centuries later in the Rome of the Renaissance. There was, however, little room for such ideals in the Rome of the ninth century, threatened, as it was, by the Saracens from without and torn asunder by the feuds of local factions. After the murder of John VIII the temporary revival of culture at Rome came to an end, and the classical tradition survived only in the cities of the South—Naples, Amalfi and Salerno— where the last representatives of Roman culture found a refuge. It was here, at the close of the ninth century, that one of the Roman exiles composed the curious elegy on the decline of Rome, which is the earliest example of those invectives against the avarice and corruption of Roman society that are so common in mediaeval literature.[10] Unlike the majority of such poems, however, it is not inspired by religious ideas. It is entirely secular and even anticlerical in tone, and has more in common with the spirit of the Italian Renaissance of the fifteenth century than with that of the Carolingian Renaissance of the North.

It was indeed only in the semi-Byzantine city-states of Italy that any independent tradition of secular culture survived. Elsewhere, throughout Central and Northern Europe, the higher culture was entirely confined to ecclesiastical circles. The cities had practically no share in it. All intellectual life was concentrated in the abbeys and in the royal or episcopal palaces which were themselves like monasteries. Although trade and town life had not entirely ceased, they were reduced to a rudimentary form, and society had become almost completely agrarian. The economy alike of the Empire and the Church was based on the ownership of land. The large estate or *villa* was organised as a little self-sufficient society, managed by a baliff according to the old system of rural administration which had in the main descended from the senatorial properties of the later Empire. The produce of such estates might support the lord and his retinue on their periodic visits, after the manner of the "one night's farm" of the Saxon and Norman charters, but more often it supplied the needs of the lord's central residence, which was the apex of the economic edifice. The Carolingian palace, as revealed by the German excavations at Ingelheim and elsewhere, was a vast rambling building, intended to house the whole retinue of the imperial court. With its porticoes, its churches and its halls, it resembled an abbey, or the old Papal palace of the Lateran, rather than the modern type of a royal residence. Above all, it was economically self-sufficient and was surrounded by the dwellings and workshops of the artisans and labourers whose crafts were necessary for the needs of the court—brewers and bakers, weavers and spinners, carpenters and workers in metal.

So, too, with the Carolingian abbey. It was no longer a colony of self-supporting ascetics; it was a great social and economic centre, the owner of vast estates, the civiliser of conquered territories, and the scene of a many-sided and intense cultural activity. The great German monasteries of the Carolingian period, whose origins were due directly or indirectly to the work of Boniface, were like the ancient temple states of Asia Minor, and played a similar part in the life of the people. In the eighth century, Fulda alone owned 15,000 plough lands; Lorsch somewhat later possessed 911 estates in the Rhineland. At Corbie, in addition to the 300 monks, there was a whole population of craftsmen and dependents grouped round the abbey. We possess in the famous ninth-century plan of St. Gall a picture of the ideal Carolingian abbey—a kind of miniature city which includes within its walls, churches and schools, workshops and granaries, hospitals and baths, mills and farm buildings.

It is impossible to exaggerate the importance of the Carolingian abbey in the history of early mediaeval civilisation. Here was an institution which was based on a purely agrarian economy and yet embodied the highest spiritual and intellectual culture of the age. The great abbeys, such as St. Gall and Reichenau, Fulda and Corbie, were not only the intellectual and religious leaders of Europe, but also the chief centres of material culture and of artistic and industrial activity. In them there was developed the traditions of learning and literature, art and architecture, music and liturgy, painting and calligraphy, which were the foundations of mediaeval culture. For that culture was in its origins essentially liturgical and centred in the Divine Office—*Opus Dei*—which was the source and end of the monastic life. And in the same way the vast wealth of the monasteries was not simply the property of the abbot and the community, as we should view it; it was the patrimony of the saint in whose name the church was dedicated. All the lands of an abbey and all its economic activity were subject to a supernatural governor and enjoyed supernatural protection. Hence the serfs of the Church were in a different category to those of other lords, and we find free men voluntarily surrendering their liberty in order to become the "Saints' Men"—"Homines Sanctorum" or "Sainteurs"—as they were called.

Under these conditions it is easy to understand how the monasteries were able to clear the forests and drain the fens and to establish flourishing settlements in places that had formerly been waste; like the Isle of Thorney, which William of Malmesbury describes in a well-known passage, standing like a Paradise in the waste of the fens with its groves and meadows, its vineyards and orchards—a miracle of nature and art.

And the monasteries were not only great agricultural centres, they were also centres of trade; and, thanks to the immunities that they enjoyed, they were able to establish markets, to coin money and even to develop a system of credit. They fulfilled in a primitive fashion the function of banks and insurance societies. Landowners could purchase pensions or become permanent residents at a monastery as oblates.[11]

Thus the Carolingian culture far outlived the Empire itself, and continued to survive in monastic centres such as St. Gall, the home of the four Ekkehards and the two Notkers, while Western Europe was plunging into the deepest anarchy and distress that it has perhaps ever known. It was owing to the work of the monasteries that the Carolingian culture was able to survive the fall of the Carolingian Empire. All through the darkness and distress of the hundred years of anarchy from 850 to 950 the great monasteries of Central Europe, such as St. Gall and Reichenau and Corvey, kept the flame of civilisation alight, so that there was no interruption in the transmission of the culture from the Carolingian period to that of the new Saxon Empire.[12]

XIII

THE AGE OF THE VIKINGS
AND THE CONVERSION OF THE NORTH

We have seen how Western Europe first achieved cultural unity in the Carolingian period. The rise of the Carolingian Empire marks the end of the dualism of culture that had characterised the age of the invasions and the full acceptance by the Western barbarians of the ideal of unity for which the Roman Empire and the Catholic Church alike stood. And thus in the new culture all the elements that constitute European civilisation were already represented—the political tradition of the Roman Empire, the religious tradition of the Catholic Church, the intellectual tradition of classical learning and the national traditions of the barbarian peoples.

Nevertheless, it was a premature synthesis, since the forces of barbarism both within and without the Empire were still far too strong to be completely assimilated. Within the limits of the Carolingian world itself, there was an almost immeasurable gap between the artificial humanism of men like Servatus Lupus and Walafrid Strabo and the mentality of the warrior noble or the peasant serf: while in the outer lands there yet remained new peoples who were still unaffected by the influence of Christianity and Roman-Christian civilisation. Hence the age of Carolingian unity was followed by a violent reaction, in which a new wave of barbarian invasion threatened to destroy all the work of Charles the Great and his predecessors, and to reduce Europe to a state of anarchy and confusion even more complete than that which followed the fall of the Roman Empire four centuries earlier.

The chief source of this external danger was to be found in Scandinavia, which from remote prehistoric times had been the centre of an active and independent movement of culture. This Nordic culture-centre had always tended to be a world apart, and since the age of the migration of peoples in the fourth and fifth centuries its isolation from the rest of Europe had been accentuated. The causes of this isolation are somewhat obscure, though no doubt the cessation of the active trading relations that had existed under the Roman Empire was one of the main factors. And it is still more difficult to explain the sudden change that caused the violent explosion of aggressive energy which characterised the period of the Viking invasions. After remaining quiescent for centuries in the narrow confines of the lands around the Baltic, the peoples of the North suddenly poured forth in a wave of conquering expansion that carried them far beyond the limits of the European world. In the course of the ninth and tenth centuries their activity extended from North America to the Caspian, and from the Arctic to the Mediterranean. They had attacked Constantinople and Pisa and North Persia and Moslem Spain, while their settlements and conquests embraced Greenland and Iceland and Russia, as well as Normandy and a great part of England, Ireland and Scotland.

The grounds of this remarkable achievement must be sought primarily in the peculiar conditions of Nordic society and culture. It was an old and in some respects highly developed culture which yet possessed few opportunities for peaceful expansion. During its centuries of isolation it had carried the art and ethics of war to a unique pitch of development. War was not only the source of power and wealth and social prestige, it was also the dominant preoccupation of literature and religion and art. The centre of the social organism was the war leader or "king," whose power rested not so much on a territorial basis as on his personal prowess and his power of attracting a following of warriors. There was no fixed law of primogeniture, and it was the ambition of every man of royal or chiefly blood to gather a *hird* of retainers, and to win renown for himself, after the fashion of Beowulf, by war and adventure and by boundless liberality to his followers.

"Beowulf, son of Scyld, was renowned in Scandinavian lands—his fame spread far and wide. So shall a young man

bring good to pass with splendid gifts in his father's possession, so that when war comes willing comrades shall stand by
him, again in his old age, the people follow him. In every
tribe a man shall prosper by deeds of love." [1]

It is true, as Professor Olrik insists,[2] that there was another
element in Northern society, the constructive labour of the
peasant and wealthy landowner "who tilled the soil and worshipped God." And this element finds its spiritual counterpart in the worship of the old deities of the earth and the
powers of fertility, the Vanir—Frey, Freya, and Njordr—
who were regarded as a different race to that of Odin, the
god of kings, and the warlike Aesir.[3] It is perhaps due to its
connection with the ancient sanctuary of this cult at Upsala
that the Swedish monarchy was able to establish its power so
early and so firmly in the fertile lands of East Sweden. Elsewhere, however, and especially in Norway, the little tribal
kingdoms seem to have been engaged in continual warfare in
which only the fittest survived, and their very existence depended, as we see in *Beowulf*, on the personal powers and
reputation of their warrior kings.

We have no direct historical evidence as to what was hap-
pening in Scandinavia in the age between the barbarian
invasions and the Viking movement. It was certainly an age
of intense political and military activity in which the stronger
kingdoms were gradually consolidating their power at the expense of their neighbours. Thus the kingdom of the Geats
was destroyed by that of the Swedes, while the Jutes and the
Heathobards were conquered by the Danes, who had already
created a powerful kingdom in the eighth century under the
leadership of King Harold Wartooth. In Norway, owing to
the character of the country, the lesser tribal unities preserved
their independence to a much later period, but the evidence of archaeology shows that the same tendencies were
at work in the little tribal kingdoms of Eastern Norway—
Romarike, Hedemark, Ringerike and Vestfold, where the
great howes or burial mounds of the prehistoric kings at
Raknehaug in Romarike, at Svei in Hedemark, and at Borre
in Vestfold, which are among the most imposing monuments
of the kind in Europe, bear witness to the increasing strength
and prestige of the royal power.

No doubt this development had some influence on the
movement of migration and colonisation that marked the Viking period, and there is no reason to question the substantial

truth of the Icelandic traditions that are recorded in such detail by Ari the Wise in his remarkable work on the settlement of Iceland.[4] But Western Norway, above all the kingdoms or aristocratic federations of Rogaland and Hordaland, had been centres of Viking activity for a century before King Harold Fairhair broke the power of the Western *hersir* or tribal chieftains at the battle of Hafrsfjord. This region had long possessed a cultural tradition of its own, which was distinguished in the fifth and sixth centuries by its aristocratic character and by the striking resemblance that it shows to the culture of Anglo-Saxon England, particularly that of the Midlands. According to Professor Shetelig[5] these peculiarities are due to the fact that Western Norway had been affected by the same wave of Germanic invasion that had brought the Anglo-Saxons to Britain and the Franks and the Burgundians to Gaul. These invaders from the South had conquered the native population and formed a ruling class which preserved its own burial rites and maintained relations with the other Germanic peoples of the West, especially those of Anglo-Saxon England. Thus Western Norway had been in contact with the British Isles for centuries before the age of the Vikings; indeed it is from these maritime relations that the country originally derived its name of Norwegr—"the North Way." Possibly the improvements in the means of navigation that took place in the seventh and eighth centuries opened the way to piratical expeditions on a larger scale. But whatever may have been the cause, the coasts of the British Isles were visited almost yearly from the close of the eighth century by the fleets of the Norwegian Vikings. The great monasteries of the islands and the coasts which were the centres of Christian civilisation in the North offered an easy and rich prey to the invaders. Lindisfarne was sacked in 793, Jarrow in 794, and Iona in 802 and 806.

But it was on Ireland that the Western Vikings concentrated their attacks. During the first half of the ninth century the whole island was invaded, so that in the words of the Irish chronicler "there was not a point in the land without a fleet." Here, too, it was the churches and monasteries that offered the easiest points of attack, and the great age of Irish monastic culture ended in wholesale slaughter and ruin. The great Norwegian leader Turgeis, who began to establish a regular Viking state in Ireland between 832 and 845, seems to have deliberately attempted to destroy Irish Christianity.

He drove out the *comarba* of St. Patrick from Armagh and made it the centre of his kingdom, while at Clonmacnoise, the great ecclesiastical centre on the Shannon, he desecrated the church of St. Ciaran and enthroned his wife, a heathen *völva* or prophetess, upon the altar. His death did little to check the development of Viking power, for in 851 Olaf the White, the son of a Norwegian king, came to Ireland and established the kingdom of Dublin, which was to continue, under the rule of Ivar, "king of all the Norsemen of Ireland and Britain," and his successors, until the twelfth century.

Thus Ireland, which had been the starting-point of the revival of Christian culture in Western Europe in pre-Carolingian times, was also the first to succumb to the new barbarian invasion, and its fate was soon shared by the Anglian Christian culture that it had done so much to create. In 835 a new series of attacks on Northern and Eastern England had been begun by the Danes, and in 867 the kingdom of Northumbria was finally destroyed. For a time it seemed as though all England would become a Viking colony. But though the independence of Wessex and Southern England was preserved by the efforts of King Alfred, the whole of Northern and Eastern England north of the Thames and Watling Street was settled by the Vikings and became known as "the Danelaw." Nor was the Scandinavian settlement limited to this area, for all the western coasts belonged to the Irish-Viking sphere of influence, and considerable territories in north-western England, such as Cumberland and the Lake District, were occupied by Norwegian colonists.

Thus, by the close of the ninth century a Norwegian maritime Empire had been formed which extended from Iceland and the Faroes to the Irish Channel and embraced all the lesser islands of the Western seas as well as a considerable part of Ireland and Northern Scotland and England.

Meanwhile, on the continent of Europe the Viking movement had followed a somewhat different course. Here it was the Danes rather than the Norwegians who took the leading part, and they had to deal not with the scattered forces of Celtic tribal society, but with the formidable power of the Carolingian Empire.

Ever since the early Merovingian period the Frankish power had been a cause of fear and distrust to the Danes, as we see from the passage in *Beowulf* in which Wiglaf relates how "the goodwill of the Merovingian king has been denied to us," since the time when Hygelac the Dane invaded Frankish territory in 520. And the tension had been increased by the Carolingian conquest of the Frisians and the Saxons, which brought the Empire into direct contact with Denmark and seemed to threaten the existence of the free pagan peoples of the North. In 808 war broke out between the two peoples. Guthred sent a fleet to ravage Frisia and threatened to attack Aachen itself. But the assassination of the Danish king in 810 put an end to the conflict, and for the next twenty years the Empire only had to deal with isolated raids of Viking bands, probably from Norway and Ireland. Charles' successor, Lewis the Pious, attempted to carry out the conversion of Scandinavia by peaceful means. He cultivated friendly relations with Harold, the son of Guthred, and finally induced him to receive baptism at Mainz in 826, together with his son and four hundred of his followers. These relations prepared the way for the missions of Ebbo and St. Anscar to Denmark and Sweden and for the establishment of Hamburg as a metropolitan see for the northern lands. But although St. Anscar was well received by the Swedish king and succeeded in founding a church at Birka in the very heart of Scandinavia, as well as several churches in Denmark, it was centuries before his work was destined to bear fruit. The dethronement of Lewis in 833 marks the beginning of a period of dynastic rivalries and civil wars which left the Empire defenceless against its Northern neighbours. The Danes established themselves in Frisia and Holland and destroyed the great port of Duurstede near Utrecht that had been for generations the centre of commercial relations with the North.

After 840 the Emperor Lothair encouraged the attacks of the Danes on his brother's territories. From this time the Viking invasions take on a new character. Viking expeditions were organised on a large scale with fleets numbering hundreds of vessels, and the western provinces of the Empire, together with England, were systematically ravaged year by year. For nearly fifty years the invasions went on increasing in intensity until all the abbeys and towns of the West from Hamburg to Bordeaux had been put to the sack and great tracts of country, especially in the Netherlands and in north-western France, were converted into desert. Even the saints themselves were forced to leave their sanctuaries, and some of the most famous relics of the West, such as the body of St. Martin or that of St. Cuthbert, travelled for years from one place of refuge to another as the tide of invasion advanced.

The efforts of the Carolingian sovereigns, above all Charles the Bald, whose dominions bore the brunt of the storm from 843 to 877, were powerless to stave off the attacks of the enemy or to prevent the dissolution of society.

The last twenty years of the century, however, saw a gradual recovery of the forces of Christendom. The hard-won victories of King Alfred in England in 878 and 885, the defence of Paris by Odo the son of Robert the Strong in 885-887, and the victory of King Arnulf in Flanders in 891 mark the turn of the tide. It was impossible to expel the invaders altogether either from England or France, but the successors of King Alfred were strong enough to establish their authority over the Danelaw, while the treaty of Charles the Simple with Rollo placed the Viking occupation of Normandy on a regular feudal basis and prepared the way for the assimilation of the Norman settlers.

Nevertheless, there was still no hope of peace for Christendom, for the Vikings were not the only enemies with which it had to contend. While the Vikings were laying waste the Western provinces, Italy and the Mediterranean coasts were a prey to the Saracens. In 827 the forces of the Aghlabite emirs who ruled in Tunisia had gained a footing in Sicily and gradually overran the whole island. Thence they went on to attack Southern Italy, and established themselves at Bari and on the River Garigliano, which they made the centres of their destructive activities for half a century. The Papal Patrimony was overrun by Moslem bands, and in 846 Rome itself was attacked, St. Peter's was sacked, and the tombs of the Apostles were violated, to the horror of the Christian world.

Meanwhile the northern coasts of the Mediterranean were exposed to the raids of Moslem pirates from Spain and the Balearic Islands, who finally established a base on the mainland at Fraxinetum, near St. Tropez. For nearly a century, from 888 to 975, this pirate stronghold was the scourge of the surrounding lands. Even the Alps were not secure, for the Saracens lay in wait at the Swiss passes and plundered the bands of pilgrims and merchants as they went down into Italy.

Finally, at the very moment when the pressure from the North had begun to decrease, Europe was threatened by a new menace from the East, the Magyars, a nomad people of mixed Finnish and Turkish origin, like the Bulgars, who had followed the track of so many former invaders from the steppes of Central Asia and South Russia to the Hungarian plain. They destroyed the new Christian kingdom of the Slavs of Moravia, and began to raid far and wide, like the Huns and the Avars before them. They ravaged the eastern part of the Carolingian realm as mercilessly as the Vikings had done in the West, and gradually extended the range of their raids until they met the rival bands of the Saracens in Italy and Provence.

Thus in the first half of the tenth century Western civilisation was reduced to the verge of dissolution. Never had it been so hard pressed even in the worst days of the eighth century, for then the attack came from the side of Islam only, while now it was from every direction. Christendom had become an island surrounded by the rising floods of barbarism and Islam. Moreover, during the earlier barbarian invasions Christendom could rely on its cultural superiority, which gave it prestige even in the eyes of its enemies. But now even this advantage was lost: for the centre of the highest culture in the West during the tenth century was to be found in Moslem Spain, and Islam was no less superior to Western Christendom in its economic and political development than in intellectual matters. In so far as commercial activity still existed in Europe, it was owing to Moslem trade, which not only embraced the whole of the Mediterranean, but extended from Central Asia to the Baltic by way of the Caspian, the Volga and the Swedish-Russian trading settlements such as Novgorod and Kiev. This intercourse explains the existence of the hoards of oriental coins, struck in the mints of Tashkent and Samarkand and Baghdad, that are so common in Scandinavia during this period, and traces of it are to be found even in England in the Goldsborough hoard and the treasure chest of the Viking army of Northumbria of 911, that was found seventy years ago near Preston, containing not only coins, but numerous ornaments of oriental design. An even more curious proof of the range of oriental influence in this age is the gilt bronze cross, now in the British Museum, which was found in an Irish bog and bears the inscription Bismillah—"in the name of Allah"—in Kufic characters.

The fate of Christendom depended not so much on its power of military resistance as on its capacity to assimilate the pagan society of the North. If the Russian Varangians had

accepted the religion of their Moslem neighbours rathe₁ than
that of the Christians, the history of Europe might have been
very different. Fortunately for Christendom, the shattered culture of Western Europe preserved its spiritual vitality and
possessed a greater power of attraction for the Northern peoples than either paganism or Islam. By the close of the tenth
century Christianity had already gained a firm foothold in the
North, and even such a typical representative of the Viking
spirit as Olaf Trygvasson had not only become a convert
himself, but set himself to spread the faith in characteristically Viking fashion.[6]

Even the recrudescence of Viking activity and the renewed
attacks on England and Ireland at this period did nothing to
check this movement. In Ireland the battle of Clontarf in
1014 finally put an end to the danger of Viking conquest,
while in England the success of the Danes only hastened the
process of assimilation. For Canute made England the centre
of his Empire and governed according to the traditions cf
his Saxon predecessors, whom he rivalled in his devotion
to the Church and in the favour that he showed to the
monasteries. His pilgrimage to Rome in 1026-1027, where
he assisted at the coronation of the Emperor Conrad, is one of
the most significant events of this period, for it marks the
incorporation of the Northern peoples into the society of
Christendom and their acceptance of the principle of spiritual unity. This finds expression in the code of laws which
Canute promulgated in England in the later years of his
reign, for it shows more completely than any document of the
age how complete was the fusion between the secular and
the religious aspects of the State and how the public law of
Christendom had become the very framework of the new
post-barbaric society that was arising in mediaeval Europe.

Thus the Viking invasions proved in the end an advantage
to Europe, since they brought new life and energy to the
somewhat anæmic and artificial civilisation of the Carolingian
world. The descendants of the Vikings became the champions
of Christendom, as we see above all in the case of the Normans, who were the leaders and organisers of the new movement of Western expansion that begins in the eleventh century. This gain was not, however, without cost, for it involved
the disappearance of the independent tradition of Nordic culture. Alike in Normandy, in England, and in Russia, the
Scandinavian settlers absorbed the culture of their environ-

ment and gradually became completely merged in the society that they had conquered. Even Scandinavia itself rapidly lost its cultural independence and became in time an outlying province of Germanic Christendom.

Only in the far West, in the Norwegian colonial territory that stretched from Greenland and Iceland to the Irish Sea, did the old traditions of the Viking Age survive and become the source of a brilliant and original culture which was entirely unlike anything that was to be found in continental Europe. Even here, however, the Nordic element did not stand alone, but came into relations with another culture which, like itself, had hitherto stood apart from the main stream of Western development—the culture of Celtic Ireland.[7] Throughout this area the Viking colonists formed the ruling class, but the mass of the population remained Celtic, and there was considerable intercourse and intermarriage between the two peoples. In this way there arose in the ninth century a mixed Celtic-Nordic culture which reacted upon the parent cultures both in Ireland and in Scandinavia. Its influence is seen most plainly in the new style of the Jellinge period in the tenth century, which produced a remarkable development of Scandinavian decorative art. Here there is no question of the source and extent of foreign influence. But it is otherwise in regard to the problem of Celtic influence in Scandinavian literature, which has always been a matter of controversy. And it is a curious thing that it has been the Scandinavian scholars who have been the chief advocates of the theory of Celtic influence, while the English writers on the subject have made it almost a point of national honour to vindicate the purely Nordic character of Scandinavian literature.

Thus Vigfusson ascribed all the greatest poetry of the Edda to a school of writers who belonged to the mixed Celtic-Nordic culture of the western islands, and likewise regarded many of the characteristics of Icelandic literature, above all the very creation of the prose saga, as due to Celtic influence and to the existence of a Celtic element in the population. Vigfusson's theory of the "Western" origin of the Eddic poems is now generally abandoned save in the case of the *Rigsthula*, which undoubtedly shows strong Irish influence. On the other hand, his view regarding the Celtic influence on Icelandic culture is still widely held, and rests on very strong arguments. Many of the settlers in Iceland came from the southern islands, bringing with them Irish wives or slaves, while some of them bore Celtic names and a few, such as the famous Aud the Wealthy, widow of Olaf the White, the King of Dublin, or Helge, the grandson of Caerbhall, King of Ossory, were actually Christians of a sort.[8] Nor did the Celtic element in the population consist only of thralls, for the *Landnamabok* described how Aud provided her Celtic freedmen with lands of their own, and the pedigrees recorded in that work and in the sagas show that some of the noblest families of Iceland had Celtic blood in their veins.[9]

Thus there seems no reason to doubt the existence of a Celtic element in Icelandic culture, which shows itself both in the character of the people and in their literary achievements. For the elements that distinguish Icelandic literature from the older tradition that is common to the Teutonic peoples, namely, the development of the Saga or prose epic and the elaborate rhymed poetry of the Skalds, are precisely those that characterise Irish literature.[10]

Nevertheless, the probability that the Icelandic genius, like that of almost every great culture that the world has seen, arose from a soil that had been fertilised by the mingling of two different races and cultural traditions does nothing to detract from the originality of its creative achievement. Even if Icelandic literature is indebted to the Celts for its use of narrative prose, nothing could be further removed from the fantastic rhetoric and magical feats of the Irish epic than the sober realism and psychological truth of the Icelandic sagas. While the former seems to take the reader back behind the Middle Ages to a vanished world, the latter seem more modern in their attitude to life and to human nature than anything in mediaeval literature.

It is true that the mature achievement of this tradition is represented by the great prose sagas of the thirteenth century—the age of Snorri and Sturla—which lies outside our period; but it is directly founded on the traditions of the Viking Age, above all, of the century from 930 to 1030, which the Icelanders themselves termed "the age of the making of the sagas." This was the age of the heroic figures whose deeds are recorded in the sagas—Vikings like Egil Skalgrimsson, lawmen like Njal, kings like Olaf Trygvasson and Olaf the Saint, and sailors and explorers like the men who colonised Greenland and discovered North America.

Moreover, this age not only lives on in the later tradition of the sagas, it is also represented by the contemporary poems of skalds like Egil Skalgrimsson and Kormac and by the completion of the older heroic poetry. Iceland was not only the creator of the saga, it was also the preserver of the Edda, and thus it is to Iceland that we owe almost everything that we know of the beliefs and the moral and spiritual ideas of the age of the Vikings. The date of the Eddic poems has long been a matter of controversy, but there can be little doubt that it coincides approximately with the whole of the Viking period. There is indeed, a wide gap between the barbaric simplicity and crudity of the more primitive poems, such as the *Lay of Atli* or the *Lay of Hamdir*, and the sublime cosmic vision of the *Volospa*, but through them all we can trace the development of the same moral ideal and the same view of reality. The Eddic conception of life is no doubt harsh and barbaric, but it is also heroic in the fullest sense of the word. Indeed, it is something more than heroic, for the noble viragos and the bloodthirsty heroes of the Edda possess a spiritual quality that is lacking in the Homeric world. The Eddic poems have more in common with the spirit of Aeschylus than with that of Homer, though there is a characteristic difference in their religious attitude. Their heroes do not, like the Greeks, pursue victory or prosperity as ends in themselves. They look beyond the immediate issue to an ultimate test to which success is irrelevant. Defeat, not victory, is the mark of the hero. Hence the atmosphere of fatalism and gloom in which the figures of the heroic cycle move. The Nibelungs, like the Atreidae, are doomed to crime and disaster by the powers behind the world, but there is no suggestion of *hubris*—the spirit of overweening confidence in prosperity. Hogni and Gunnar, or Hamdis and Sorli, are conscious that they are riding forth to death, and they go to meet their fate with open eyes. There is no attempt, as in the Greek view of life, to justify the ways of gods to man, and to see in their acts the vindication of external justice. For the gods are caught in the same toils of fate as men. In fact, the gods of the Edda are no longer the inhuman nature-deities of the old Scandinavian cult. They have been humanised, and in a sense spiritualised, until they have become themselves the participants in the heroic drama. They carry on a perpetual warfare with the powers of chaos, in which they are not destined to conquer. Their lives are overshadowed by the knowledge of an ultimate catastrophe—the Doom of the Gods—the day when Odin meets the Wolf.

Here only is there room for some kind of a theodicy, since the apparently arbitrary conduct of the gods to the heroes may be explained as due to their need for human allies. As for instance in the *Eiriksmal,* where Odin allows Eric to perish before his time, "because it is not surely to be known when the grey wolf shall come upon the seat of the Gods."

This unique view of the world finds its highest expression in the great Nordic apocalypse of the *Volospa,* which was probably composed by an Icelandic poet at the very close of the Viking period. In this poem the crudities of the old pagan mythology have been replaced by an almost philosophic conception of nature, which is probably due to the contact with the higher culture of Christendom. The opening lines[11] especially, describing the primeval chaos, bear a striking resemblance to the Old High German verses of the Wessobrunner Prayer. "Earth was not, nor high Heaven, nor hill nor tree. The sun shone not, the moon gave not light, nor the glorious sea. Then was there Naught, unending, unwending, and one Almighty God, mildest of men." [12]

And so, too, the final description of the Doom of the Gods seems to have taken some of its colouring from the Christian presentation of the Last Judgment. Nevertheless, there are elements in the poem which belong neither to the world of Christian thought nor to that of Scandinavian nature religion. Above all, it is strange to find in the *Volospa* an idea which seems to us so difficult and recondite as that of the Eternal Return—the rebirth of the world and the repetition of all that has gone before.

> *The Aesir meet on Ida meadows:*
> *Tell over once again mighty exploits of old,*
> *Con ancient runes of Odin's graving.*
>
> *Wondrous strange, on the sward are found*
> *Mid the grass, long after, the golden pieces,*
> *The draughts they had owned, in the dawn of days.*[13]

But throughout the Eddic poems we are constantly being surprised by the mixture of profound thought and primitive mythology, of sublime heroism and barbaric cruelty, which seems to characterise the Viking mind. In the same way it is difficult for us to reconcile the savage brutality of the hero of Egils Saga with the intense personal feeling of his great lyric on the death of his sons—the *Sonatorrek,* the composition of which, according to the saga, restored to him his will to live, after he had resolved to commit suicide.[14] And this contradiction is no less marked in the history of the Icelandic society itself, in which the harshest possible environment produced so remarkable a development of culture.

It is indeed one of the miracles of history that this desolate island, settled by pirates and adventurers who revolted against the social constraint even of Viking Norway, should have produced a high culture and a literature which is, of its kind, the greatest in mediaeval Europe. It is as though New England had given birth to Elizabethan literature or French Canada to that of the Grand Siècle. But as W. P. Ker has said, the apparent anarchy of Icelandic society is deceptive. "The settlement of Iceland looks like a furious plunge of angry and intemperate chiefs, away from order into a grim and reckless land of Cockayne. The truth is that these rebels and their commonwealth were more self-possessed, more clearly conscious of their own aims, more critical of their own achievements than any commonwealth on earth since the fall of Athens." [15] It was an intensely aristocratic community in which almost every family possessed a great social tradition, and its very remoteness and lack of material wealth led to the intensive cultivation of its traditions and of the resources of its interior life.

It almost seems to justify the extreme claims of nationalist separatism when we find this Ultima Thule of the habitable world, this society which had voluntarily exiled itself from the European unity, producing, nevertheless, the earliest and most precocious fruit of modern European culture. Yet the amazing achievement of the native Nordic genius must not blind us to the fact that Icelandic culture in its mature development did owe something very essential to the world outside. The influence of Christianity on Iceland was not, as some writers would have us believe, a superficial and external element in the life of the people: it was of fundamental importance for their culture. It is true that the acceptance of Christianity by the Althing in 1000, as recorded in the *Islendingabok*, does appear rather a lukewarm and "political" affair, and that the apostles of the new faith, such as Thangbrand and even Olaf Trygvasson himself, are not precisely models of evangelical morality. But neither was Constantine, nor Theodosius, nor Charlemagne. The lawlessness and individualism of Viking society were naturally unfavourable to the strict observance either of the moral or the ceremonial law of the Church and must have produced many queer types of Christian, such as Thormod the poet, who made a vow that he would fast on nine feast days and eat meat on nine fast days if he succeeded in slaying his enemy, and who replied to the scandalised protest of St. Olaf's master-cook by saying that "Christ and I shall be good friends enough if there be no more than half a sausage to part us." [16]

But this is only one side of the picture. The conversion of Iceland was not merely a matter of political expediency; it was the acceptance of a higher spiritual ideal, as is shown by the attitude of Hialte, the Christian spokesman at the Althing of 1004: "The heathen men summoned a great gathering and there they agreed to sacrifice two men out of each Quarter and call upon the heathen gods that they would not suffer Christendom to spread over the land. But Hialte and Gizor had another meeting of Christian men and agreed that they too would have human sacrifices as many as the heathen. They spoke thus: 'The heathen sacrifice the worst men and cast them over rocks or cliffs, but we will choose the best of men and call it a gift of victory to our Lord Jesus Christ, and we will bind ourselves to live better and more sinlessly than before, and Gizor and I will offer ourselves as the gift of victory of our Quarter.' " [17]

In fact, the higher elements in the Icelandic culture itself, as represented by men like Njal, the peacemaker, and Gisli Sursson and the author of the Volospa, had already outgrown the barbarism of the old pagan society with its practice of human sacrifice and infanticide and its insistence on the duty of blood revenge.

The Viking ideal was by itself too destructive and sterile to be capable of producing the higher fruits of culture. It acquired its higher cultural value only after it had accepted the Christian law and had been disciplined and refined by a century and more of Christian civilisation. Between the age of the Vikings and the civil wars and feuds of the Sturlung period, there intervenes an age of peace and piety during which the leaders of the people were churchmen like the great bishop Gizor the White, and St. John of Holar and St. Thorlac of Scalholt. As the Christne Saga writes, "Bishop Gizor (1082-1118) kept such peace in the land that there was no great feud between the chiefs, and the carrying of arms was almost laid aside. Most of the men of worship were clerks and hallowed priests, albeit they were chiefs." This was the society that created the new literary tradition, and it is well to remember that its founders, Saemund the Historian and Ari the Wise, were both of them priests and scholars, the former having even made his studies at Paris. It is to Ari that we owe not only our knowledge of the beginnings of Iceland and its institutions, but the creation of the literary style which made possible the work of Snorri Sturlason and the great Saga writers. But this Christian Icelandic culture, like that of the Anglian kingdom of Northumbria four hundred years before, is essentially transitory. It is the point at which the dying world of the barbaric North comes into momentary contact with the new consciousness of Christian Europe. It is followed by a sudden decline in which the anarchic element in northern society, which could no longer find an outlet in external aggression, turns inwards and destroys itself. Here, as in Norway, the aristocratic class that was the heir and guardian of the old traditions was swept away by civil wars and confiscations, and with the thirteenth century the Viking world sinks into the peaceful stagnation of an impoverished peasant society.

XIV

THE RISE OF THE MEDIAEVAL UNITY

The storm of barbarian invasion that fell upon Europe in the ninth century seems sufficient of itself to explain the premature decline of the Carolingian Empire and the dissolution of the newly-acquired Western unity. Nevertheless, it is easy to exaggerate its importance. It was far from being the only influence at work; indeed, it is almost certain that the fortunes of the Carolingian Empire would have followed a similar course, even if it had not had to undergo the attacks of the Vikings and the Saracens.

The germs of decay were inherent in the Carolingian state from its origins. For in spite of its imposing appearance, it was a heterogeneous structure without an internal and organic principle of unity. It claimed to be the Roman Empire, but it was in fact the Frankish monarchy, and so it embodied two contradictory principles, the universalism of the Roman and Christian traditions on the one hand, and the tribal particularism of barbaric Europe on the other. Consequently, in spite of its name, it bore little resemblance to the Roman Empire or the civilised states of the old Mediterranean world, it had much more in common with those barbaric Empires of the Huns and the Avars and the West Turks which were the ephemeral products of military conquest and which succeeded one another so rapidly during these centuries on the outskirts of the civilised world.

The Roman Empire of the Carolingians was a Roman Empire without the Roman law and without the Roman le-

gions, without the City and without the Senate. It was
a shapeless and unorganised mass with no urban nerve centres
and no circulation of economic life. Its officials were neither
civic magistrates nor trained civil servants, but merely territorial magnates and semi-tribal war leaders. And yet it was
also the embodiment and representative of an ideal, and this
ideal, in spite of its apparent failure, proved more durable
and persistent than any of the military or political achievements of the period. It outlived the state to which it had
given birth and survived through the anarchy that followed,
to become the principle of the new order which arose in the
West in the eleventh century.

The champions of this ideal were the great Carolingian
churchmen, who played so large a part in the administration
of the Empire and the determination of the imperial policy
from the time of Charles the Great to that of his grandson
Charles the Bald.

While the counts and secular magnates for the most part
represented local and territorial interests, the leaders of the
ecclesiastical party stood for the ideal of a universal Empire
as the embodiment of the unity of Christendom and the
defender of the Christian faith. Agobard of Lyons even
ventures to attack the traditional Frankish principle of personal law and to demand the establishment of a universal
Christian law for the universal Christian commonwealth. In
Christ, he says, there is neither Jew nor Gentile, Barbarian
nor Scythian, neither Aquintanians, nor Lombards, nor Burgundians, nor Allemanni. "If God has suffered in order that
the wall of separation and enmity should be done away and
that all should be reconciled in His Body, is not the incredi-
ble diversity of laws that reigns not only in every region or
city, but in the same household and almost at the same table,
in opposition to this divine work of unity?" [1]

Thus the Emperor was no longer the hereditary chieftain
and war leader of the Frankish people; he was an almost
sacerdotal figure who had been anointed by the grace of God
to rule over the Christian people and to guide and protect
the Church. This involves, as we have seen, a strictly theocratic conception of kingship, so that the Carolingian Emperor was regarded, no less than the Byzantine Basileus, as
the vicar of God and the head of the Church as well as of the
state. Thus Sedulius Scotus (c. 850) speaks of the Emperor
as being ordained by God as His vicar in the government of

the Church and as having received power over both orders
of rulers and subjects, while Cathulf goes so far as to say
that the king stands in the place of God over all his people,
for whom he has to account at the Last Day, while the
bishop stands in the second place as the representative of
Christ only.[2]

But the Carolingian theocracy differed from the Byzantine
in that it was a theocracy inspired and controlled by the
Church. There was no lay bureaucracy such as existed in the
Eastern Empire; its place was taken by the episcopate, from
whose ranks the majority of the Emperor's advisers and ministers were drawn. Consequently, as soon as the strong hand
of Charles the Great was removed, the theocratic ideal led to
the exaltation of the spiritual power and the clericalisation
of the Empire rather than to the subordination of the Church
to the secular power.

The leaders of the clerical party were men who had played
an important part in the inauguration of the new Empire,
above all, Charles the Great's nephews, Adalhard and Wala
of Corbie, and Agobard of Lyons. During the early years
of Lewis the Pious, in spite of the temporary disgrace of
Adalhard in 814, their ideals were in the ascendant. In 816
the sacred character of the Empire was solemnly reaffirmed
by the coronation of Lewis by Pope Stephen at Rheims, and
in the following year the unity of the Empire was secured
by the Constitution of Aix, which set aside the old Frankish
rules of succession in favour of the Roman principle of un-
divided sovereignty. Lothair was to succeed his father as sole
Emperor, and though his brothers Pepin and Lewis received
in appanage kingdoms in Aquitaine and Bavaria, they were
strictly subordinated to the imperial supremacy.

This settlement represented the triumph of the religious
ideal of unity over the centrifugal forces in the national life;
and consequently when Lewis, under the influence of his
second wife, the Empress Judith, attempted to set it aside,
so as to provide a third kingdom for their child, Charles, he
met with the determined resistance not only of Lothair and
the other interested parties, but also of the leaders of the
ecclesiastical party. For the first time the Church intervened
decisively in European politics by the part that it played in
the dramatic events which culminated in the temporary deposition of Lewis the Pious in 833. The importance of this
episode has been obscured by the natural sympathy that his-

torians have felt for the unfortunate Lewis, deserted by his
followers and humiliated by his children after the manner
of King Lear, and they have consequently seen in the events
at Colmar, "the Field of Lies," nothing but a shameful act of
treachery dictated by selfishness and greed. Nevertheless, the
movement of opposition to Lewis was not simply the work
of time-serving prelates and courtiers; it was due to the
action of idealists and reformers who stood for all that was
highest in the Carolingian tradition; men such as Agobard,
and Wala, Paschasius Radbertus, the theologian, Bernard of
Vienne, and Ebbo of Rheims, the apostle of the North. The
disinterestedness and sincerity of these men is evident
from the writings of St. Agobard himself and of Paschasius
Radbertus, who was also a personal witness of the events and
whose life of Wala—the *Epitaphium Arsenii*—is regarded by
Manitius as one of the most remarkable works of the Carolingian age.[3]

Agobard was the representative of the Western tradition
of Tertullian and St. Augustine in its most uncompromising
form,[4] and he is remarkable for the vigour with which he
denounced popular superstitions, such as the belief in wiz-
ards and the practice of the ordeal, and maintained the rights
of the Church and the supremacy of the spiritual power. Wala
equally stood for the same principles, but in a less uncompromising fashion. He regarded the misfortunes of the Empire as due above all to the growing movement of secularisation that caused the Emperor to usurp the rights of the
Church, while the bishops devoted themselves to affairs of
state. This, however, did not prevent him from intervening in
the question of the imperial succession, for the unity and
peace of the Empire was in his eyes no mere question of
secular policy. It was a moral issue, and therefore one on
which it was the right and the duty of the Church to pro-
nounce, even if this involved passing judgment on the Emperor himself. Consequently, when Pope Gregory IV, who
had accompanied Lothair to Colmar, hesitated to infringe the
traditional Byzantine conception of the imperial prerogative, it was Wala and Radbertus who reassured him[5] by re-
minding him of his right as Vicar of God and St. Peter to
judge all men and be judged by none, and eventually per-
suaded him to take the leading part in the proceedings which
culminated in the deposition of the Emperor.[6]

This episode marks the emergence of a new claim to the

supremacy of the spiritual over the temporal power; and to the Church's right of intervention in the affairs of the state, which foreshadows the later mediaeval development. And it is significant that it originated not with the Papacy itself, but with the Frankish clergy, and was closely connected with the new theocratic conception of the state that was implicit in the Carolingian Empire. The state was no longer regarded as something distinct from the Church with independent rights and powers. It was itself a part, or rather an aspect, of the Church, which was, in the words of the letter of the bishops to Lewis the Pious in 829, "a single body divided under two supreme figures—that of the king and that of the priest." Thus the state could no longer be identified with the world and regarded as essentially unspiritual; it becomes itself an organ of the spiritual power in the world. Nevertheless, the older conception had entered so deeply into Christian thought, above all through the writings of St. Augustine, that it could not be entirely superseded, and thus throughout the Middle Ages, while the state insisted on its divine right as the representative of God in temporal affairs, it was always apt to be regarded by religious minds as a profane and worldly power that had no part in the sacred inheritance of the spiritual society.

In the Carolingian age, no doubt, so long as the Empire remained united, the Emperor was actually regarded as the representative of the principle of unity and the leader of the whole society. But with the division of the Carolingian inheritance among the sons of Lewis this ceased to be the case, and henceforward it was the episcopate that became the guardian of the imperial unity and the arbitrator and judge between the rival princes. The chief representative of this tendency in the second half of the ninth century was the great metropolitan of the West Frankish kingdom, Hincmar of Rheims, who was a redoubtable champion alike of the rights of the Church against the secular powers and of the cause of peace and unity in the Empire. But the same principles were admitted by the rulers themselves, notably by Charles the Bald, who recognises his dependence on the ecclesiastical power in the most unequivocal terms in the manifesto that he issued in 859, when an attempt was being made to depose him. He appeals to the sacred character of the authority that he had received as anointed king, and adds, "From this consecration I ought to be deposed by none, at least not without the hearing and judgment of the bishops by whose ministry I have been consecrated king, for they are the Thrones of God on whom God sits and by whom He passes judgment. To their paternal correction and chastising judgment I have always been ready to submit and do at present submit myself." [7]

Here we see the coronation ceremony which had previously been of very secondary importance elevated into a new position as the ultimate basis of the royal power. In fact it is on this that Hincmar himself bases his argument for the supremacy of the spiritual power, for since it is the bishops that create the king, they are superior to him, and his power is an instrument in the hands of the Church, to be guided and directed by it towards its true end. But Hincmar's ideal of a theocratic Empire controlled by an oligarchy of metropolitans involved a conflict on the one hand with the universal authority of the Holy See, and on the other with the independent claims of the local episcopate. It was in the interests of the latter that the False Decretals, issued under the name of Isidore Mercator, were compiled, probably at Le Mans or elsewhere in the province of Tours between the years 847 and 852. These are the most important of all the forgeries of the Carolingian period, but they are by no means an exceptional phenomenon, for the scholars of that age devoted themselves to the forgery of ecclesiastical and hagiographical documents with no less enthusiasm and no more moral scruple than the Renaissance scholars showed in imitating the works of classical antiquity. Their attitude to history was indeed so radically different from our own that it is equally difficult for us to condemn or to excuse them. In the case of the False Decretals, however, the motive is clear enough. The author wished to establish by detailed and unequivocal evidence the rights of the local episcopate to appeal directly to Rome against their metropolitans, and to safeguard the independence of the Church against the secular power. But great as was their importance for the subsequent development of canon law and for the progress of ecclesiastical centralisation in the Middle Ages, it is impossible to regard them as directly responsible for the increased prestige of the Papacy in Western Europe in the ninth century. They were a result rather than a cause of that development, which had its roots in the conditions that we have just described.

And still less can we attribute any real influence on Papal policy to the other great forgery of the period—the Donation of Constantine—for it seems to have been unknown to the Popes of the ninth century, and it was not until the middle of the eleventh century that it was first used at Rome in support of the wider papal claims. It is indeed still very uncertain when or where it was composed and for what object. The old view that it was concocted at Rome in the eighth century (c. 775) in order to secure the independence of the states of the Church, is now sometimes questioned, and it seems possible that it dates from the same period as the False Decretals. Perhaps the most plausible view is that it was the work of that able and sinister man, Anastasius the Librarian, during the period after 848, when he was in exile from Rome and was intriguing with Lewis II for the papal chair.[8] Such an act agrees well enough with the measureless ambition and the historical interests of that unscrupulous scholar, though at first sight it seems inconsistent with his connection with Lewis II. Nevertheless, the latter was ready enough to exalt the Papacy when it served his purpose, especially against the rival claims of the Byzantine Empire, and it was actually he who first asserted the view, adopted by the later mediaeval canonists, that the Emperor owes his dignity to his coronation and consecration by the Pope.[9]

Thus the new position of social hegemony in Western Europe that the Papacy acquired at this period was thrust upon it from without rather than assumed by its own initiative. As Dr. Carlyle writes with regard to the rise of the Temporal Power, "Any one who studies the Papal correspondence and the Liber Pontificalis in the eighth century will, we think, feel that the leadership of the Roman *respublica* in the West was forced upon them (the Popes) rather than deliberately sought. It was only slowly and reluctantly that they drew away from the Byzantine authority, for after all, as civilised members of the Roman state, they preferred the Byzantine to the barbarian." [10] In the same way in the ninth century the Papacy submitted to the control of the Carolingian Empire and even accepted the Constitution of 824, which made the Emperor the master of the Roman state and gave him practical control over the appointment of the Pope. Nevertheless, the bond of association with the Carolingian Empire of itself increased the political importance of the Papacy, and as the Empire grew weaker and more divided, the Papacy came to be regarded as the supreme representative of Western unity. Thus there was a brief period between the political effacement of the Papacy under Charlemagne and Lothair and its enslavement to local factions in the tenth century, when it seemed prepared to take the place of the Carolingian dynasty as the leader of Western Christendom. The pontificate of Nicholas I (858-867) foreshadows the future achievements of the mediaeval Papacy. He withstood the greatest men of his time, the emperors of the East and West, Hincmar, the leader of the Frankish episcopate, and Photius, the greatest of Byzantine patriarchs, and he successfully asserted the spiritual authority and independence of the Holy See even when the Emperor Lewis II attempted to impose his will by the use of armed force.

His successors were incapable of maintaining so lofty a position. Nevertheless, under John VIII (872-882), the Papacy was the one remaining bulwark of the Carolingian Empire, and it was due to the personal initiative of the Pope that Charles the Bald was crowned Emperor in the year 874, and Charles the Fat in 881. This final restoration of the Empire was, however, little more than an empty gesture. It was as different from the Empire of Charlemagne as the feeble and epileptic Charles the Fat was unlike his magnificent ancestor. In fact, the Empire no longer represented political realities and was in no position to act as the guardian of the Church and of civilisation. "We have looked for light," wrote the Pope, "and behold darkness! We seek succour, and we dare not emerge from the walls of the city in which there reigns an intolerable storm of persecution, because neither our spiritual son, the Emperor, nor any man of any nation brings us help." In 882 John VIII fell a victim to his enemies and Rome became the scene of a carnival of murder and intrigue which reached its climax in the ghoulish farce of 896, when the corpse of Pope Formosus was dragged from its tomb and submitted to a mock trial by his successor Stephen VI, who was himself to be murdered a few months later. Thus Papacy and Empire alike slid down into the abyss of anarchy and barbarism which threatened to engulf the whole of Western civilisation.

It is difficult to exaggerate the horror and confusion of the dark age that followed the collapse of the Carolingian experiment. The acts of the synod of Troslé in 909 give us some idea of the despair of the leaders of the Frankish church at the prospect of the universal ruin of Christian society. "The cities," they wrote, "are depopulated, the monasteries ruined and burned, the country reduced to solitude." "As the first men lived without law or fear of God, abandoned to their passions, so now every man does what seems good in his own eyes, despising laws human and divine and the commands of the Church. The strong oppress the weak; the world is full of violence against the poor and of the plunder of ecclesiastical goods." "Men devour one another like the fishes in the sea."

In fact the fall of the Empire involved not only the disappearance of the scarcely achieved unity of Western Europe, but the dissolution of political society and the breaking up of the Carolingian states into a disorganised mass of regional units. Power fell into the hands of anyone who was strong enough to defend himself and his dependents from external attack. This was the origin of the new local and semi-national dynasties that make their appearance in the latter part of the ninth century owing to the work of men like Robert the Strong, the founder of the Capetian house, who fought strenuously against the Vikings of the Loire and the Seine; like Bruno, Duke of Saxony, who defended his land against the Danes and the Wends; or Boso of Provence, who was crowned king by the bishops and nobles of Burgundy in 879, because they needed a protector against both the Vikings of the North and the Saracens of the Mediterranean. But these kingdoms were no less weak and insecure than the Carolingian states, since they were exposed to the same centrifugal forces that destroyed the Empire. During the second half of the ninth century the local officials had emancipated themselves from the control of the central government, and the offices of count and duke had become hereditary benefices and usurped all the privileges of royalty. In fact the count was for all practical purposes the king of his *pagus*, or canton. The one principle of the new society was the law of force and its correlative—the need for protection. Personal freedom was no longer a privilege, for the man without a lord became a man without a protector. Thus fealty and homage became the universal social relations, and the ownership of land became bound up with a complex of rights and obligations, both personal, military and juridical. In the same way the churches and monasteries were forced to find protectors, and these "advocates"—*Vögte, avoués*—acquired practical control over the lands and tenants of their clients. In short, the state and its public authority had become absorbed in the local territorial power. Political authority and private property were merged together in the new feudal relation, and the rights of jurisdiction and the duty of military service ceased to be universal public obligations and became annexed to the land as privileges or burdens of a particular tenure.

But though this evolution towards feudalism was the characteristic feature of the age, the feudalism of the tenth century was far from being the elaborately organised and symmetrical system that we find in Domesday Book or in the Assizes of Jerusalem. It was a much looser and more primitive organisation, a kind of compromise between the forms of an organised territorial state and the conditions of tribal society. The artificial administrative centralisation of the Carolingian period had disappeared, and there remained only the bare elements of barbaric society—the bonds of land and kinship and that which united the chief and his warriors. Thus the social bond that held feudal society together was the loyalty of warriors to their tribal chieftain rather than the public authority of the state; indeed, the society of the tenth century was in some respects more anarchic and barbarous than the old tribal society, for except in Germany, where the ancient tribal organisation still preserved its vitality, the traditional law and social spirit of the tribal society had disappeared, while the culture and political order of the Christian kingdom was too weak to take their place.

Nevertheless, the Church remained and continued to keep alive the traditions of higher civilisation. In so far as intellectual culture and civic life still survived, they existed in close dependence on the ecclesiastical society. For the state had lost all contact with the urban tradition and had become completely agrarian. The kings and nobles lived a semi-nomadic existence, subsisting on the resources of their lands and passing on from one estate to another in turn. Such a society had no use for towns, save for purely military purposes, and the so-called towns that came into existence at this period, like the *burgs* of Flanders and Germany and the *burhs* of Anglo-Saxon England, were in fact primarily fortresses and places of refuge, like the tribal strongholds of an earlier period. The old cities, on the other hand, were now almost wholly ecclesiastical in character. In the words of Professor Pirenne, "a theocratic government had completely replaced the municipal regimen of antiquity." They were ruled by the bishop and owed their importance to his cathedral and court and to the monasteries that lay within the city walls, or like St. Germain-des-Prés at Paris, and Westminster in London, in their immediate vicinity. They were the centre of administration of the diocese and of the episcopal and monastic estates, and their population consisted almost entirely of the clergy and their dependents. It was to provide for their needs that the market existed, and the great feasts of the ecclesiastical year attracted a large influx of population from outside. It was in fact a sacred city rather than a political or commercial organism.[11]

In the same way, it was the Church, not the feudal state, that was the true organ of culture. Learning, literature, music and art all existed primarily in and for the Church, which was the representative of the Latin tradition of culture and order as well as of the moral and spiritual ideals of Christianity.

Moreover, all the social services which we regard as natural functions of the state, such as education and poor relief and the care of the sick, were fulfilled, in so far as they were fulfilled at all, by the action of the Church. In the Church every man had his place and could claim the rights of spiritual citizenship, whereas in the feudal state the peasantry had neither rights nor liberty and was regarded mainly as property, as part of the livestock that was necessary for the equipment of an estate.

It is impossible to understand early mediaeval culture on the analogy of modern conditions, which are based on the conception of the single all-inclusive society of the sovereign state. There were in fact two societies and two cultures in early mediaeval Europe. On the one hand, there was the peace-society of the Church, which was centred in the monasteries and episcopal cities and inherited the tradition of later Roman culture. And, on the other hand, there was the war-society of the feudal nobility and their following, whose life was spent in incessant wars and private feuds. Although the latter might be affected personally by the influence of the religious society, whose leaders were often their own kinsmen, they belonged socially to a more primitive order. They were the successors of the old tribal aristocracies of barbarian Europe, and their ethos was that of the tribal warrior. At the best they preserved a certain rude measure of social order and protected their subjects from external aggression. But in many cases they were purely barbarous and predatory, living in their strongholds, as a mediaeval chronicler writes, "like beasts of prey in their dens," and issuing forth to burn their neighbours' villages and to hold the passing traveller to ransom.

The vital problem of the tenth century was whether this feudal barbarism was to capture and absorb the peace-society of the Church, or whether the latter could succeed in imposing its ideals and its higher culture on the feudal nobility, as it had formerly done with the barbarian monarchies of the Anglo-Saxons and the Franks.

At first sight the prospects seemed even more unfavourable than they had been in the age that followed the barbarian invasions, for now the Church itself was in danger of being engulfed in the flood of barbarism and feudal anarchy. Princes and nobles took advantage of the fall of the Empire to despoil the churches and monasteries of the wealth that they had accumulated during the previous period. In Bavaria, Arnulf carried out a wholesale secularisation of church lands, as Charles Martel had done in the Frankish kingdom at the close of the Merovingian period, and the Bavarian monasteries lost the greater part of their possessions.[12] In the West things were even worse, since the monasteries had been almost ruined by the ravages of the Northmen; and the feudalisation of the West Frankish kingdom left the Church at the mercy of the new military aristocracy, who used its resources to create new fiefs for their followers. Hugh Capet was lay abbot of most of the richest abbeys in his dominions, and the same policy was followed on a smaller scale by every local potentate.

Thus the development of feudalism had reduced the Church to a state of weakness and disorder even greater than that which had existed in the decadent Merovingian state before the coming of St. Boniface. Bishops and abbots received investiture from the prince like other feudatories and held their benefices as "spiritual fiefs" in return for military service. The higher offices had become the prerogative of the members of the feudal aristocracy, many of whom, like Archimbald, the tenth-century Archbishop of Sens, wasted the revenues of their sees on their mistresses and boon companions. Even in the monasteries the rule of chastity was no longer strictly observed, while the secular clergy lived openly as married men and often handed on their curés to their sons.

Worst of all, the Church could no longer look to Rome for moral guidance and spiritual leadership, for the Papacy itself had fallen a victim to the same disease that was attacking the local churches. The Holy See had become the puppet of a demoralised and truculent oligarchy, and under the rule of Theophylact and the women of his house, above all, the great Marozia the Senatrix, mistress, mother and murderess of Popes, it reached the lowest depths of degradation.

Nevertheless, the state of affairs was not so hopeless as one might conclude from the spectacle of all these scandals and abuses. They were the birth-pangs of a new society, and out of the darkness and confusion of the tenth century the new peoples of Christian Europe were born. The achievements of the Carolingian culture were not altogether lost. Their tradition remained and was capable of being applied anew to the circumstances of the regional and national societies wherever there was any constructive force that could make use of them. Above all, the forces of order found a rallying-point and a principle of leadership in the Carolingian ideal of Christian royalty. The kingship was the one institution that was common to the two societies and embodied the traditions of both cultures. For while the king was the lineal successor of the tribal chieftain and the war leader of the feudal society, he also inherited the Carolingian tradition of theocratic monarchy and possessed a quasi-sacerdotal character owing to the sacred rites of coronation and anointment. He was the natural ally of the Church, and found in the bishops and the monasteries the chief foundations of his power. And this dual character of mediaeval kingship is represented by two sharply contrasted types of ruler. There are the war-kings, like Sweyn of Denmark, or Harold Hadrada, whose nominal profession of Christianity does not prevent them from following in all things the traditions of the barbarian warrior; and there are the peace-kings and royal saints, like Wenceslas of Bohemia, and Edward the Confessor, and Robert II of France, who are entirely the servants of the spiritual society and live the life of crowned monks. But it is rare to find either element existing in so pure a form as in these examples, and the normal type of mediaeval royalty embodies both characters, as we see in the case of monarchs like St. Olaf and Canute, the Saxon emperors, and the great kings of Wessex.

The last are of peculiar importance, since they were the

first to attempt the task of national reconstruction in the spirit of the Carolingian tradition and to inaugurate that alliance between the national monarchy and the national church which is the characteristic feature of the period. So complete was this fusion in Wessex that the synods and councils of the Anglo-Saxon church became merged in the secular assemblies, and the ecclesiastical legislation of the tenth and eleventh centuries is the work of the king and his council, in which, however, the churchmen took the most prominent place. In the same way it was the king who took the initiative in the reform of the Church and in the restoration of monastic life which had been almost destroyed by the Danish invasions. Moreover, it is in Wessex, even more clearly than elsewhere, that we can trace the growth of a new vernacular culture on the basis of the Carolingian tradition under the patronage of the national monarchy. For King Alfred's remarkable translations of St. Gregory and Orosius and Boethius and Bede, which he carried out with the help of foreign scholars, "Plegmund my archbishop, and Asser my bishop, and Grimbald and John, my mass priests," actually represent a deliberate attempt to adapt the Christian classical culture, which had been confined to the international world of Latin culture, to the needs of the new national culture.[13] "For it seems good to me," he writes in his preface to St. Gregory's *Pastoral Care*, or "*Herd Book*," "that we also should turn some of the books that all men ought to know into that language that we can all understand, and so bring it about, as we easily may with God's aid if only we have peace, that all the youth of England, sons of free men who have the wherewithal, shall be set to learning before they are fit for other things, until they can read English writing well; and let those whom one wishes to educate further and to advance to a higher rank afterwards be instructed in the Latin language."

The work of restoration which was inaugurated by Alfred and his successors in the Anglo-Saxon kingdom was carried out on a far larger scale and with more permanent results by the Saxon kings in Germany. Indeed it is possible that the latter owed something to the example of their English predecessors, for Henry the Fowler allied himself to the house of Alfred by the marriage of his son Otto I with the daughter of Athelstan, and there are features in his policy in which historians have seen the influence of Anglo-Saxon precedents.[14] Nevertheless, Henry himself was an unlettered barbarian, who cared nothing for culture, who showed little favour to the Church, and who ruled Germany as the warrior leader of a tribal confederation. His power rested not on the universal claims of the Carolingian monarchy, but on the loyalty of his fellow Saxons, who still preserved their old tribal organisation and traditions in a purer form than any of the other peoples of Germany. The strength of this tribal feeling may be seen in Widukind's *History of the Saxons*, which is inspired throughout by a spirit of purely tribal patriotism, although it is the work of a monk of Corvey, the headquarters of ecclesiastical culture in the region, and dates from after the revival of the Empire.[15]

It was Henry's son Otto I who was the first to recover the Carolingian tradition and unite it with the tribal patriotism of the Saxon people. In contrast to his father, he was not satisfied with his election by the secular magnates, but took care to be crowned and anointed according to the solemn ecclesiastical rites at Aix, the old capital of the Empire, and he inaugurated the policy of close co-operation with the Church which was to make the episcopate the strongest foundation of the royal power. To an even greater extent than under the Carolingian Empire the episcopate became an organ of secular government. For the bishop was no longer merely a coadjutor and overseer of the local count; he had absorbed the functions and privileges of the latter and had begun to acquire the dual character of the mediaeval prince-bishop, the ruler of an ecclesiastical principality. This system was, of course, irreconcilable with the spiritual independence of the Church and the canonical principle of episcopal election, since it was essential for the ruler to keep the appointment of bishops in his own hands, as they had become the only reliable instruments of royal administration. In Lorraine, for example, the dukedom was held by Bruno, the Archbishop of Cologne, the brother of Otto I, and it was the bishops who controlled the disorderly feudal nobility and maintained the royal authority throughout the whole territory.

Nevertheless, this fusion between the Church and the royal power did not merely result in the secularisation of the former; it also lifted the monarchy out of the restricted environment of the tribal polities and brought it into relation with the universal society of Western Christendom. The Papacy, for all its weakness and degradation, remained the head of the Church, and the ruler who wished to control the Church, even in his own domains, was forced to secure the co-operation of Rome. And even apart from this the whole weight of Carolingian precedent and tradition forced the new kingdom towards Rome and the imperial crown.

Modern nationalist historians may look on the restoration of the Empire as a regrettable sacrifice of the true interests of the German kingdom to an impracticable ideal. But for the statesmen of the time Christendom was just as much a reality as Germany, and the restoration of the Carolingian monarchy in Germany found its natural fulfillment in the restoration of the Christian Empire. It is true that an interval of thirty-seven years had gone by since the death of the last nominal emperor, but for the greater part of that time Rome had been in the power of Alberic, the greatest of the house of Theophylact, who had been strong enough to keep possible rivals at a distance and to appoint a succession of Popes who were not unworthy of their office. His son, the infamous Pope John XII, was, however, incapable of taking his father's place and was driven to follow the example of the Popes of the eighth century, and call on the German king for help against the kingdom of Italy.

Consequently Otto I was undertaking no novel adventure, but merely treading a well-worn and familiar path when he answered the appeal of the Pope, like so many rulers before him, and entered Italy in 961 to receive the imperial crown. But none the less his coming produced a profound change in the European situation. It brought Northern Europe once more into contact with the civilised world of the Mediterranean from which it had been so long divorced. For Italy, in spite of its political disorder, was now at last entering on a period of economic and cultural revival. The rich trading cities of the South and the Adriatic—Naples, Amalfi, Salern Ancona and Venice—were in close relation with the high civilisation of the Eastern Mediterranean and were large Byzantine in culture, and their influence had a stimulating effect on the economic and social life of the rest of the peninsula, especially on the cities of the Lombard plain and of Romagna.

And this revival of Italian culture was accompanied by a reawakening of national feeling and of the old civic traditions. Venice was arising in the splendour of her youth under the first of her great doges, Peter Orseolo II, while even rulers like Alberic and Crescentius attempted to recall the memory of Rome's past greatness.

In the cities of Italy the old traditions of secular culture still survived. They alone in the West still possessed lay schools in which the grammarians kept alive the old ideals of the classical schools of rhetoric. They produced scholars, such as Liudprand of Cremona, Leo of Vercelli, and Stephen and Gunzo of Novarra, who rivalled the monastic scholars of the North in their learning, and far surpassed them in the quickness of their wits and the sharpness of their tongues, as we see in the amazing epistle in which Gunzo overwhelms an unlucky monk of St. Gall, who had ventured to criticise his grammar, with a torrent of mingled erudition and abuse. The persistence of classical and even pagan influences in Italian culture is also shown in the curious story of Vilgard, the grammarian of Ravenna, who was a martyr to his belief in the literal inspiration of the sacred poets, Horace, Virgil and Juvenal, and appears in a more attractive form in the charming little poem "*O admirabile Veneris idolum*" composed by an unknown clerk of Verona. No doubt this only represents one aspect of Italian culture, which was by no means lacking in religious elements. The very poet whom I have just mentioned was, according to Manitius, also the author of "*O Roma Nobilis*," that classic expression of the Christian ideal of Rome, and the same ideal inspires the remarkable poem on the procession on the feast of the Assumption—*Sancta Maria quid est?*—dating from the time of Otto III, which is almost the only literary product of the Roman culture of that age which we possess.[16]

Nevertheless, as in the fifteenth century, the revival of Italian culture and its complete independence of the North were undoubtedly accompanied by a movement of religious decline and moral disorder. The Holy See had become the slave of nepotism and political factions, and had lost its international position in Christendom. And its situation was the more perilous inasmuch as the Church north of the Alps was being affected by the new moral ideals of the movement of monastic reform and had begun to set its own house in order. At the council of Saint-Basle de Verzy in 991 the French bishops openly declared their belief in the bankruptcy of the Papacy. "Is it to such monsters (as Pope John XII or Boniface VII), swollen with their ignominy and devoid of all knowledge human or divine, that the innumerable priests of God throughout the world who are distinguished by their knowledge and virtues should lawfully be submitted?" asks their spokesman, Arnoul of Orleans. "We seem to be witnessing the coming of Antichrist, for this is the falling away of which the apostle speaks, not of nations but of the churches." [17]

If Italy had remained isolated from Northern Europe, Rome would have naturally gravitated towards the Byzantine Empire, as was indeed the deliberate policy of Alberic and other leaders of the Roman aristocracy, and there would have been a real danger that the eleventh century would have witnessed a schism, not between Rome and Byzantium, but between the old world of the Mediterranean and the East and the young peoples of Northern Europe. Actually, however, this danger did not materialise. The Northern movement of reform did not turn against the Papacy, as in the sixteenth century, but became its ally and co-operated with it to renew the religious life of Western Christendom; and the first representative of this movement to occupy the Papal chair and to prepare the way for the new age was the very man who was the representative of the Gallican party at the council of Saint-Basle and recorded its anti-Roman pronouncements, Gerbert of Aurillac.

This change, however, could never have taken place had it not been for the existence of the Western Empire. It was the coming of the Empire that rescued the Papacy from its servitude to local factions and restored it to Europe and to itself. It is true that the restoration of the Empire seemed at first to mean nothing more than the subjugation of the Papacy to a German prince in place of a local magnate. Nevertheless, the new conditions inevitably changed the horizon of imperial policy and brought with them wider and more universal aims. The Empire gradually lost its Saxon character and became an international power. Otto I married the Burgundian-Italian Queen Adelaide, while their son Otto II was the husband of a Greek princess, Theophano, who brought with her to the West the traditions of the Byzantine imperial court. Thus the offspring of their marriage, Otto III, united in his person the twofold tradition of the Christian Empire in its Carolingian and Byzantine form. From his mother and from the Calabrian Greek, Philagathus, he received the influence of the higher culture of the Byzantine world, while his tutor, Bernward of Hildesheim, at once a scholar, an artist and a statesman, represented all that was best in the Carolingian tradition of the North. Moreover, he was intensely sensitive to the higher spiritual influences of the time as we see from his personal friendship with St. Adalbert of Prague, and his relations with the leading ascetics of Italy, St. Romuald and St. Nilus.

With such a character and such an upbringing it is not surprising that Otto III should have conceived an imperialism that was Byzantine rather than Germanic, and that he should have devoted his life to the realisation of its universal claims and ideals. It was in pursuance of this end that he broke with the tradition of centuries by making his youthful cousin Bruno Pope, instead of a member of the Roman clergy. But it was not in Bruno, but in Gerbert, the most learned and brilliant scholar of the age, that he found a true kindred spirit who was capable of co-operating with him in his life's work. Hitherto he had been conscious of the inferiority of Western culture in comparison with Greek civilisation and refinement. It was Gerbert who taught him that it was the West and not Byzantium that was the true heir of the Roman tradition and who inspired him with the desire to recover this ancient inheritance. "Let it not be thought in Italy," wrote Gerbert, "that Greece alone can boast of the Roman power and of the philosophy of its Emperor. Ours, yea ours, is the Roman Empire! Its strength rests on fruitful Italy and populous Gaul and Germany and the valiant kingdoms of the Scythians. Our Augustus art thou, O Caesar, the emperor of the Romans who, sprung of the noblest blood of the Greeks, surpasses the Greeks in power, controls the Romans by right of inheritance and overcomes both alike in wisdom and eloquence." [18]

Consequently when the early death of Bruno made it possible for Gerbert to succeed him as Pope Sylvester II, Otto proceeded with his help to carry out his plans for the renewal of the Empire and the restoration of Rome to its rightful place as the imperial city and the centre of the Christian world. His attempt, and still more the Byzantine forms in which it was embodied, has, it is true, aroused the derision of modern historians, who see in it nothing but a piece of childish make-belief, cloaked in Byzantine forms.[19] But in reality Otto's policy, though without political results, had far more historical significance than any of the practical achievements of contemporary politicians, for it marks the emergence of a new European consciousness. All the forces that went to make up the unity of mediaeval Europe are represented in it—the Byzantine and Carolingian traditions of the Christian Empire and the ecclesiastical universalism of the Papacy, the spiritual ideals of monastic reformers, such as St. Nilus and St. Romuald, and the missionary spirit of St. Adalbert, the Carolingian humanism of Gerbert, and the national devotion of Italians like Leo of Vercelli to the Roman idea. Thus it marks the point at which the traditions of the past age flow together and are merged in the new culture of the mediaeval West. It looks back to St. Augustine and Justinian, and forward to Dante and the Renaissance. It is true that Otto III's ideal of the Empire as a commonwealth of Christian peoples governed by the concordant and interdependent authorities of Emperor and Pope was never destined to be realised in practice; nevertheless, it preserved a kind of ideal existence like that of a Platonic form, which was continually seeking to attain material realisation in the life of mediaeval society. For the ideal of Otto III is precisely the same ideal that was to inspire the thought of Dante, and throughout the intervening centuries it provided an intelligible formula in which the cultural unity of mediaeval Europe found conscious expression. Nor was it as sterile in practical results as it is usually supposed, for the short years of Otto and Gerbert's joint rule saw the rise of the new Christian peoples of Eastern Europe. It was due to their action, inspired in part by Otto's devotion to the memory of his Bohemian friend St. Adalbert, that the Poles and the Hungarians were freed from their dependence on the German state-church and given their own ecclesiastical organisation which was the indispensable condition for the independence of their national cultures.

This marks a vital modification in the Carolingian imperial tradition. The unity of Christendom was no longer conceived as the unity of an imperialist autocracy, a kind of Germanic Tsardom, but as a society of free peoples under the presidence of the Roman Pope and Emperor. Hitherto conversion to Christianity had involved political dependence and the destruction of national tradition, and this is the reason why the Wends and the other Baltic peoples had offered so stubborn a resistance to the Church. But the close of the tenth century saw the birth of a new series of Christian states extending from Scandinavia to the Danube. The eleventh century saw the passing of Northern paganism and the incorporation of the whole of Western Europe into the unity of Christendom. And at the same time the long winter of the Dark Ages had reached its end, and everywhere throughout the West new life was stirring, new social and spiritual forces were awakening, and Western society was emerging from the shadow of the East and taking its place as an independent unity by the side of the older civilisations of the oriental world.

CONCLUSION

It is impossible to draw an abrupt line of divison between one period and another, above all in the history of so vast and complex a process as the rise of a civilisation; and consequently the date which I have chosen to mark the end of this survey is a matter of practical convenience rather than of scientific definition. Nevertheless there is no doubt that the eleventh century marks a decisive turning-point in European history—the end of the Dark Ages and the emergence of Western culture. The previous revivals of culture in the age of Justinian and that of Charlemagne had been partial and temporary, and they had been followed by periods of decline, each of which seemed to reduce Europe to a lower stage of barbarism and confusion than it had known before. But with the eleventh century a movement of progress begins which was to continue almost without intermission down to modern times. This movement shows itself in new forms of life in every field of social activity—in trade and civic life and political organisation, as well as in religion and art and letters. It laid the foundations of the modern world not only by the creation of institutions that were to remain typical of our culture, but above all by the formation of that society of peoples which, more than any mere geographical unit, is what we know as Europe.

This new civilisation was, however, still far from embracing the whole of Europe, or even the whole of Western Europe. At the beginning of the eleventh century Europe was still, as it had been for centuries, divided up between four or five distinct culture-provinces, of which Western Christendom appeared by no means the most powerful or the most civilised. There was the Nordic culture of north-western Europe, which was just beginning to become part of Christendom, but still preserved an independent tradition of culture. In the South there was the Western Moslem culture of Spain and North Africa, which embraced practically the whole basin of the Western Mediterranean. In the East, the Byzantine culture dominated the Balkans and the Aegean and still possessed a foothold in the West through South Italy and the Adriatic and the Italian trading cities, such as Venice and Amalfi and Pisa; while further north, from the Black Sea to the White Sea and the Baltic, the world of the Slavs, the Balts and the Finno-Ugrian peoples was still mainly pagan and barbarous, though it was beginning to be affected by influences from the Byzantine culture of the South, the Nordic culture of Scandinavia and the Moslem culture of Central Asia and the Caspian.

Thus the culture that we regard as characteristically Western and European was confined in the main within the limits of the former Carolingian Empire, and found its centre in the old Frankish territories of Northern France and Western Germany. In the tenth century it was, as we have seen, hard pressed on every side and even tended to contract its frontiers. But the eleventh century saw the turn of the tide and the rapid expansion of this central continental culture in all directions. In the West the Norman Conquest took England out of the sphere of the Nordic culture that had threatened for two centuries to absorb it, and incorporated it into the continental society; in the North and East it gradually dominated the Western Slavs and penetrated Scandinavia by its cultural influence; while in the South it embarked with crusading energy on the great task of the reconquest of the Mediterranean from the power of Islam.

In this way the peoples of the Frankish Empire imposed their social hegemony and their ideals of culture on all the surrounding peoples, so that the Carolingian unity may be regarded without exaggeration as the foundation and starting-point of the whole development of mediaeval Western civilisation. It is true that the Carolingian Empire had long lost its unity, and France and Germany were becoming more and more conscious of their national differences. Nevertheless they both looked back to the same Carolingian tradition, and their culture was compounded of the same elements, though the proportions were different. They were still in essence the Western and East Frankish realms, though, like brothers who take after different sides of their family, they were often more conscious of their difference than of their resemblance. In both cases, however, the cultural leadership lay with the intermediate regions—the territories of the Empire that were most Latinised, and those in France where the Germanic element was strongest: Northern France, Lorraine and Burgundy, Flanders and the Rhineland. Above all, it was Normandy, where the Nordic and Latin elements stood in sharpest contrast and most immediate contact, that was the leader of the movement of expansion.

It was this middle territory, reaching from the Loire to the Rhine, that was the true homeland of mediaeval culture and the source of its creative and characteristic achievements. It was the cradle of Gothic architecture, of the great mediaeval schools, of the movement of monastic and ecclesiastical reform and of the crusading ideal. It was the centre of the typical development of the feudal state, of the North European communal movement and of the institution of knighthood. It was here that a complete synthesis was finally achieved between the Germanic North and the spiritual order of the Church and the traditions of the Latin culture. The age of the Crusades saw the appearance of a new ethical and religious ideal which represents the translation into Christian forms of the old heroic ideal of the Nordic warrior culture. In *The Song of Roland* we find the same motives that inspired the old heathen epic—the loyalty of a warrior to his lord, the delight in war for its own sake, above all the glorification of honourable defeat. But all this is now subordinated to the service of Christendom and brought into relation with Christian ideas. Roland's obstinate refusal to sound his horn is entirely in the tradition of the old poetry, but in the death scene the defiant fatalism of the Nordic heroes, such as Hogni and Hamdis, has been replaced by the Christian attitude of submission and repentance.

"Towards the land of Spain he turned his face, so that Charles and all his army might perceive that he died as a valiant vassal with his face towards the foe. Then did he confess him in right zealous wise and hold forth his glove to heaven for his transgressions." [1]

It is true that the heroic ideal had already found expression in the literature of the Christian peoples, above all in the noble Lay of Maldon with its great lines: "Thought shall be harder, heart the keener, courage the greater, as our might lessens." But here there is as yet but slight trace of Christian sentiment.[2] The old tradition still survives intact. Indeed, throughout the Dark Ages, Western Society had been characterised by an ethical dualism that corresponds to the dualism of culture. There was one ideal for the warrior and another for the Christian, and the former still belonged in spirit to the barbaric world of northern paganism. It was not until the eleventh century that the military society was incorporated into the spiritual polity of Western Christendom by the influence of the crusading ideal. The institution of knighthood is the symbol of the fusion of Nordic and Christian traditions in the mediaeval unity, and it remains typical of Western society from the time of *The Song of Roland* to the day when its last representative Bayard, "the good knight," died like Roland with his face to the Spaniards at the passage of the Sesia, in the age of Luther and Machiavelli. For the Middle Ages are the age of Nordic Catholicism, and they endured only as long as the alliance continued between the Papacy and the North—an alliance which had been inaugurated by Boniface and Pepin and consolidated by the work of the northern movement of ecclesiastical reform in the eleventh century, which had its source in Lorraine and Burgundy. This alliance was first broken by another Boniface and another king of the Franks at the close of the thirteenth century, but though it never wholly recovered its strength it remained the corner-stone of Western unity, until the time when the Papacy became completely Italianised and the peoples of the North ceased to be Catholic.

But though mediaeval culture was the culture of the Christian North, its face was turned, like Roland's, to the Islamic South, and there was not a land from the Tagus to the Euphrates in which the northern warriors had not shed their blood. Norman princes ruled in Sicily and Antioch, Lorrainers in Jerusalem and Edessa, Burgundians in Portugal and Athens, Flemings in Constantinople; and the ruins of their castles in the Peloponnese and Cyprus and Syria still bear witness to the power and enterprise of the Frankish barons.

This contact with the higher civilisation of the Islamic and Byzantine world had a decisive influence on Western

Europe and was one of the most important elements in the development of mediaeval culture. It showed itself, on the one hand, in the rise of the new aristocratic courtly culture and the new vernacular literature, and, on the other, in the assimilation of the Graeco-Arabic scientific tradition and the rise of a new intellectual culture in the West.[3] And these influences remained in the ascendant until they were checked by the Renaissance of the classical tradition, which coincided with the Turkish conquest of the East and the separation of Western Europe from the Islamic world. With the ending of the Middle Ages, Europe turned its back on the East and began to look westward to the Atlantic.

Thus the mediaeval unity was not permanent, since it was based on the union of the Church and the Northern peoples, with a leaven of oriental influences. Nevertheless its passing did not mean the end of European unity. On the contrary, Western culture became more autonomous, more self-sufficient and more *occidental* than ever before. The loss of spiritual unity did not involve the separation of the West into two exclusive and alien cultural units, as would almost certainly have been the case if it had occurred four or five centuries earlier. In spite of religious disunion, Europe retained its cultural unity, but this was now based on a common intellectual tradition and a common allegiance to the classical tradition rather than on a common faith. The Latin grammar took the place of the Latin Liturgy as the bond of intellectual unity, and the scholar and the gentleman took the place of the monk and the knight as the representative figures of Western culture. The four centuries of Nordic Catholicism and oriental influence were followed by four centuries of Humanism and occidental autonomy. To-day Europe is faced with the breakdown of the secular and aristocratic culture on which the second phase of its unity was based. We feel once more the need for spiritual or at least moral unity. We are conscious of the inadequacy of a purely humanist and occidental culture. We can no longer be satisfied with an aristocratic civilisation that finds its unity in external and superficial things and ignores the deeper needs of man's spiritual nature. And at the same time we no longer have the same confidence in the inborn superiority of Western civilisation and its right to dominate the world. We are conscious of the claims of the subject races and cultures, and we feel the need both for protection from the insurgent forces of the

oriental world and for a closer contact with its spiritual traditions. How these needs are to be met, or whether it is possible to meet them, we can at present only guess. But it is
well to remember that the unity of our civilisation does not
rest entirely on the secular culture and the material progress
of the last four centuries. There are deeper traditions in
Europe than these, and we must go back behind Humanism
and behind the superficial triumphs of modern civilisation, if
we wish to discover the fundamental social and spiritual
forces that have gone to the making of Europe.

NOTES

INTRODUCTION

[1] There is a still lower depth that has been discovered by those modern writers who seem to regard the past as a kind of menagerie stocked with strange beasts whose peculiarities are exhibited by the show-man-biographer to the public on the payment of rather a large fee.

[2] Cf. his "Pro monachis," printed in his *Ausgewählte Kleine Schriften*, and his son's preface to that volume.

[3] A glance at any of the books dealing with royal descents will show that a considerable portion of the English middle classes can claim some direct descent not merely from Edward III or Henry II, but from Charlemagne and St. Vladimir, and Boleslav of Poland and the leaders of the Vikings!

THE ROMAN EMPIRE

[1] Mommsen, *History of Rome*, Eng. trans. V, 102.

[2] E.g., the thesis of Strzygowski in *Altai-Iran* and his more recent books.

[3] The auxiliary troops attached to the legion were, on the other hand, raised from the less Romanised population of the outlying provinces. But they also were commanded by Roman officers and received rights of citizenship at the end of their twenty-five years of service.

[4] In Egypt the *artaba* of corn, which had been worth seven or eight drachmæ in the second century, cost no less than 120,000 drachmæ in the time of Diocletian. Rostovtzeff, *Social and Economic History of the Roman Empire*, p. 419.

[5] Rostovtzeff, *op. cit.*, chs. X and XI.

[6] *Journal of Egyptian Archæology*, VI, 164.

[7] M. Aurel, I, 14 (Long's trans.).

[8] E.g., the lines of Prudentius, *contra Symmachum*, II, 816-819: "Romanism differs from barbarism as a man differs from an animal and as he that has speech from the dumb and as Christianity differs from paganism." Cf. also the letter of Gregory the Great to Leontius (*Epp.* XI, 4).

[9] There is, however, one striking exception, the work of Salvian, *De Gubernatione Dei*, which is an uncompromising condemnation of the vices of Roman society and even to some extent an apology for the barbarians. There was, as I have shown elsewhere, an undercurrent of hostility to the Roman Empire and to secular civilization in the Christianity of that age which finds its strongest expression among the Donatists but is not entirely absent from the writings of St. Augustine. Cf. *A Monument to St. Augustine*, pp. 36 and 52-64.

[10] Dumque offers victis proprii consortia juris
Urbem fecisti quod prius orbis erat.
Rutil, Itin, 63.

[11] Haec est in gremio victos quae sola recepit
Humanumque genus communi nomine fovit.
Claudian On the Second Consulate of Stilicho, 150.
Cf. Boissier, *La Fin du Paganisme*, II, 137, p. 252 (ed. 7).

[12] *Contra Symmachum*, II, 578-636.

THE CATHOLIC CHURCH

[1]   Qualis Berecyntia mater
Invehitur curru Phrygias turrita per urbes
Laeta deum partu, centum complexa nepotes
Omnis caelicolas, omnis supera alta tenentis.
Aen., VI, 785.

[2] St. Cyprian, *Ep.* LXXVI, trans. R. E. Wallis.

[3] In recent years particular attention has been devoted to the Mandaeans or "Christians of St. John," of Southern Babylonia, the only one of these sects that has survived to modern times. Lidzbarski and Reitzenstein have attempted to prove that this sect was originally connected with the Essenes and with the disciples of John the Baptist, and consequently that the Mandaean writings have an important bearing on the question of Christian origins. S. A. Pallis, however, has shown (in his *Mandaean Studies*, 1919) that the parallels with Judaism are superficial and of relatively recent origin and that Mandaeanism is essentially a Gnostic sect which subsequently, in Sassanian times, came under the influence of Zoroastrian ideas. He also rejects the earlier theory of Brandt that the fundamental stratum in Mandaean beliefs is based on ancient Babylonian religion.

[4] *I Peter* ii. 9.

[5] So clear is this, that Sohm went so far as to regard this epistle as the starting-point of the juridical conception of the Church, which in his view abruptly replaced the earlier "charismatic" view. But, as Harnack points out, the conception of a divine apostolic authority is as old as the Church itself and appears clearly enough in the decree of the Council of Jerusalem. *Acts* xv, 23-27.

[6] *I Clement*, XX, XXXVII, XL-XLIV, etc.

[7] "By its (the Roman Church's) tradition and by its faith announced to men, which has been transmitted to us by the succession of bishops, we confound all those who in any way by caprice or vainglory or by blindness and perversity of will gather where they ought not. For to this Church, on account of its higher origin, it is necessary that every Church, that is, the faithful from all sides, should resort, in which the tradition from the Apostles has always been preserved by those that are from all parts" (Irenaeus, *Against Heresies*, III, iii).

The expression "propter potentiorem principalitatem" which I have translated as "higher origin" is somewhat disputed. It has often been translated as "more powerful headship" or as "preeminent authority" (*e.g.*, in the Ante-Nicene Library translation, Vol. I, p. 261). I think there can be little doubt that principalitas = ἀρχαιότης and refers to the origins of the see, as in the passage of Cyprian, *Ep.* LIX, 13—"navigare audent ad Petri cathedram et Ecclesiam principalem unde unitas sacerdotalis exorta est," where "principalem" means the original or earliest church.

It is the same argument that Optatus and St. Augustine were to use against the Donatists, as in the lines:

Numerate sacerdotes vel ab ipsa Petri sede,
et in ordine illo patrum quis cui successit videte:
ipsa est petra quam non vincunt superbae infernorum portae.
Psalmus c. partem Donat. 18.

[8] The question has recently been discussed by Mr. Norman Baynes in the Raleigh Lecture for 1929. He maintains that the dominant motive in Constantine's career was his "conviction of a personal mission entrusted to him by the Christian God," that he "definitely identified himself with Christianity, with the Christian Church and the Christian creed"; and that he believed the prosperity of the Empire to be bound up with the unity of the Catholic Church. Thus the Byzantine ideal of a Roman Empire founded on the orthodox faith and united with the orthodox Church has its source in the vision of Constantine. *Constantine the Great and the Christian Church* by N. H. Baynes; *Proceedings of the British Academy*, Vol. XV. (with very full bibliographical notes on the subject).

[9] *Oration in Praise of Constantine*, XVI.

[10] *Contra Celsum*, III, 29, 30. Cf. Battifol, *l'Eglise Naissante*, ch. vii.

[11] St. Hippolytus is the last Roman Christian to write in Greek. Novatian in the middle of the third century already writes Latin,

although Greek probably remained the liturgical language until the following century.

[12] Harnack writes: "In all cases it was a political institution, invented by the greatest of politicians, a two-edged sword which protected the endangered unity of the Church at the price of its independence." (*History of Dogma*, Eng. trans., III, 127.)

[13] Cf. H. Gelzer, *Die Konzilien als Reichsparlamente* in *Ausgewahlte Kleine Schriften* (1907). He argues that the Councils followed the precedent of the ancient Senate in their arrangement and forms of procedure.

[14] Dom Cabrol has shown how the liturgical cycle was evolved from the local ceremonies connected with the Holy places at Jerusalem in the fourth century. The ceremonies of Holy Week at Rome were in origin an imitation of this local cycle, and the group of churches round the Lateran at Rome, St. Maria Maggiore, Sta. Croce in Gerusalemme, St. Anastasia, etc., in which these ceremonies were performed, reproduced the sanctuaries of the holy places at Jerusalem. Cabrol, *Les Origines Liturgiques, Conf. VIII.*

[15] "Que l'on eût été bien inspiré, si au lieu de tant philosopher sur la terminologie, d'opposer l'union physique a l'union hypostatique, les deux natures qui n'en font qu'une à l'unique hypostase qui régit les deux natures, on se fût un peu plus préoccupé de choses moins sublimes et bien autrement vitales. On alambiquait l'unité du Christ, un mystère; on sacrifiait l'unité de l'Eglise, un devoir." Duchesne, *Eglises Séparées*, p. 57.

[16] The backwardness and isolation of the West in theological matters is shown by the fact that St. Hilary himself admits that he had never heard of the Nicene faith until the time of his exile in A.D. 356. (*De Synodis*, 91.)

[17] We may also note the introduction of liturgical poetry into the West by Hilary and Ambrose.

[18] The letter is given in Greek by Athanasius, *History of the Arians*, 44. I follow Tillemont's French version in *Memoires*, Tom. VII, 313.

[19] *Contra Constantium imperatorem*, 5.

[20] *De Fide*, II, xvi. 136, 142 (trans. H. de Romestin).

[21] Ambrose, *Ep. XXIV*, 4, 5.

[22] Cf. the whole of his Oration in Praise of Constantine. *E.g.*, he writes, "Let me lay before thee, victorious and mighty Constantine, some of the mysteries of His sacred truth: not as presuming to instruct thee who art thyself taught of God; nor to disclose to thee those secret wonders which He Himself not through the agency or work of man, but through our common Saviour and the frequent light of His Divine presence has long since revealed and unfolded to thy view; but in the hope of leading the unlearned to the light of truth and displaying before those who know them not, the causes and motives of thy pious deeds." *Cap. XI.*

[23] Ambrose, *Ep. LI*, 11.

²⁴ *History of Dogma* (Eng. trans.), III, 226. He goes on to say, "Yet this nimbus was not sufficiently bright to bestow upon its possessor an unimpeachable authority; it was rather so nebulous that it was possible to disregard it without running counter to the spirit of the universal Church." The Greek ecclesiastical historians, Socrates and Sozomen, both of them laymen and lawyers, are impartial witnesses to the position accorded to the Roman see at Constantinople in the fifth century, as Harnack notes (*ibid.*, note 2). Cf. Batiffol, *Le Siège Apostolique*, 411-416.

THE CLASSICAL TRADITION
AND CHRISTIANITY

[1] *Sat.* xv, 110-112.
[2] This ideal of a liberal education dates from the Sophists themselves, above all from Hippias of Elea, but it was not until the time of Martianus Capella and the writers of the later Empire that the number of the Liberal Arts was definitely fixed. The subdivision between the Trivium and the Quadrivium is later still, and is probably due to the Carolingian Renaissance. On the other hand, the mediaeval idea of the Liberal Arts as essentially propaedeutic— a preparation for theology—is very ancient, since it goes back to Posidonius and Philo, from whom it passed to the Christian scholars of Alexandria. Cf. Norden, *Die antike Kunstprosa*, pp. 670-679.
[3] 1 *Corinthians* i. 20-27.
[4] Tertullian, *De Testimonio Animae*, 1. (Translated by Roberts and Donaldson.)
[5] Aug. *Epist.* XVI.
[6] *Philocalia* XIII, i. (Trans. W. Metcalfe.)
[7] Gregory Thaumaturgus, *Panegyric of Origen*, xiii. (Trans. W. Metcalfe.)
[8] His chief work—the *Symposium of the Ten Virgins*—is an elaborate imitation of a Platonic dialogue.
[9] *Dialogus de claris oratoribus* 30.
[10] *Epist.* XXII. Cf. Rufinus, *Apol.* II, 6, and St. Jerome's answer. *Apol.* I, 30-31, III, 32.
[11] From the preface to the *Hebraicae Quaestiones in Genesim*, Cavallera. St. Jerome, *app.* P., p. 105. "If such a man as Cicero," he says, "could not escape criticism, what wonder if the dirty swine grunt at a poor little man like me!"
[12] Rufinus, *Apol.* II, 8.
[13] E.g., Erasmus speaks of Jerome as "that heavenly man, of all Christians beyond question the most learned and the most eloquent. . . . What a mass there is in his works of antiquities, of Greek literature, of history! and then what a style! What a mastery of language, in which he has left not only all Christian authors far

behind him, but seems to vie with Cicero himself."—*Ep.* 134, trans. Nichols (=*e.p.* 141 ed. Allen).

Like the humanists, Jerome pillories his opponents under sobriquets drawn from classical literature. Rufinus is Luscius Lavinius or Calpurnius Lanarius (from Sallust), Pelagius and his supporters are Catiline and Lentulus. In the famous quarrel between Poggio and Francisco Filelfo the latter actually appeals to the precedents of Jerome and Rufinus in order to justify the violence of his invectives. Cf. his letters, printed in the Appendix to Walser's *Poggius Florentinus*, Nos. 40 and 42.

[14] *Peristephanon*, II, 433.

[15] *Peristephanon*, II, 517.

[16] *Peristephanon*, IV, 197.

[17] *Sermo*, 141.

[18] Cf., *e.g.*, *de Trinitate*, VIII, iii.

[19] Aug. *Confessions*, V, iii. Cf. X, xxxv.

THE BARBARIANS

[1] Professor Macalister writes: "A Tuath was a community of people, not necessarily united by ties of blood, and therefore, *not* to be called a tribe, which is *always* a misnomer WHEREVER used in reference to Celtic Ireland." (*The Archaeology of Ireland*, p. 25). But, as we have pointed out, the tribe is not necessarily a union of kinsfolk. In the majority of cases it consists, as in Ireland, of a number of such groups or septs.

[2] The importance of the Celtic element in Dacia and the Danube lands is well shown by Parvan (*Dacia*, by V. Parvan Ch. IV., "Carpatho-Danubians and Celts").

[3] Parvan (*op. cit.*, p. 166) insists particularly on the co-operation of Celtic and Roman elements in the culture of the Empire in Central Europe. "Once again a great Celtic unity crossing Northern Italy made its appearance in Europe, but this time Rome was the gainer. From Lugdunum in Gaul to Sirmium near the mouth of the Theiss we see one world making use of one great line of communication upon which all other highways, whether the Celtic Rhine or Danube, or from Latin Italy, converge. Every country traversed by this mighty route flourished the more because it shared in the prosperity of the whole."

[4] H. Shetelig, *Préhistoire de la Norvège*, 154-159. (Oslo, 1926.)

[5] Cf. Rostovtzeff, *Iranians and Greeks in South Russia*.

THE BARBARIAN INVASIONS
AND THE FALL OF THE
EMPIRE IN THE WEST

[1] Recent continental writers, such as Dopsch (*Grundlagen*, I, 341-5), Schumacher (III, 273, etc., 351-6), suggests that the Germanic *Hufe* or Hide may be derived from the *Sors* of the Roman settler, which consisted of separate allotments of agricultural land, with rights of pasture and common.

[2] The Sarmatian graves even contain objects of Chinese origin, such as jadite sword-hilts and, in one case, a Chinese bronze mirror.

[3] The Romans had already begun to recognise the importance of heavy cavalry. Constantius II owed his victory at Mursa in 351 to his cuirassiers, the "Cataphracts."

[4] Cf. C. Jullian, *Histoire de Gaule*, Vol. VII, chap. vii.

[5] *Ep.* 123, 15-16.

[6] Orosius, VII, 48.

[7] Greg. Tur., II, 37.

[8] Thurlow Leeds, *Archaeology of Anglo-Saxon Settlements*, pp. 58, etc., and R. Smith, *Guide to Anglo-Saxon Antiquities*, pp. 25 and 34.

THE CHRISTIAN EMPIRE
AND THE RISE OF THE
BYZANTINE CULTURE

[1] This parallelism is discussed with full bibliographical notes by E. Kornemann, in Gercke and Norden, Vol. III (*Die römische Kaiserzeit*, Appendix 4, *New Rome and New Persia*).

[2] Cf. Eusebius, *Oration on the Tricennalia of Constantine*, cap. ii.

[3] Byzantine silver plate dating from the sixth century has been found at Perm in Eastern Russia.

[4] The life of St. John the Almoner, by Leontios of Neapolis, mentions the case of a corn-ship which was driven as far west as Britain and which returned with a cargo of tin at the beginning of the seventh century.

[5] So numerous were these that Ammianus Marcellinus complains that the imperial transport service was quite disorganised by the bands of bishops travelling hither and thither in government conveyances. (Am. Marcell., XXI, 16, 18.)

[6] *Codex Theodosianus*, XVI, 1, 2.

[7] The civil diocese was a group of provinces under the authority of a vicar. Of the five dioceses of the East, Egypt, with five provinces, corresponds to the Patriarchate of Alexandria, the Orient with fifteen provinces to the Patriarchate of Antioch, while Asia, Pontus

and Thrace, with a total of twenty-eight provinces, finally went to form the Patriarchate of Constantinople.

[9] E.g., the *Dionysiaca* of Nonnus of Panopolis (fifth century); the *Rape of Helen* by Kolluthus of Lycopolis (sixth century); the *Hero and Leander* of Musaeus, and the lost epics of Tryphiodorus.

[9] *Le Système du Monde*, Vol. I, chs. v and vi; Vol. II, ch. x, etc.

[10] E.g., the verses of Agathias and Theaetetus Scholasticus on Priapus of the Anchorage, *Anth. Pal.*, X, 14 and 16, and the dedication to Pan by Agathias, *Anth. Pal.*, VI, 79.

[11] He even influenced the West through early mediaeval chronicles such as the eighth century *Chronicon Palatinum*. Cf. Krumbacher, pp. 327-331.

THE AWAKENING OF THE EAST
AND THE REVOLT OF THE
SUBJECT NATIONALITIES

[1] *Syriac Documents* in *Ante-Nicene Christian Library*, Vol. XX, p. 129.

[2] *Syriac Documents*, p. 114.

[3] *Op. cit.*, p. 121.

[4] The *Parabolani* were originally a kind of ambulance corps whose business it was to care for the sick and the pestilence-stricken. But they justified their title—"the venturesome" or "the reckless"—by acting as the ringleaders of the mob of Alexandria in every religious disturbance, and were a constant source of anxiety to the civil authority. Cf. *Codex Theodosianus*, XVI, 2.

[5] Some modern historians, such as E. Schwartz, tend to exaggerate the political motive in Athanasius' policy and to depict him primarily as an ambitious hierarch. But there is no doubt that he found his most powerful ally in the national feeling of the Egyptian populace. As Duchesne writes, "Tout ce que l'Egypte comptait d'honnêtes gens était pour lui. C'était le défenseur de la foi, le pape légitime, le père commun; c'était aussi, grande recommendation, l'ennemi, la victime du gouvernement. . . . Sauf quelques dissidents qui ne se montraient que derrière les uniformes, la population était entièrement à ses ordres." *Histoire ancienne de l'Eglise*, II, 268.

[6] *The Rhythms of Ephrem the Syrian*, trans. J. Morris in the *Oxford Library of the Fathers*, pp. 102, 95, 87.

THE RISE OF ISLAM

[7] On the origins of this South Arabian civilisation, cf. my *Age of the Gods* (1928), pp. 78-9, 115-116, 410.

2 Compare *Sura IX*, 90-105. E.g., "The Arabs of the desert are most stout in unbelief and dissimulation, and it is not likely that they should be aware of the laws which God has sent down to his apostle."

3 Quoted in Browne's *Hist. of Persian Lit.*, I, 188-189.

4 *Sura IX*, 102. Tr. Rodwell.

5 The Isaurians who originated from Germanicea in Commagene.

6 Between 685 and 741 there were five Syrian Popes—John V, Sergius I, Sisinnius, Constantine and Gregory III.

THE EXPANSION OF MOSLEM CULTURE

1 Ibn Hazm (994-1064), who as a Spaniard was partial to the Umayyad family, wrote as follows: "The Umayyads were an Arabic dynasty, they had no fortified residence or citadel; each of them dwelt in his villa where he lived before becoming Khalif; they did not wish that the Moslems should speak to them as slaves to their masters, nor kiss the ground before them, or their feet. . . . The Abbasids, on the contrary, were a Persian dynasty, under which the Arab tribal system, as regulated by Omar, fell to pieces, the Persians of Khorasan were the real rulers and the government became despotic as in the days of Chosroes." Quoted by de Goeje in *Encyclopædia Britannica*, Volume 5, p. 426 (11th edition).

2 Von Kremer, *Kulturgeschichtliche Streifzüge*, pp. 41-42, quoted by E. B. Browne, *History of Persian Literature*, I, 307.

3 He was known to mediaeval Europe as Johannitius, and his Introduction to Galen was one of the first Arabic books to be translated into Latin.

4 Authors of the *Liber Trium Fratrum*, translated by Gerard of Cremona.

5 His treatise on Algebra was translated by Robert of Chester in 1145, while the translation of his arithmetical work *Algorismi de numeris Indorum* was probably due to Adelhard of Bath. His astronomical tables, the Khorasmian tables (trans. 1126) were also of great importance in the history of mediaeval science.

6 His introduction to astronomy, *De scientia astrorum*, was translated by Plato of Tivoli in 1116. It was from him also that the West derived its first knowledge of Trigonometry.

7 His essays are like the set pieces of the classical schools of rhetoric, imaginary pleadings or arguments on such subjects as the superiority of negroes to whites or the contest between autumn and spring. Both the Rhetoric and the Poetics of Aristotle were known to the Arabs.

3 Duhem, *Le système du Monde*, IV, p. 314.

9 Carra de Vaux, *Les Penseurs de l'Islam*, II, pp. 145-146.

10 Salamiyya, near Homs.

[11] According to Druse teaching, al Hakim's habit of riding upon an ass typifies his relation to the earlier revelations. The ass represents the Speakers or Prophets of the previous dispensations!

[12] Browne, *Literary History of Persia*, II, 235.

[13] Carra de Vaux, *Les Penseurs de l'Islam*, IV, 102-115, from Dieterici, *Die Abhandlungen der Ikwân es-Safâ in Auswahl*, Leipzig, 1883-86, esp. pp. 594-596. *Cf.* Dieterici, *Die Philosophie bei dem Arabern*, Part VIII, pp. 85-115.

THE BYZANTINE RENAISSANCE
AND THE REVIVAL OF
THE EASTERN EMPIRE

[1] We must except Theophilus, the last of the Iconoclastic emperors, who took a genuine interest in art and culture and was the patron of two Iconoclast scholars, Leo of Thessalonica and his brother the Patriarch John.

[2] At the same time, the Paulician heresy reached the Bulgarians from the Armenian colonists near Philippopolis, and gave birth to the Slavonic sect of the Bogomils. It rapidly spread throughout the Balkans, especially in Bosnia, where it became for a time the national religion, as well as to Russia (as early as 1004), and at a later date to Western Europe.

[3] It is right, they said, that in the Church things should follow the course of the sun, and that they should have their origin in the same part of the world where God Himself deigned to be revealed in human form. S. Greg. Naz., *Carmen de vita sua*, 1690-1693.

[4] Viz., the Arian schisms, 343-398; that concerning St. John Chrysostom, 404-415; the Acacian schism, 484-519; Monethelitism, 640-681; the Iconoclasts, 726-787 and 815-843. Thus the seeds of strife are to be found neither in the eleventh nor the ninth centuries, but as far back as the time of the Arian Controversy, "that abominable and fratricidal war, which," as Duchesne writes, "divided the whole of Christendom from Spain to Arabia, and ended after sixty years of scandal only to leave to future generations the germs of schisms of which the Church still feels the effects." (*Histoire ancienne de l'Eglise*, II, 157.)

[5] An even more extreme instance of this insistence on points of ritual is to be found in the rubric that appears in the old editions of the Lenten Triodion on the Sunday before Septuagesima. "On this day the thrice accursed Armenians keep their disgusting fast which they call Artziburion. But we eat daily cheese and eggs, in refutation of their heresy." N. Nilles, *Kalendarium Utriusque Ecclesiae*, II, p. 8. The same tendency characterised the Russian Church in modern times, and its greatest crisis arose out of the liturgical reforms of the Patriarch Nikon.

[6] So far from supporting the reforming movement in the Eastern

Church, the Papacy was partly responsible for the appointment of the boy patriarch Theophylact, which was one of the most discreditable episodes in the history of the Byzantine Church in the tenth century.

[7] E.g., the Patriarchs Photius, Tarasius (784-806), Sisinnius (996-998) and Michael Cerularius himself.

THE WESTERN CHURCH AND THE CONVERSION OF THE BARBARIANS

[1] *Ep.* X, 20, tr. Dudden, *Gregory the Great*, II, 38.

[2] *Hom. in Ezech.*, II, vi, 22-23. Trans. Dudden, *op. cit.*, II, 19-20. Cp. the letter of St. Columban to Pope Boniface IV (*Ep.* V).

[3] Largior existens angusto in tempore praesul
Despexit mundo deficiente premi.
H. Grisar, *Rome and the Popes in the Middle Ages*, Vol. III, p. 185 (Eng. trans.).

[4] "St. Augustine's theory of the Civitas Dei was in germ that of the mediaeval papacy without the name of Rome. In Rome itself it was easy to supply the insertion and to conceive of a dominion still wielded from the ancient seat of government, as world-wide and almost as authoritative as that of the Empire. The inheritance of the imperial traditions of Rome, left begging by the withdrawal of the secular monarch, fell as it were into the lap of the Christian bishop."—Professor C. H. Turner in *Camb. Med. Hist.*, Vol. I, p. 173.

[5] S. Leon. Mag. *Sermones*, 82. Cp. Prosper, *de Ingratis*, 51 ff. So, too, Columbanus contrasts the wider sway of Christian Rome with that of the pagan Empire. "We Irish," he writes, "are specially bound to the See of Peter, and however great and glorious Rome itself may be, it is only this See that is great and renowned for us. The fame of the great city was spread abroad over the rest of the world, but it only reached us when the chariot of the Church came to us across the western waves with Christ as its charioteer and Peter and Paul as its swift coursers." *Epistle to Pope Boniface* (ep. v).

[6] There was also a current of foreign influence that derives from St. Ninian's foundation of Whithern in Galloway and is represented in Ireland by St. Enda of Aran, but it is secondary in importance to the tradition of Llancarvan and Clonard.

[7] Ryan, *Irish Monasticism*, pp. 179-184. So unique was the position held by St. Bridget that some legends even went so far as to assert that she herself had received episcopal orders!

[8] There is also evidence for the existence of non-monastic tribal bishops, for the laws seem to take for granted that every *tuath* should possess a bishop of its own, who occupies a position second

to that of the king. (Ryan, *op. cit.*, p. 300, n. 2.) These *tuath* bishoprics were the origin of the later mediaeval Irish sees, but in early times they were of far less importance than the great monastic jurisdictions, and their authority was weakened by the existence of the numerous wandering bishops such as those of whom St. Boniface complains on the continent in the eighth century.

[9] Jonas, *Vita Columbani*, I, 17.

[10] In some cases in Brittany, the menhir itself was christianised by the addition of a small cross.

[11] Quoted from the Leonine Sacramentary by Grisar (*op. cit.*, III, 285). Grisar also draws attention to the remarkable coincidence between the Lesson from Isaiah in the Mass for the Ember Wednesday in Advent and the verses of Ovid to Ceres on the Feriae Sementivae (*Fasti*, I, v. 597 ff).

[12] A most remarkable example of the survival of the old fertility magic in a Christian dress has been preserved in the elaborate Anglo-Saxon charm for barren land. Mass is sung over four sods from the four quarters of the field, incense and blessed salt is placed in the body of the plough, and as the first furrow is driven the ploughman repeats the following invocation to the Mother Goddess:

> "Hail to thee, Earth, mother of men!
> Be fruitful in God's embrace
> Filled with food for the use of men."

Anglo-Saxon Poetry, trans. R. K. Gordon (Everymans Library), pp. 98-100.

[13] According to Dom Chapman, St. Benedict drew up his Rule as an official code for Western monasticism at the suggestion of Pope Hormisdas and Dionysius Exiguus, and he sees traces of its influence in the monastic legislation of Justinian (*Novella*) and in the writings of Cassiodorus. This view, however, involves serious difficulties. Cf. Chapman, *St. Benedict and the Sixth Century* (1929), and Dom Cabrol's criticisms in the *Dublin Review*, July, 1930.

[14] This is the view of Bröndsted, *Early English Ornament*, p. 92. Professor Baldwin Brown, on the other hand, ascribes the Lindisfarne Book to native Anglian genius.

[15] E.g., the following passage from *The Wanderer*: "Thus did the Creator of men lay waste this earth, till the old work of giants stood empty, free from the revel of castle dwellers. Then he who has thought wisely of the foundations of things, and who deeply ponders this dark life, wise in his heart, often turns his thoughts to the many slaughters of the past and speaks these words: 'Whither has gone the horse? Whither has gone the rider? Whither has gone the giver of treasure; Whither the place of feasting? Where are the joys of hall? Alas the bright cup! Alas, the warrior in his corslet! Alas, the glory of the prince! How that time has passed away, grown dark under the shadow of night, as if it had never been," Gordon, *op. cit.*, p. 82. Cp. also *The Ruin*, *Deor*, *The Seafarer*, etc.

[16] R. G. Collingwood, *Roman Britain* (first ed.), p. 101.
[17] Cf. Thurlow Leeds, *The Archaeology of the Anglo-Saxon Settlements*, pp. 70-71.
[18] *Epistola ad Egbertum*. The lay monasteries of which Bede speaks in this letter may have been a Celtic institution, but they were also common in Spain in the sixth century, and St. Fructuosus of Braga refers to them in his monastic rule.
[19] Cf. W. Braune. *Angelsächsisch und Althochdeutsch*, in *Beiträge zur Geschichte der deutschen Sprache*, ed. Paul and Braune, XLIII, 361-445 (1918).
[20] Abridged from *Ep. XLIX* (to Pope Zacharias, ed. Giles, I, 101-105).

THE RESTORATION
OF THE WESTERN EMPIRE
AND CAROLINGIAN RENAISSANCE

[1] *Libri Carolini*, I, 1, 3; II, 11, 19; III, 15, etc. Alcuin, *Ep*. 198, etc. He writes that there are three supreme powers in the world—the Papacy at Rome, the Empire at Constantinople, and the royal dignity of Charles, and of these the last is the highest since Charles is appointed by Christ as the leader of the Christian people. (Cf. *Cambridge Mediaeval History*, II, 617.)
In accordance with these ideas Alcuin substituted *imperium christianum* for *Romanorum* in his revision of the liturgical books.
[2] Under the Carolingians the Capella became a kind of Holy Synod as well as taking an important share in the secular administration. The Capella was originally the body of ecclesiastics who guarded the cloak (capa) of St. Martin, the palladium of the Frankish kingdom, and who were consequently in close attendance on the court.
[3] Fustel de Coulanges, *Les transformations de la royauté franque*, p. 588.
[4] This attitude was maintained by Charles in his later years and by his successor, Lewis the Pious, who attempted to play the part of mediator in 824-825 between the Byzantine Empire and the Papacy. Even as late as 870 Hincmar still rejected the Second Council of Nicaea and regarded the Council of Frankfurt as œcumenical and orthodox.
[5] The greatest scholars of the Carolingian period, with the exception of Alcuin and Theodulph, were all either monks or pupils at Fulda, e.g., Einhard, Rabanus Maurus, who was abbot from 822-842, and his pupils, Walafrid Strabo, and Servatus Lupus.
[6] Fulda for example was largely an Anglo-Saxon colony and the copying school, which was one of the most important on the continent, still used insular script of the English type.
[7] Similar basilicas had already been built in England by Wilfred

and Benedict Biscop, and they were the normal type of church in Merovingian Gaul.

[8] Cf. A. Goldschmidt *German Illumination* (*Carolingian period*), pp. 7-10.

[9] "*Sed togata quiritum more seu trabeata latinitas suum Latium in ipso latiali palatio singulariter obtinebat.*" Johannes Diaconus, *Vita Gregorii*, II, 13, 14. Cf. J. H. Dudden, *Gregory the Great*, I, 283.

[10] *Poetae Aevi Carolini*, ed. Traube, III, 555.

> Nobilibus quondam fueras constructa patronis;
> Subdita nunc servis heu male Roma ruis.
> Deseruere tui tanto te tempore reges
> Cessit et ad Graecos nomen honosque tuus.
> In te nobilium rectorum nemo remansit
> Ingenuique tui rura Pelasga colunt.
> Vulgus ab extremis distractum partibus orbis
> Servorum servi nunc tibi sunt domini.

[11] Cf. Berlière, *l'Ordre Monastique*, pp. 103-106 and notes.

[12] We possess in the famous Chronicle of St. Gall by Ekkehard the Fourth (eleventh century), a remarkably vivid picture of the social and intellectual life of a great abbey during this period. It shows that the abbey and its school were at the height of their prosperity during the age when conditions in Western Europe as a whole were at their worst, *i.e.*, from 892 to 920.

THE AGE OF THE VIKINGS
AND THE CONVERSION OF THE NORTH

[1] *Anglo-Saxon Poetry*, trans. R. K. Gordon, p. 4.

[2] A. Olrik, *Viking Civilisation*, pp. 102-103.

[3] We must, however, remember that in Viking times it was not Frey but the warrior Thor who was regarded as the god of the farmers.

[4] The historian of the Normans, Dudo, attributes the Viking movement to a crisis of over-population, caused by the practice of polygamy. There is no doubt that this did have a certain influence, as we see in the case of the struggle between Eric Bloodaxe and the other sons of Harold Fairhair, but it was restricted to the ruling class of kings and chiefs, from whom the Viking leaders were usually drawn.

[5] H. Shetelig, *Préhistoire de Norvège*, pp. 183-188.

[6] Denmark had already accepted Christianity in the reign of Harold Bluetooth (950-986), which also marks the establishment of a powerful and united Danish State.

[7] Professor Olrik writes, "Considered as a whole, this Irish element in Scandinavian culture is a phenomenon in itself, which does not coincide with the principal current of the Christian movement as it passes over Europe. It appears rather as an enrichment and expansion of the native North European stage of civilisation than

as a part of the new trend accompanying the introduction of Christianity. In so far as it swept away a portion of the ancient heritage, this tendency might have made a breach for the entrance of the new main current; and furthermore certain Christian impulses did emanate from Ireland. But in at least equal measure this Irish influence contributed to the production of a special civilisation which somewhat impeded the rapid absorption of the North into Christian Europe." *Viking Civilisation,* p. 120.

[8] Ari writes of Helge, "He was very mixed in his faith. He put his trust in Christ and named his homestead after Him, but yet he would pray to Thor in sea voyages and in hard stresses and in all those things that he thought were of most account to him." *Landnamabok,* III, xiv, 3.

[9] Cf. the index to the first volume of Vigfusson and Powell's *Origines Islandicae,* in which all the Celtic names are marked with an asterisk.

[10] Cf. Olrik, V*iking Civilisation,* pp. 107-120, where the author gives a general statement of the case for Irish influence on Scandinavian literature, which he regards as established in the case of the saga and probable in the case both of the later heroic poetry and of the new "court poetry" of the Skalds. It is true that the Skaldic poetry has its beginnings in Western Norway, but as Professor Olrik notes, "the first known skald, Bragi Boddason, had an Irish wife and uses at least one Irish word in his *Ragnarsdrapar,*" while the system of rhyme recalls that of Irish poetry (*op. cit.,* p. 120).

[11]

[11] Of old was the age when Ymir lived:
Sea nor cool waves nor sand there were;
Earth had not been nor heaven above
But a yawning gap and grass nowhere.

The sun, the sister of the moon from the south
Her right hand cast over heaven's rim;
No knowledge she had where her home should be,
The moon knew not what might was his,
The stars knew not where their stations were.
                                    (Trans. Bellows.)

[12] W. P. Ker, *The Dark Ages,* p. 240.

[13] Trans. B. S. Philpotts, in *Edda and Saga,* p. 137.

[14] Here are the concluding stanzas in which Egil finds compensation for his misfortunes in the thought of his art. (The epithets in the first verses refer to Odin. The sister of the Wolf is Hel, goddess of death.)

Worship I not, then, Vilir's Brother,
The Most High God, of my own liking.
Yet Mimir's friend hath to me vouchsafed
Boot for my bale that is better, I ween.

Mine Art He gave me, the God of Battles,
Great Foe of Fenrir, a gift all faultless,
And that temper that still has brought me
Notable foes mid the knavish-minded.

All's hard to wield now. The Wolf's right sister
—All Father's Foes—on the sea-ness stands.
Yet will I be glad, with a good will,
And without grief, abide Hell's coming.
> Trans. E. R. Eddison, *Egils Saga*, p. 193 (1930).

[15] W. P. Ker, *The Dark Ages*, p. 314.
[16] Thormod Saga in *Origines Islandicae*, II, 705.
[17] Christne Saga, viii, 7, in *Origines Islandicae*, I, pp. 400-401.

THE RISE OF THE MEDIAEVAL UNITY

[1] *Monumenta Germaniae Historica: Epistolae* (ed. Dümmler), III, 159, *seq*. Cf. Hincmar, *de raptu viduarum*, c, xii.

[2] Carlyle, *Mediaeval Political Theory in the West*, I, 259-261. Cathulf's view is no doubt derived from Ambrosiaster *Quaestiones Veteris et Novi Testamenti* 35 (cf. *op. cit.*, I, 149).

[3] Manitius, *Geschichte des lateinischen Literatur des Mittelalters*, I, 405-406.

[4] Agobard was one of the few scholars of the period to study the works of Tertullian. Cf. Manitius, *op. cit.* I, 386.

[5] "Wherefore we give him some writings supported by the authority of the Holy Fathers and of his predecessors which none may gainsay, that his was the very power of God and the Blessed Peter, and he had authority towards all peoples for the Christian faith and the peace of the Churches for preaching the gospel and attesting the truth, and in him was all the supreme authority of living power of St. Peter by whom it is necessary that all be judged inasmuch as he himself is judged by none."—Radbertus, *Epitaphium Arsenii*, II, 16.

[6] Radbertus writes, "*Tunc ab eodem sancto viro* (*sc. Gregorio*) *et ab omnibus qui convenerant adjudicatum est quia imperium tam praeclarum et gloriosum de manu patris ceciderat ut Augustus Honorius* (*Lothair*) . . . *eum releveret et acciperet*," *op. cit.*, II, 18. This, however, does not refer to the solemn judgment by the bishops which took place at Soissons two months later under the leadership of Ebbo and Agobard. By that time both Wala and the Pope had withdrawn in disapproval.

[7] *Monumenta German. Hist.*, Sect. II, Vol. II, No. 300, cap. 3, in Carlyle, *Political Theory*, Vol. I, 252.

It was at this time that the coronation ceremony and office assumed the developed form that was to be universal throughout the West during the Middle Ages and which survives to-day only in England. The sacred rite of coronation and anointing is of immemorial antiquity in the Near East, but it is uncertain how it first reached the West. It first appears in Spain in the seventh century, and probably about the same time in the British Isles. The oldest existing order is that in the Pontifical of Egbert (ascribed to the eighth century), and it was apparently from England, and not from Spain, that the rite was introduced into the Frankish realm in 750.

[8] Cf. Schnürer, *Kirche und Kultur*, II, 31-34. The earlier date is, however, maintained by Levison, *Konstantinische Schenkung und Sylvester Legend* in *Miscellanea Ehrle II*, Rome, 1924. Another view is that of Grauert, who argues that it was the work of Hilduin of St. Denys about the year 816.

[9] In the letter of Lewis to the Emperor Basil preserved in the *Chronicon Salernitanum*. Cf. Carlyle, *op. cit.*, I, 284.

[10] Carlyle, *Mediaeval Political Theory*, I, 289.

[11] "Henceforth the towns were entirely under (the bishops') control. In them was to be found, in fact, practically only inhabitants dependent more or less directly upon the Church. . . . Their population was composed of the clerics of the cathedral church and of the other churches grouped near by; of the monks of the monasteries which, especially after the ninth century, came to be established, sometimes in great numbers, in the see of the diocese; of the teachers and students of the ecclesiastical schools; and finally of servitors and artisans, free or serf, who were indispensable to the needs of the religious group and to the daily existence of the clerical agglomeration." H. Pirenne. *Mediaeval Cities*, p. 66.

[12] The abbey of Tegernsee lost no less than 11,746 of its 11,860 estates (*mansus*) (Hauck, *Kirchengeschichte Deutschlands*, II, 9, note 3).

[13] A similar service was performed a century later in Germany by Notker Labeo (d. 1022), the famous teacher of the school of St. Gall. He translated the works of Boethius, including his version of Aristotle's *Categories*, Martianus Capella, and several other books. But Notker stands almost alone, since the revival of classical studies on the continent increased the supremacy of Latin, and the influence of Anglo-Saxon culture, which had always been favourable to the vernacular, was on the wane.

[14] Notably with regard to the resemblance of his regulations regarding the burgs and fortresses of the Wendish Mark to Edward the Elder's legislation about the *burhs* of the Danelaw. Cf. *Cambridge Mediaeval History*, III, p. 183 and note.

[15] This assimilation of barbaric elements by the dominant monastic culture is also to be seen in the *Waltharius* of Ekkehard the First, of St. Gall (c. 920-930), a remarkable attempt to recast the native tradition of German heroic poetry in the classical forms of the Latin epic. But here the influence of Christian ideas is stronger

and points towards the coming of the new literatures of mediaeval Christendom.

[16] Printed in Novati, *L'influsso del Pensiero Latino sopra la Civiltà Italiana del Medio Evo*, pp. 127-130.

[17] Gerberti, *Acta concilii Remensis* (*Monumenta Germ. Hist. Script.*, III, 672). Fleury, *Histoire ecclésiastique*, L, LVII, cc. xxi-xxvi.

[18] *Lettres de Gerbert*, ed. J. Havet, No. 187, p. 173.

[19] The Byzantine element in Otto's court was not due to an artificial imitation of exotic ceremonial, as some modern historians have supposed. It was the natural result of the semi-Byzantine tradition of tenth-century Rome and of the Empire itself. Thus Charles the Bald appeared in Byzantine dress at the assembly of Ponthion in 876 as a sign that he had received the imperial crown. Cf. Halphen *La Cour d'Otton III à Rome, Ecole française de Rome*, in *Mélanges d'archéologie et d'histoire*, XXV, 1905.

CONCLUSION

[1] *The Song of Roland*, tr. J. Crosland, lines 2360-2365. Cp. lines 2366-2396.

[2] It is true that the dying speech of Brythnoth strikes a religious note: "I thank Thee, O Lord of the Peoples, for all those joys which I have known in the world. Now, gracious Lord, I have most need that Thou shouldst grant good to my spirit, that my soul may journey to Thee, may pass in peace into Thy keeping, Prince of Angels." But the moral climax of the poem is found, not here, but in the last words of "the old companion": "I am old in age; I will not hence, but I purpose to lie by the side of my lord, by the man so dearly loved."—*Anglo-Saxon Poetry*, tr. R. K. Gordon, pp. 364-367.

[3] I have discussed these aspects of mediaeval culture in an article on *The Origins of the Romantic Tradition* in *The Criterion*, Vol. XI (1932), pp. 222-248, and in two articles on *The Origins of the European Scientific Tradition* in *The Clergy Review*, Vol. II (1931), pp. 108-121 and 194-205.

INDEX

Christopher Dawson

Christopher Henry Dawson was born in 1889 in Wales and educated at Winchester and Trinity College, Oxford. From 1930 to 1936 he was lecturer in the history of culture at University College, Exeter. He became editor of the Dublin Review in 1940. Among his other publications are *The Age of the Gods, Progress and Religion, The Spirit of the Oxford Movement, The Modern Dilemma, Mediaeval Religion, Religion and Culture,* and *Religion and the Rise of Western Culture.*